DeFi Risk & Reward

DeFi Risk & Reward

Navigating the Wild West of Finance

Othman Verdan

Mindful Pages

Published in 2026

ISBN: 9789374598924 (PB)
ISBN: 9789374597033 (eBook)

Published by

Mindful Pages
Imprint of Alpha Editions LLC
312 W. 2nd St #1834
Casper, WY 82601, USA

This book was developed using advanced writing tools to support the drafting and ideation process. All content has been thoughtfully curated, refined, and reviewed to ensure quality and relevance.

Content

Introduction viii

Chapter 1 What DeFi Really Is 1

Chapter 2 Smart Contracts and Code Risk 37

Chapter 3 Liquidity Pools and AMMs 67

Chapter 4 Lending, Leverage and Liquidations 100

Chapter 5 Yield Farming Without the Fairy Dust 131

Chapter 6 Security, Custody and Operational Hygiene. 162

Chapter 7 Stablecoins and Peg Risk 188

Chapter 8 Governance, Tokens and Power 216

Chapter 9 Volatility, Sizing and Behaviour 244

Chapter 10 Building Your DeFi Playbook 270

About the Author 300

Introduction

The collapse began quietly, as most collapses do. Blocks continued to tick forward, validators dutifully signed, dashboards still displayed the pleasant greens of borrowed confidence. Then, in the space of an hour, the numbers slipped, the collateral buffer thinned, and the liquidation bots that were meant to protect the system froze under the weight of their own incentives. By dawn, a protocol once hailed as the future of decentralised credit had evaporated into a forensic spreadsheet of transactions, frozen chat logs, and belated recriminations. Its code had been audited twice. The assurances had been plentiful. The assumptions—only visible in hindsight—were fatal. A different story unfolds at the same moment: a token triples in price, and social feeds fill with triumphant screenshots. Yet the so-called yield fuelling this ascent does not come from innovation or value creation; it comes from traders paying a premium for speed, frontrunning, and fleeting opportunities carved out of microstructure quirks. For the few who understand this, the rally is less a sign of strength than a reminder that markets often reward misunderstanding before correcting it with brutal clarity. These two scenes, though superficially opposed, speak to the same paradox. Decentralised finance makes risk legible in code while multiplying the pathways through which error, misaligned incentives, or human overconfidence can cascade. What once remained buried within balance sheets, service agreements, and institutional opacity now appears as parameters, contracts, and liquidations visible to anyone willing to look. But visibility is not comprehension. Transparency does not guarantee safety. And code, for all its promise of impartiality, cannot neutralise the oldest drivers of financial excess: greed, fear, coordination failure, and the catastrophic power of assumptions left unexamined. This book begins from a simple conviction: DeFi is neither the utopia its evangelists proclaim nor the scam its detractors insist upon. It is an evolutionary stage of finance—raw, experimental, occasionally reckless, but also unusually honest about the trade-offs embedded within its systems. To navigate it well, one must learn to read incentives rather than headlines; to grasp how protocols generate returns without being seduced by the theatre of numbers; to translate volatility into position sizes, controls, and exit rules that serve as tools rather than talismans. The promise of this book is not that it will make you fearless, but that it will help you become appropriately afraid, and therefore capable of acting with clarity rather than impulse.

In the early decades of the twentieth century, financial speculation became a public sport for the first time. Crowds gathered at brokerage houses to watch tickers spit out streams of hope and ruin in thin paper ribbons. Newspapers chronicled the exploits of traders who saw the economy as a game of nerve and timing. Yet beneath the frenzy lay a more enduring transformation: markets had become accessible before they had become comprehensible. DeFi mirrors this historical moment with uncanny fidelity. A decentralised protocol can be used by anyone long before it is understood by most. The friction that once slowed participation—clerks, forms, waiting periods—has dissolved into a few signatures on a wallet. Opportunity, risk, and error now travel at the speed of computation. The historical parallel is not an indulgence; it is a warning. Whenever distribution outpaces understanding, markets generate both possibility and peril in equal measure. What differentiates those who thrive from those who drown is not technological sophistication but the discipline to ask better questions.

The central question this book confronts is deceptively direct: **what, precisely, is DeFi?** It is not, as marketing often implies, a set of apps for speculative yield. Nor is it simply the crypto-native variant of shadow banking. At its core, DeFi replaces platforms with protocols—human intermediaries with automated rules. The shift sounds subtle but carries consequences as profound as the transition from handwritten ledgers to double-entry bookkeeping. When the rules of a financial system live in code rather than institutional charters, the nature of trust changes. Instead of relying on the integrity or solvency of firms, one relies on the correctness and incentive alignment of the contracts that govern how assets move. This is an appealing shift, but it is also an unforgiving one. Code does not care about intent. It cares about execution.

Yet even understanding protocols in isolation is insufficient. DeFi's defining strength—and its defining vulnerability—is composability. Protocols plug into one another like financial Lego, forming stacked dependencies in which the failure of one layer can ripple upwards into sudden instability. A lending market relies on a price oracle maintained by another protocol; that oracle may rely on decentralised exchange pools whose liquidity thins under stress; those pools may rely on liquidity providers whose incentives shift when yields elsewhere become more attractive. Composability is a marvel of open architecture, but it is also a map of potential contagion. To participate wisely, one must understand not only how a mechanism works, but how it behaves within an interconnected ecosystem.

This is why tokens, often dismissed as speculative chips, matter more than their price charts suggest. Tokens serve as coordination tools: they shape behaviour, distribute power, incentivise participation, and occasionally distort judgement. A token that grants governance rights embeds political structure into code; one that grants fee discounts shapes user behaviour; one that emits inflationary rewards underwrites temporary liquidity that evaporates when the music stops. Understanding a protocol without understanding its token is like studying a constitution without studying the electorate. Incentives, not ideals, determine outcomes.

Yield, too, must be stripped of its mystique. In traditional finance, yield arises from identifiable economic activity: lending capital, bearing risk, providing liquidity, underwriting uncertainty. In DeFi, those same principles hold, yet they are frequently obscured by token emissions that create the illusion of return without underlying value. This book will teach you to distinguish engineered yield—fees from traders, funding rates, risk transfer—from circular yield, where the only source of return is the inflationary distribution of tokens destined to collapse under their own weight. In doing so, you will begin to see markets as they are rather than as they present themselves.

This transformation in perception is urgent. DeFi no longer sits at the edges of finance as a curiosity for technologists and thrill-seekers. It has grown into an experimental testbed where ideas about collateral, liquidity, credit, and governance are being rewritten in real time. Institutions that once dismissed it as fringe now explore its architecture for inspiration, competition, or convergence. Regulators confront the challenge of governing systems without borders, CEOs of exchanges ponder integration with protocols that threaten to disintermediate them, and policymakers debate how to classify assets that behave like neither securities nor currencies in any familiar sense. To ignore DeFi is to ignore a crucial frontier of financial innovation; to embrace it blindly is to invite avoidable trouble.

Yet the urgency is not merely economic or technological; it is profoundly human. Behind every liquidation event or governance vote lies a story of decision-making under uncertainty. Behind every exploit lies a chain of assumptions about trust, coordination, and the limits of automation. DeFi exposes, with uncomfortable clarity, the psychological habits that have shaped finance for centuries: the tendency to chase returns without questioning their source, the belief that systems can be optimised into safety, the allure of narratives that promise liberation from traditional structures without acknowledging their essential functions. In this sense, DeFi is not a break from history but its continuation on a faster clock.

A recurring motif in this book is the *frontier*. Not the romantic frontier of folklore, but the true one: a place where rules are emerging, not settled; where opportunity attracts both innovators and opportunists; where the absence of established institutions creates space for creativity and chaos in equal measure. The frontier is not for the reckless; it is for those who approach uncertainty with curiosity, discipline, and humility. DeFi is this kind of frontier. It is neither a lawless wilderness nor a curated marketplace; it is a space where participants must build their own frameworks for risk, due diligence, and control.

As the chapters unfold, you will learn to interpret smart contracts not as impenetrable artefacts but as systems with understandable threat surfaces. You will learn why audits are necessary but insufficient, why upgradability is a double-edged sword, and why bug bounty programmes often reveal more about a protocol's culture than its code. You will explore how liquidity pools set prices, why impermanent loss persists despite its misleading name, and how concentrated liquidity transforms passive positions into active strategies with operational consequences. You will see how lending markets function, why liquidations matter, and how leverage can turn composability into a source of systemic fragility.

You will also encounter the subtler dimensions of participation: custody practices that separate competence from calamity; governance structures that distribute power in ways that resemble both democracies and oligarchies; stablecoins that promise predictability yet harbour their own varieties of peg risk; and behavioural tools that support rational decision-making when markets lurch between exuberance and panic. These elements form a coherent playbook, not a set of heuristics. What emerges is a rigorous way of seeing—one that connects incentives, mechanics, and behaviour into a single lens.

As you read, the initial paradox that opened this introduction will gain new clarity. DeFi makes risk visible, yet visibility alone cannot protect you. Code can encode rules, but it cannot encode prudence. Markets can automate settlement, but they cannot automate judgement. The responsibility shifts to the participant—more power, more freedom, and more consequences for misunderstanding either.

The final question, then, is not whether DeFi will survive. It will. The more interesting question is what form it will take as the experiments stabilise, failures accumulate into wisdom, and the architecture matures. Will decentralised networks become the financial commons of the digital age, or will they be subsumed into hybrid systems where institutions and protocols co-govern value? Will tokens evolve into sophisticated instruments of coordination, or will they fragment communities into factions competing for influence? Will stablecoins become the de facto settlement layer of the internet, or will their fragility invite regulatory reshaping?

This book does not claim to predict these outcomes. Its purpose is more modest and more useful: to equip you with the intellectual tools, analytical instincts, and practical frameworks needed to navigate whichever future emerges. What follows is neither evangelism nor scepticism, but a grounded, unvarnished account of how decentralised finance works, why it fails, where it innovates, and how to participate without surrendering to speculation or fear.

You hold, in essence, a guide to the frontier. Not a map—because the terrain is still being drawn—but a method for reading the landscape, evaluating its risks, and recognising its possibilities. If approached with discipline, DeFi can be liberating; if approached carelessly, it can be unforgiving. The choice, and the responsibility, lies with each participant.

Let us proceed.

Chapter 1
What DeFi Really Is

The first thing a newcomer notices on-chain is the absence of the usual furniture of finance. No brokers. No bank clerks. No compliance officers glancing over forms. Instead, there is a quiet, almost unsettling impersonality: a wallet connects, a transaction signs, and value moves. The shift feels trivial at first, a sleight of software that replaces one interface with another. Yet beneath this apparent simplicity lies a profound reordering of how financial systems function, who they depend on, and what trust means. A trader once spent half a morning waiting for a broker to confirm a limit order; now, an automated market maker stands ready to quote a price at any hour, indifferent to who approaches or why. A lender once relied on a credit department to evaluate risk; now, a protocol decides eligibility based solely on collateral fed to it, line by line, in code. The form is digital, but the change is deeply structural.

Consider the first time someone realises that a decentralised exchange has no order book in the traditional sense—no human making markets, no high-frequency algorithms competing for placement, not even a matching engine humming behind the scenes. There is only a pool of liquidity and a mathematical curve. Trades are executed not by negotiation but by computation. Price is not determined by two parties bargaining; it is determined by a formula adjusting balances with every interaction. It is a financial world built not on the discretion of intermediaries but on the predictability of mechanisms. For many, this is a revelation. For others, it feels like stepping into a marketplace where the stalls rearrange themselves automatically, without vendors present. But it is in these absences—these missing people, missing processes, missing points of friction—that the true meaning of DeFi begins to take shape.

The paradox is that this removal of intermediaries does not diminish the need for trust; it simply relocates it. You no longer trust the firm—you trust the code. You trust the mechanism to behave as advertised, to execute without favour or fatigue, to handle edge cases with the same rigour as routine ones. This is the heart of what distinguishes DeFi from its centralised counterparts. Financial relationships that were once held together by reputation, regulation, and legal frameworks are now mediated by smart contracts whose authority derives from logic rather than licence. To understand DeFi, one must understand this inversion. It is not merely a technical shift—it's a shift in the emotional texture of financial life. Fear migrates. Confidence migrates. So do failure modes.

Yet understanding a protocol in isolation is a bit like analysing a single gear without noticing the machine it powers. DeFi's defining trait—and the reason its successes and failures are often so dramatic—is composability. Protocols plug into one another with the ease of children's building bricks, each exposing functions that others can call, rely on, or assume will behave in stable ways. A decentralised exchange provides prices; a lending protocol consumes these prices; a yield aggregator deposits user funds into the lending protocol; a structured product builds on the aggregator. Each layer depends on the stability of the layers beneath it, even when the participants interacting with the top layer remain entirely unaware of what lies below. This stack is a marvel of permissionless innovation, but it is also a precarious tower of assumptions. When one component falters—a mispriced oracle, a thin liquidity pool, an unexpected governance change—the consequences propagate with a speed that would make traditional institutions shudder.

This interdependence is not a flaw of DeFi; it is its natural consequence. Open systems invite collaboration, competition, and re-use. They also expose every assumption to stress tests far more brutal than any institution would design intentionally. To navigate this world well, one must cultivate the habit of looking past the glossy interface to the chain of dependencies behind it. The question is no longer "Does this protocol work?" but "What does this protocol rely on to work?" Those who grasp this distinction survive; those who ignore it learn quickly, often painfully.

Tokens, too often caricatured as mere speculative assets, play a more subtle role in this architecture. They are the coordination tools of decentralised systems: part access key, part membership badge, part economic incentive. To hold a governance token is to hold a voice—unequal, perhaps, and often contested—within a collective mechanism. To hold a utility token is to hold a right to participate, to pay fees, to earn discounts, to align oneself with the rules of the system. Much of DeFi culture treats tokens like lottery tickets, yet their true importance lies in how they organise behaviour. A protocol with a poorly designed token is like a city with chaotic zoning laws: activity happens, but not always in the places or ways intended.

The distribution of these tokens matters even more. Who receives them, in what quantities, with what expectations, determines whether a protocol evolves into a community-run endeavour or a playground for insiders. Fee rebates, governance incentives, vesting schedules, emissions curves—these are not decorative elements but the political economy of DeFi. They shape the choices people make: when to provide liquidity, whether to remain loyal, how actively to participate in governance, when to exit. In a world where trust is horizontal rather than hierarchical, incentives become the currency of coordination.

All of this leads to one of the most misunderstood aspects of DeFi: yield. For many newcomers, the numbers look almost mythic—returns so high that they seem either miraculous or fraudulent. Occasionally, they are both. But at its core, yield in DeFi derives from the same economic principles that shape yield in any financial system: fees from facilitating transactions, premiums for bearing risk, payments for providing liquidity, returns earned through funding markets or risk transfer. These streams are real, measurable, and often robust. The danger arises when genuine sources of yield are drowned out by emissions—tokens printed in the hope of attracting attention, liquidity, or momentum. Emissions can create temporary excitement but rarely create durable value. The challenge for any discerning participant is to distinguish between yield that emerges from economic activity and yield that emerges from self-referential inflation. The former endures; the latter evaporates.

Understanding what DeFi really is, then, requires abandoning two common misconceptions: the belief that it is a speculative casino, and the belief that it is a frictionless utopia. It is neither. It is a system of protocols rather than platforms, mechanisms rather than institutions, incentives rather than commands. It is also a place where novelty outpaces comprehension, where risk accumulates in unexpected corners, where transparency coexists with opacity of understanding. The territory demands a different style of attention—closer, more mechanical, yet also more philosophical. What does it mean to trust a system whose rules are written not in statute but in Solidity? What does it mean to participate in an economy where your most important counterparties may be algorithms rather than individuals? What does it mean when financial coordination becomes modular, programmable, and subject to remixing by anyone with sufficient skill?

These are not abstract questions. They shape every decision a participant makes, from the tokens they hold to the protocols they touch. They shape how systems grow, how they fail, and how they recover. And they shape, in ways still unfolding, the future architecture of global finance.

The pages that follow will dissect these foundational elements—protocols, composability, tokens, and yield—not as isolated concepts but as interlocking forces. You will see how automated contracts replace institutional trust, how layered dependencies form the skeleton of on-chain economies, how tokens transform governance into a publicly visible game of incentives, and how yield arises from mechanisms rather than miracles. By the end of the chapter, these ideas will no longer appear as jargon or marketing slogans. They will feel like the structural beams of a financial system that rewrites the assumptions of the last century.

For now, hold on to a single idea: DeFi is not defined by the interfaces you click or the tokens you trade. It is defined by the architecture beneath them. The more clearly you can perceive that architecture—the rules, the incentives, the mechanisms, the interdependencies—the more confidently you can navigate the frontier ahead. The chapter begins there: at the shift from platforms to protocols, from trust in firms to trust in mechanisms, from the familiar world of intermediaries to the stranger, more revealing world of automated rules.

Protocols, Not Platforms

When Uniswap launched its first public version in November 2018, inside a small co-working space in Brooklyn, the contrast with the incumbents it quietly challenged was stark. On the screens of traders in London, Singapore and Chicago, order books refreshed hundreds of times per second, each line reflecting a human decision, an algorithm's micro-prediction, or the quiet presence of a market-maker smoothing imbalances. At Uniswap's modest debut, there was no order book at all. No quotes waiting to be hit, no service desk to call, no broker to reassure a nervous participant. There was only a contract on Ethereum, a pool of assets, and a formula—$x \cdot y = k$—executing trades with absolute indifference. For many who tested it in those early weeks, the experience felt eerie. Finance had lost its people. Code had taken the chair reserved for the intermediary. It did not promise fairness; it promised rules.

This was not the first time finance had been reconfigured by mechanism. The Chicago Board Options Exchange, founded in April 1973, transformed how risk was priced by imposing formal contracts where informal agreements once dominated. But even CBOE depended on brokers, clerks and specialists to enforce its structure. Uniswap, and the broader class of automated market makers it inspired, relocated enforcement entirely into software. The contract accepted liquidity, quoted prices, and settled trades without consulting anyone. A trader in Tokyo at 2 a.m. encountered exactly the same logic as a trader in Lagos at midday. The code did not negotiate. It executed. Five words capture its authority: *the mechanism replaces the intermediary.*

What this shift reveals is that DeFi alters the locus of trust. In traditional markets, trust is anchored in firms: their capital, their legal accountability, their operational competence. A participant may distrust a broker but rely on the exchange, or vice versa; confidence is distributed across institutions. In a protocol-driven system, trust is anchored in how the rules are written and how faithfully they run. If the smart contract is sound, the participant is safe within its boundaries. If it is flawed, no brand reputation or compliance department can compensate. The trust relationship becomes narrower, sharper, more brittle. A single line of logic can determine outcomes that, in an institutional setting, would involve committees, controls and discretion. The motif here—*the mechanism*—threads through every corner of decentralised finance.

Uniswap V1's removal of order books is a vivid demonstration of how mechanisms behave when freed from human mediation. Yet it is only one illustration. MakerDAO's launch of the DAI stablecoin in December 2017—an experiment combining collateral, governance and automated stability rules—showed that entire financial services could be delivered without an operating company in the conventional sense. There was a community, there were contributors, but there was no helpdesk to phone when markets turned. What users trusted was the architecture: collateral thresholds, liquidation penalties, governance safeguards. The platform as a firm disappeared; the protocol as a rule-set took its place.

To understand why this matters, it helps to recognise that intermediaries in traditional finance do more than match orders or process transactions. They absorb risk, mediate information, and maintain continuity when systems strain. A broker who sees clients panic may slow execution; a clearing house under pressure may extend settlement windows; an exchange may halt trading to limit disorder. Smart contracts do none of these things. They do not soothe, delay or reconsider. They execute precisely as written. When a lending protocol on Ethereum liquidates a borrower because its collateral crossed a threshold by a fraction of a percentage point, the mechanism does not inquire whether the move was temporary or whether the borrower misclicked. It acts. This mechanical impartiality is what draws some participants and unsettles others.

Named examples show both strengths and limitations. On 12 March 2020, during the global sell-off tied to the spread of COVID-19, MakerDAO's liquidation auctions malfunctioned when gas prices on Ethereum spiked. Keepers—the independent actors responsible for bidding on collateral—failed to participate in time. Several auctions cleared at zero bids, leaving users under-compensated and the system temporarily insolvent. The rules worked, but their reliance on external behaviour created fragility. Conversely, when Curve Finance launched its stablecoin-optimised AMM in January 2020, its pricing logic weathered extreme market turbulence with notable stability. The mechanism's design—using multiple curves to minimise slippage among assets intended to trade near parity—absorbed stress with predictable grace. The counter-example sharpens the point: mechanisms are powerful, but they are only as resilient as the assumptions they embed.

These examples demonstrate why naming the mechanism matters. Although participants often speak casually of "using a platform" or "trading on an exchange", DeFi encourages a different mental model. You interact not with a platform but with a protocol. You rely not on a company but on a contract. The distinction appears semantic until a failure occurs. When a centralised exchange suffers a system outage, regulators can demand accountability and customers can pursue remedies. When a smart contract misfires due to a logic flaw, the fallout is governed by the rules of the mechanism itself. Programmable certainty replaces institutional recourse.

Trust becomes a design variable. This is not an abstraction; it manifests in behaviours visible on-chain. When a contract is immutable, adoption often grows slowly until audits, bounties and real-world usage build confidence. When a contract is upgradable via proxy patterns, users examine the admin keys or timelocks to understand who can alter the rules and how quickly. A lending protocol with a four-hour timelock elicits different risk assessments from one with a three-day delay. A decentralised exchange governed by a multisig controlled by five known individuals is perceived differently from one governed by thousands of token-holders. Each design communicates a trust structure, and users behave accordingly: they deposit, hesitate, withdraw or demand higher returns based on those signals.

The replacement of intermediaries with rules also changes what "failure" looks like. In traditional settings, failure is often discretionary—a misjudgement, a lapse in oversight, a mispriced instrument. In protocol settings, failure is mechanical. The liquidation either triggers or it does not. The price oracle either updates or it stalls. The governance vote either passes or it fails to reach quorum. Everything hinges on the mechanism. A participant who understands this sees incidents not as anomalies but as disclosures of the system's implicit assumptions.

Consider also how protocols interact. The mechanism does not exist alone; it sits within a web of other mechanisms. A decentralised exchange may rely on oracles, which rely on data aggregation, which rely on liquidity elsewhere. A lending market may accept a token whose value is influenced by governance decisions in another protocol. When Compound integrated Uniswap LP tokens as collateral in September 2020, it opened the door to positions whose risk depended on two protocols simultaneously. This composability is a defining strength of DeFi, but it also magnifies the significance of the mechanism. Each protocol inherits assumptions from the ones beneath it. To trust the stack, you must trust not just one rule-set but many.

Yet mechanisms are not neutral. They encode preferences, power and politics. Automated market makers privilege liquidity providers in certain ways; lending protocols privilege over-collateralised borrowers; governance mechanisms privilege voters with higher token balances. These rules shape behaviour: who supplies liquidity, who borrows, who participates, who abstains. They are not natural laws; they are chosen architectures. Naming them is the first step in evaluating their consequences.

A well-known limitation of mechanism-based systems lies in their inability to adapt to context not foreseen by designers. In late 2021, when gas fees surged on Ethereum, smaller participants were priced out of interacting with several protocols. The mechanism had no provision for "fairness" in the colloquial sense. It simply charged what the network demanded. The counterpoint is that this rigidity also prevents favouritism: a user with £10,000 experiences the same rules as a user with £10 million. Reconciling these forces reveals the heart of the matter: DeFi mechanisms create equality of rules, not equality of outcomes.

A second limitation is that mechanisms, unlike institutions, struggle with ambiguity. For example, during the TerraUSD collapse in May 2022, no protocol could reinterpret events or offer extraordinary measures. Positions unwound as written. Some observers argued that the rigidity of mechanisms made the system safer by preventing discretionary bailouts; others argued it made the system harsher by ignoring human intent. Neither view is entirely wrong. Both underscore that mechanism-centric finance operates on a plane where compassion and judgement are absent by design.

Yet these limitations coexist with strengths that traditional systems cannot replicate. Mechanisms make behaviour inspectable. Anyone can audit a protocol's rules, observe its flows and replicate its logic. Decisions become legible. Incentives become predictable. The opacity of balance sheets, bilateral arrangements and institutional cultures gives way to a form of transparency that, while not perfect, is unprecedented in finance. Participants may misinterpret what they see, but they are not denied access to the view.

This inspectability gives rise to a new form of literacy. The competent participant does not merely ask whether a protocol is safe but examines how the mechanism behaves across scenarios. They look at liquidity depth, oracle responsiveness, governance participation rates, admin key structures, gas sensitivities. These are not hobbyist curiosities; they are the behavioural metrics of mechanisms. Trust shifts from belief to examination.

A second quiet motif—the mechanism as *architecture*—captures a deeper implication. Architecture shapes what is possible. A cathedral invites certain forms of gathering and discourages others; a narrow alley shapes movement differently from a public square. Protocols, likewise, structure economic behaviour. They define who can act, how quickly they can act, and what constraints govern those actions. When users interact with AMMs instead of order books, when they borrow through algorithmic lending instead of credit adjudication, when they vote in governance rather than petitioning a support desk, their behaviour is channelled through architecture. And architecture, once established, is difficult to unbuild.

This returns us to the core question: how does trust migrate when intermediaries vanish? Trust does not disappear; it recalibrates. It moves from institutional character to mechanical clarity. It moves from human discretion to predictable enforcement. It moves from brand reputation to code review. Some find this shift liberating—rules without negotiation, access without permission. Others find it precarious—rules without recourse, consequences without empathy. The truth lies not in choosing one narrative over the other but in understanding the trade-offs that mechanisms impose.

The final consideration is pragmatic. When a professional or researcher engages with DeFi, they are not evaluating a company; they are evaluating a mechanism: its logic, its limits, its dependencies, its incentives. A thoughtfully designed mechanism can enable financial activity at a global scale with minimal friction. A poorly designed one can collapse under stress or invite manipulation. The difference is not semantic; it is structural.

What remains unresolved is how far society will allow mechanisms to govern financial life without the buffers, exceptions and interpretive capacities of institutions. Will the rigidity of rules produce fairness or brittleness? Will the absence of intermediaries produce empowerment or exposure? The question is not theoretical. It is the question every participant confronts when they click "confirm" and commit value to a contract that cannot hear them, understand them or negotiate with them. The mechanism waits. The decision is yours.

Composability and the Stack

When Compound integrated Uniswap's liquidity pool tokens as collateral in September 2020, a subtle but consequential shift occurred. A user depositing an ETH–DAI LP token into Compound was, in effect, mortgaging a position built on another protocol, whose price depended on a constant-product curve running on Ethereum, which itself relied on oracles to keep external prices aligned. One action—a deposit—touched at least three layers: the lending market, the automated market maker, and the oracle infrastructure. At Compound's office in San Francisco that month, engineers traced how liquidations might cascade if any underlying layer mispriced the LP token. The prospect was clear. A controlled system could turn reflexive. Risk could climb the stack.

This phenomenon—the ease with which one protocol plugs into another—defines decentralised finance. It is the quiet engine behind its speed of innovation. It is also the quiet source of its most critical fragilities. Ethereum's architecture allowed Compound to use Uniswap LP tokens without negotiation, licensing or human coordination. Everything was permissionless. Everything was modular. Lego bricks clicked into place with reassuring ease. But Lego bricks also topple if the base weakens. That is the paradox: the very openness that fuels growth seeds systemic risk. Five words capture the motif: *the stack remembers everything.*

Composability reveals itself first through behaviour rather than theory. Look at a user interacting with a yield aggregator built in London in late 2021. They deposit USDC. That aggregator routes funds to Aave, which supplies liquidity to a borrower whose collateral is priced by Chainlink oracles. The aggregator simultaneously stakes the claim token it receives into a vault that uses Curve's pools to manage stablecoin exposure. One click; five dependencies; dozens of implicit assumptions. Show the flow, name the layers, examine the implications. The user sees yield. The system sees a stack.

The first claim is simple: composability accelerates innovation. You can measure this in development velocity. In January 2020, before AMMs dominated stablecoin trading, Curve's founder Michael Egorov introduced a new pricing curve tailored for low-volatility assets. Because Curve exposed its contracts openly, by mid-2020 multiple yield products integrated its pools without formal partnership. Developers in Berlin, Singapore and Buenos

Aires stitched Curve into lending markets, arbitrage systems and structured vaults. The mechanism spread not through boardrooms but through lines of code imported from public repositories. The implication is straightforward. Innovation compounds when the components are modular, inspectable and open. Yet this freedom carries cost: fewer barriers to entry also mean fewer buffers against unintended coupling.

The second claim: composability introduces systemic fragility through dependency chains. Show it through a concrete case. On 14 November 2020, the protocol Value DeFi suffered a multi-layer exploit that combined flash loans from Aave, price manipulation on Curve, and a vulnerability in its own logic. The attacker stitched protocols together as easily as a developer would in a legitimate integration. The mechanism behaved correctly at each layer; the composition did not. A single vector propagated through pricing, collateral assessment and execution logic within minutes. It demonstrated how stacked assumptions could unravel when stressed. The implication is clear. Each layer may appear sound when isolated, yet fragile when synchronised.

A counter-example helps clarify limits. Consider the behaviour of Aave during the May 2021 market drawdown. ETH fell sharply. Liquidations surged. Yet Aave's dependence on Chainlink's time-weighted oracles—updated with deliberate pacing—acted as a stabiliser. The stack resisted reflexivity; liquidations proceeded in an orderly fashion. Here, the composition of lending + oracle + collateral logic produced resilience rather than fragility. Reconciling these cases reveals an underlying principle: whether composability strengthens or weakens a system depends on how tightly the layers couple and how predictable each component's behaviour remains under stress.

The stack becomes clearest when traced through price. Prices in DeFi are not monolithic. They emerge from multiple layers: liquidity pools broadcast ratios, oracles aggregate data, lending markets read these feeds, and derivatives protocols build positions on top of them. Each layer transforms a signal. Each transformation adds latency, friction or amplification. In February 2021, during a period of extreme volatility on Binance Smart Chain, PancakeSwap's AMM pricing momentarily diverged from external markets by several percentage points. Protocols relying on these pools for internal price discovery cascaded the distortion upwards. Liquidations occurred against inflated or deflated valuations. The market did not experience a failure of any single mechanism; it experienced a failure of synchronisation across the stack.

Composability also creates new forms of liquidity behaviour. Liquidity becomes *layered*—not merely sitting in pools, but locked as collateral, wrapped into tokenised claims, or staked in multi-step strategies. One can see this in the behaviour of Curve's 3pool during late 2022, when large shifts in USDT/USDC/DAI balances signalled upstream stress from centralised issuers. The pool's imbalance affected the stablecoin pegs; the peg movements affected lending health factors; and those health factors influenced liquidation volumes. Each metric was traceable on-chain, yet the interpretation required stack literacy. The motif returns: *the stack remembers everything.* What looks like a minor imbalance at one layer can propagate quietly until it becomes a liquidity event elsewhere.

Equally important are governance dependencies. When Yearn integrated with multiple protocols—Balancer, Curve, Aave—it inherited their parameter choices, their admin key design, their timelocks, and their governance risks. A decision taken by voters in another protocol's forum could alter Yearn's risk without Yearn's direct involvement. In April 2022, when a governance vote in one integrated protocol altered emissions without wide communication, several vaults saw abrupt shifts in returns. The behaviour was rational, the outcome predictable, yet the coordination failure showed how governance itself becomes part of the stack.

A limitation emerges. If everything is composable, coordination becomes complex. Developers must track changes across multiple protocols, understanding not only the logic but the intentions of maintainers. A counter-example helps illuminate. When Lido introduced stETH in December 2020, its designers foresaw that the token would be widely used as collateral. They communicated assumptions transparently, built upgrade paths with community oversight, and established metrics—coverage ratios, withdrawal queues—to help downstream protocols evaluate risk. This clarity reduced uncertainty in the stack. Reconciling this with more chaotic integrations suggests that composability rewards clear signalling. It punishes opacity.

Metrics help make these dynamics visible. Liquidation volume signals stress. Oracle update frequency signals data reliability. Pool depth signals exit capacity. Governance quorum rates signal political resilience. Each metric maps to a layer. The professional who learns to read these signals sees not a flat market but a stack of systems interacting in real time. What looks like volatility becomes a chain of decisions. What looks like failure becomes a misaligned interface between components.

Historical parallels illustrate how modular systems behave under coupling. The 1987 Black Monday crash saw portfolio insurance strategies reinforce selling pressure because many funds used similar models. Mechanisms interacted. In DeFi, recursion can emerge even more quickly. In June 2022, a large borrower on Aave used stETH as collateral. A discount emerged between stETH and ETH on Curve. That discount affected health factors. Liquidation fears influenced liquidity providers, who rotated out of certain assets. Again, the stack remembered everything: collateral logic, AMM pricing, borrower behaviour. Each action was rational; the composition amplified stress.

Yet composability is not inherently destabilising. It also enables unprecedented transparency. A researcher in Oxford or Nairobi can inspect every layer of a protocol stack, replay events, model contagion pathways and evaluate assumptions. No equivalent exists in traditional finance, where exposure webs lie inside bilateral contracts or internal books. Composability, in this sense, is both microscope and accelerant. It reveals structure and accelerates interaction.

The architectural motif is unavoidable. A protocol stack is not a loose collection of components; it is a built environment. It shapes movement. It channels behaviour. It privileges some actions and makes others costly. Just as a city's road layout determines traffic patterns, a DeFi stack's architecture determines how information, liquidity and risk flow. When the base layer is robust, the structure above can flourish. When the base layer thins—through shallow liquidity, slow oracles or opaque governance—the entire arrangement becomes precarious.

Composability also influences time. Protocols operate at different speeds. AMMs adjust prices instantly. Oracles update in intervals. Governance operates in days. Liquidations occur in seconds. When layers with different temporal rhythms connect too tightly, mismatches emerge. A governance decision may lag behind a market move; an oracle update may lag behind an AMM; a lending protocol may liquidate based on out-of-date prices. These are not abstractions; they manifest in liquidations, parameter misfires and user losses. Time becomes part of the stack.

Professional users often gravitate toward the elegance of composability, but elegance can obscure responsibility. When one protocol integrates another, it inherits its behaviour. When a developer plugs into a data feed, they inherit its assumptions. When an institution builds a product on top of multiple protocols, it inherits their governance cycles, oracle latencies and liquidity bottlenecks. The stack asks a simple question: do you understand what you are inheriting?

This leads to the final tension. Composability grants extraordinary creative power. It allows a handful of engineers to build financial architectures once reserved for global institutions. But it also exposes every design choice to the scrutiny—and consequence—of the stack. No protocol operates alone. Every contract touches another. Every assumption propagates. The system remembers.

The unresolved question sits at the edge of every integration: which dependencies strengthen the design, and which turn a clean architecture into a precarious tower? The decision is not trivial. It defines whether composability becomes a tool for resilience or a vector for contagion.

Tokens as Coordination Tools

In October 2020, at a cramped workspace near Shoreditch High Street in London, the decentralised exchange dYdX released an audited report tracing how its new liquidity mining programme reshaped user behaviour within weeks. The data startled even the team. Traders who had rarely placed more than a handful of positions per day suddenly executed dozens. Previously inactive accounts reawakened with near-scripted regularity. The cause was unambiguous: the newly introduced DYDX token, distributed automatically according to trading volume and open interest. A token had changed the cadence of a market. It had not altered the mechanics of trading. It had altered the incentives. And with that, it altered behaviour.

Tokens in decentralised finance are often treated as mere prices on a screen—assets to be charted, debated or speculated upon. Yet their deeper function is not as instruments of wealth but as instruments of coordination. They set the tempo. They shape participation. They distribute power. To understand DeFi, you must understand tokens not as chips in a casino but as coded signals that nudge, constrain and mobilise users. The motif here is simple and quiet: *the token behaves like a script*. It cues action. Participants follow.

The first claim emerges clearly when seen before it is named. In December 2020, Uniswap's fee discount schedules showed that users holding UNI increased their pool engagement by measurable margins during periods of governance debate. The behaviour was visible on-chain: wallets that previously provided thin liquidity began committing larger clips—£10,000 here, £50,000 there—

whenever discussions about fee switches intensified. Show the behaviour, name the mechanism, explain the effect. Holding a token was not just owning an asset; it was gaining a contingent right within a collective decision. The implication is substantial. Tokens give economic actors reasons to act beyond price speculation.

Distribution is the second element, and its weight becomes obvious when traced through a specific case. When SushiSwap launched in August 2020, its SUSHI token was emitted on an aggressive schedule, rewarding early liquidity providers far more than later ones. The result was a dramatic migration of assets from Uniswap to SushiSwap over a span of days. Behaviour followed distribution. The structure of incentives pulled liquidity like a gravitational field. Yet when the emission rate tapered, liquidity partially returned. This oscillation—visible in the daily total value locked metrics recorded by multiple analytics platforms—demonstrated how token scheduling shapes expectations, commitments and reversals. It also revealed a broader truth: distribution is political. It determines who benefits first, who governs next, and who remains after incentives cool.

A credible counter-example sharpens the concept. In February 2022, ENS—the Ethereum Name Service—distributed ENS tokens to users based on historical ownership of .eth domain names. This airdrop did not meaningfully alter how most users behaved operationally. They continued to register names, update records and maintain renewals at similar frequencies to prior months.

Distribution alone did not transform behaviour. Why? Because the token's utility—governance—did not materially affect the day-to-day function of naming. The script lacked cues. The motif returns: *the token behaves like a script.* It only shapes the scene when the script demands performance.

Reconciling these cases illustrates a central principle. Tokens influence behaviour when two ingredients align: distribution and utility. Distribution sets who receives them and in what proportions; utility defines what those recipients can do with them. Without utility, distribution is noise. Without distribution, utility is gated. Both matter because tokens coordinate. They create expectations. They signal priorities. They embed incentives in programmable form.

Utility, like distribution, becomes visible through concrete actions. When Binance introduced BNB in 2017 with fee discounts on its exchange, users quantifiably shifted trading patterns. The Binance annual report (2019) recorded reduced taker fees and higher trading volumes among accounts holding BNB. The relationship was not mysterious. Participants compared fees, measured savings and committed trades through the discounted path. The token shaped behaviour because its utility aligned with a clear metric—fee reduction—visible at every execution. The implication extends beyond centralised contexts. Fee rebates, governance rights, access privileges and collateral eligibility function similarly on-chain. They turn holding into participating.

Governance rights add a political dimension. When MakerDAO granted MKR holders the authority to adjust stability fees or collateral parameters, it transformed the token from a speculative asset into a vote-bearing share of a monetary mechanism. In April 2021, when MKR holders voted to increase the debt ceiling for new collateral types, wallets with only modest balances submitted ballots. This wasn't abstract governance; it resulted in measurable changes to DAI supply within hours. Behaviour mapped governance. Governance mapped incentives. A token became an instrument of collective economic action.

Yet governance also exposes limitations. Low voter participation remains common. A study by Gauntlet (May 2022) found that turnout in major DeFi governance proposals often hovered between 3 and 10 per cent of outstanding voting tokens. This metric reveals a behavioural truth: tokens do not guarantee engaged governance. They only offer the possibility. Participation depends on costs, context, clarity and coordination. The script is on the table, but many choose not to perform. Reconciling this with earlier examples indicates that utility must be both meaningful and accessible. If a token grants rights that users deem too abstract, they will disengage.

Distribution also encodes power. A protocol where 60 per cent of voting tokens sit with ten wallets broadcasts a political structure, even if unspoken. That distribution shapes behaviour in visible and measurable ways. Smaller holders hesitate to challenge proposals. Large holders coordinate privately. Delegates emerge to interpret a system too large for individual voters. These behaviours are not theoretical. They occur in governance forums, Discord discussions and snapshot voting records. A participant studying them sees a political economy forming in real time.

A second motif—*the script becomes a map*—helps illuminate how token utility guides long-term behaviour. If a token grants access to a lending discount, the map points users toward borrowing. If it increases yield for stakers, the map points toward longer lock-ups. If it grants voting power, the map points toward governance engagement. Each utility draws a route. Participants take it when incentives and expectations align.

Yet tokens can misfire. A distribution that rewards mercenary liquidity may attract capital that vanishes when yields fall. A utility that promises governance influence may be undermined by low turnout or concentrated holdings. A token intended to stabilise behaviour may instead create reflexivity, as users buy in anticipation of votes that drive price. The risk becomes visible in trading patterns—spikes around governance deadlines, surges in liquidity during emissions, sudden departures when incentives change. These are not abstract failures; they are behavioural signatures.

A counter-example to overdependence on token incentives can be seen in Bitcoin's early history. In January 2009, when Satoshi Nakamoto mined the genesis block, Bitcoin had no market value, no exchange listing, no fee rebates, no governance votes. Its distribution was rudimentary. Yet a small cohort of adopters still contributed hash power, discussed protocol changes on forums, and maintained the network. Their coordination arose not from token utility but from ideology and experimentation. Behaviour preceded incentive. This does not invalidate the role of tokens in DeFi; it clarifies their limits. Tokens amplify and organise behaviour, but they do not create commitment where none exists.

Returning to DeFi, the interplay of distribution and utility becomes particularly clear when examining staking. When Lido launched stETH in December 2020, it offered holders a tokenised claim representing staked ETH. Utility came from liquidity: stETH could be traded, used as collateral or integrated into structured products. Distribution remained tied to deposits. The result was a cycle of behaviour that could be traced through daily issuance and integration events. When borrowing markets made stETH attractive collateral, deposits surged. When liquidity imbalances widened—as they did in May 2022—users adjusted positions with almost choreographed timing. The token had become both script and map, directing movement across the stack.

Metrics anchor this behaviour. One can track governance participation, staking ratios, emission schedules, lock-up durations, liquidity depth, fee savings and collateral usage. Each tells a story of coordination. When governance participation rises, the script is compelling. When emission schedules flatten, mercenary behaviour recedes. When lock-ups lengthen, expectations stabilise. When liquidity deepens, coordination strengthens. This is why tokens matter. They do not simply represent value; they organise it.

Yet the architecture of tokens raises unresolved tensions. A system that coordinates through incentives risks over-fitting behaviour to short-term rewards. A system that coordinates through rights risks capturing power in the hands of early adopters. A system that coordinates through access risks exclusion. The designer must choose trade-offs: concentrate distribution or spread it, weight governance by stake or by identity, reward short-term liquidity or long-term commitment. Each decision produces a distinct behavioural pattern.

The unresolved question shadows every protocol launch: what behaviour should the token script, and what behaviour will it script unintentionally? The two rarely match perfectly. The gap between design and action is where real coordination emerges.

Where Yield Comes From

In June 2020, when Compound opened distribution of its COMP token from its headquarters in San Francisco, the protocol's metrics shifted almost instantly. Total value supplied doubled within forty-eight hours. Borrowing followed, expanding by comparable magnitude. Commentators described the surge as a renaissance. Yet the team's internal dashboards told a quieter story: net protocol income—the spread between interest paid by borrowers and interest earned by suppliers—barely moved. The newfound "yield" that users celebrated did not come from economic activity. It came from emissions. Code was distributing tokens, not redistributing value. The scene captured a paradox with unusual clarity. When numbers rise, it is not always clear who is paying.

To trace genuine yield, one must step away from the noise of token rewards and watch what markets actually do. A decentralised exchange collects fees when traders swap assets, regardless of price direction. A lending protocol earns through interest rate differentials derived from borrower demand. A derivatives venue produces funding payments between long and short positions based on imbalance. These are economic functions older than any blockchain. They persist because they reflect real costs or real demand. The motif to carry through this section—*who pays?*—reveals the difference between durable yield and theatrical yield.

The first claim is best shown, not told. On 15 September 2020, Uniswap's fee tracker for the ETH/USDC pair recorded one of its largest single-day fee accruals of the quarter. This was not due to incentives or emissions. It was because traders moved size through the pool as Ethereum's price swung. The contract charged 30 basis points per trade, producing fees measured block by block. Show the behaviour; name the mechanism; explain the implication. Liquidity providers earned because traders demanded immediacy. That demand created cost. Users paid. Yield emerged.

The opposite dynamic surfaces when incentives mask the absence of genuine flow. When Yield Farming Protocol YFII launched in July 2020, its emissions structure attracted vast short-term deposits. But on-chain analytics showed low trade volume across its integrated pools. Fees stayed thin. Emission-driven yields—sometimes quoted above 1,000 per cent annualised—were being paid in freshly minted tokens with no corresponding cash flow. The protocol distributed dilution, not earnings. Once emissions slowed, capital retreated. This is circular yield: a flow that depends not on service provision but on continual token creation. The motif returns: *who pays?* In circular systems, the answer is often nobody in particular—or everybody through dilution.

A counter-example deepens the distinction. When dYdX expanded its perpetuals exchange in April 2021, funding payments became a material driver of returns for liquidity providers. Funding rates emerged from an observable mechanism: when perpetual prices diverged from spot prices, one side of the market compensated the other to maintain balance. Traders, not the protocol, paid. Funding flips—daily or hourly—became a visible rhythm. One can measure them. One can model them. Crucially, they originate in market misalignment, not token emissions. Comparing this with emission-driven events exposes a core principle: real yield arises from economic friction or economic service.

The second claim concerns risk transfer. Lending protocols cannot generate yield unless someone is willing to borrow. Borrowers, in turn, pay because they expect returns elsewhere—leverage, arbitrage, or liquidity access. In March 2021, during a period of strong enthusiasm for collateralised stablecoin strategies, Aave's borrow demand for USDT spiked. This drove interest rates higher and produced meaningful returns for suppliers. The behaviour of users—borrowing to pursue external strategies—created yield for other users. Risk transferred from lender to borrower, priced according to market conditions. No new tokens were minted to conjure income. The yield came from a risk decision made by identifiable actors.

Consider a limitation: not all borrow-driven yield is sustainable. In November 2021, during a surge in levered stETH strategies, borrowing demand temporarily inflated supply yields for ETH-denominated loans. Yet this yield depended almost entirely on recursive borrowing loops—borrowing ETH to buy stETH to use as collateral to borrow more ETH. When markets corrected in 2022, the unwinding of these loops caused yields to collapse. Reconciling this limitation with earlier examples leads to a structural insight. Borrow-driven yield is real, but it can be fragile when built on reflexive strategies rather than economic demand such as arbitrage or stablecoin liquidity needs.

Another source of yield lies in liquidity provision itself. AMMs reward liquidity because liquidity reduces slippage and enables trading. But the yield comes from the fees traders pay, not from the pool's existence. In late May 2021, during a weekend of high activity, Curve's 3pool recorded daily fees exceeding £1 million. The metric was public, verifiable, and linked directly to stablecoin trading. Liquidity providers earned because the pool served a purpose: it allowed stablecoins to be swapped with minimal deviation from peg. Fee flow matched usage. Nothing circular. Nothing speculative. Behaviour—trading—created compensation.

Contrast this with pools that remain unused. During parts of 2022 and 2023, several smaller Uniswap pools, designed for exotic tokens, accrued negligible fees for days at a time. Liquidity providers who committed capital to these pools earned near-zero real yield. The pool existed. The mechanism worked. But without flow, there was no income. This is a natural test for economic yield. If users do not transact, liquidity providers do not earn. If borrowers do not borrow, lenders do not earn. If traders do not imbalance perpetual markets, funding does not accrue. Real yield is tied to behaviour, not design.

Insurance-like mechanisms offer another vantage. When Nexus Mutual, founded in 2019 in London, expanded its cover offerings to exchange risks and protocol smart contract risks, it priced cover based on assessed risk and claim probability. Members staked NXM to underwrite the risks. Premiums paid by users created yield for those underwriters. Again, *who pays?* The insured. What drives yield? Risk transfer layered onto quantifiable behaviour such as cover purchase volume, historical claim rates and asset exposure. This form of yield resembles traditional underwriting but is delivered through mechanism rather than institution.

The architecture of real yield becomes clearer when tracking metrics over time. Fee revenue, borrow interest, funding payments and insurance premiums fluctuate with identifiable drivers: volatility, demand, liquidity and risk appetite. These drivers leave signatures—volume spikes, borrow utilisation charts, funding rate oscillations, premium curves. They reveal not just activity but causality. The professional who reads these patterns sees yield not as a rate but as a story: someone pays for immediacy, someone pays for leverage, someone pays for certainty.

The motif returns—*who pays?*—and directs attention to a subtle point. In markets where no one appears to pay, something else is happening. Either an issuer is printing tokens to subsidise activity, or value is being redistributed from late participants to early ones. When emissions drive yield, the payer is the future holder of the token whose value may be diluted. Such systems may serve as bootstrapping tools, attracting early liquidity or participants, but they do not produce sustainable return. They are accelerants, not engines.

A notable example of emissions used responsibly comes from Liquity, launched in April 2021, which distributed LQTY tokens to stability providers and borrowers but capped distribution at launch. There were no perpetual emissions. The system relied primarily on redemption fees and borrowing fees that fluctuated according to utilisation. Users paid. Yield emerged. The absence of circularity made the mechanism more predictable. Compare this with protocols where emissions were uncapped. When inflation exceeds demand, token prices fall, and yield collapses even as the emission rate remains high. This behaviour is visible in long-term charts of several DeFi tokens post-2021.

A counter-example from traditional markets helps clarify distinctions. When exchanges such as CME or ICE generate revenue, they do so through contract fees tied to trading volume. These revenues are stable because they reflect structural demand: hedging, speculation, arbitrage. They do not depend on distributing stock to traders. The similarity to AMM fee revenue is evident. The difference is simply decentralisation. Behaviour creates yield, not dilution.

The deeper implication is that yield is not a mystery. It is a function of cost, demand and risk. A borrower pays to access liquidity. A trader pays to transact quickly. An underwriter earns for assuming risk. A liquidity provider earns when flow is high. A staker earns when securing a network has measurable cost. Every genuine yield source matches a service to a payer.

Yet this clarity does not solve the hardest question. When protocols blend both real yield and emissions, how does one determine which component dominates? How does one measure economic durability? How does one compare fee revenue from volatile trading to stable funding payments in subdued markets? The answer is rarely obvious. It sits at the intersection of design, behaviour and time.

The tension remains unresolved. When viewing a yield figure on a dashboard—20 per cent, 80 per cent, 200 per cent—the critical question lingers: who pays? And for how long?

Chapter 2
Smart Contracts and Code Risk

The breach lasted twelve minutes. On a grey morning in April 2022, auditors poring over the post-mortem of the Beanstalk Farms exploit tried to reconstruct how a governance contract had been drained of more than £150 million with a single proposal and a flash loan. The chain of events was humiliatingly simple. A hostile actor borrowed voting power, passed a malicious upgrade, and siphoned funds before the community even realised a vote had begun. No passwords were stolen. No servers were compromised. The code did exactly what the code allowed. The rules held, and yet the system failed. For many observers, the shock was not that an exploit had occurred—DeFi history is punctuated with them—but that it had occurred without violating a single line of logic. The attack unfolded inside the rules.

Smart contracts promise a cleaner world: transparent rules, automated execution, a financial architecture free from the ambiguities of paperwork or the temperaments of human intermediaries. Yet the very forces that make them elegant also make them unforgiving. A mechanism that cannot bend cannot forgive. A rule that cannot interpret cannot protect. When a bug exists, it executes. When a privilege exists, it may be used. When an assumption fails, it fails absolutely. The frontier that once felt liberating begins to feel surgical: a landscape where precision governs everything, and imprecision costs dearly. The paradox is sharp. The more faithfully a contract executes, the more catastrophic a flaw becomes.

This chapter turns to that paradox. Smart contracts are among the most powerful tools in decentralised finance, but they are also its most brittle components. Their threat surface is both visible and elusive—visible because the code is open, elusive because vulnerabilities often emerge from interactions rather than lines. Re-entrancy, integer miscalculations, oracle manipulation, privilege escalation: these are familiar words in audit reports, but each hides an ecosystem of failure modes. Some are obvious. Many are quietly interdependent, the kind of risks that only reveal themselves under pressure, as if the contract were a bridge that appears sturdy until a particular pattern of traffic crosses it at the wrong speed.

One of the enduring motifs in this chapter is that of the *boundary*. A smart contract is a boundary drawn in code—between what it can do and what it must never do; between users and maintainers; between automated behaviour and privileged intervention. Reading a threat surface is an act of tracing these boundaries. Where can state change occur? Who can trigger it? Which external contracts does this one trust? Which assumptions about price, timing or behaviour remain implicit and untested? The reader who learns to inspect these edges acquires something akin to architectural vision: the ability to see where weight rests, where pressure accumulates, and where a single weakness can compromise the full structure.

Audits, too, exist at the boundary between confidence and complacency. They offer expertise, but not certainty. Their presence is comforting, but their omissions are equally instructive. Most professionals read an audit summary with the relief of seeing "no critical issues found." Few pause to consider what a cluster of "low severity" issues might mean under stress or composability, or how a finding marked as "informational" may become consequential when a protocol interacts with another with subtly different assumptions. Auditors assess code; they cannot assess how users or rival protocols will behave months later. To learn to read audit reports is to learn to read silence—to ask what was not covered, what assumptions were accepted, what privileges remained intact.

The question of upgradability adds yet another layer of tension. A contract that cannot be upgraded is pure in its finality but dangerous in its inflexibility. A contract that can be upgraded is safer in theory but riskier in practice, because the upgrade path itself becomes a point of trust. Proxy patterns, multisigs, timelocks: these are political tools disguised as technical patterns. They determine who can alter the rules, how changes occur, and how much warning users receive. An emergency pause function might save a protocol during an exploit, yet its very existence signals that someone, somewhere, holds a key to the machine. Trust migrates again—from code to its custodians, from mechanism to governance.

Bug bounty programmes occupy a different corner of this landscape. They turn the capacity for harm into an incentive for disclosure. When well designed, they reveal not only vulnerabilities but culture: whether a team rewards research generously, publishes clear post-mortems, treats white-hat actors as collaborators rather than adversaries. Chaos testing—those moments when teams simulate attacks or commission adversarial reviews—exposes a deeper truth. Smart contracts behave differently under fire than under casual inspection. The way a system handles edge cases, rate limits, extreme market movements or adversarial queries reveals layers of risk invisible during calm periods. This is the "live fire" aspect of decentralised systems: they are battle-tested not in labs but in the wild, where incentives are real and adversaries are unrelenting.

Stepping back, the chapter explores something elemental about mechanism-driven finance. Code shifts the locus of trust not by eliminating risk but by reformatting it. Instead of trusting an institution to behave correctly, one trusts a mechanism to behave consistently. The difference is subtle but profound. Institutions fail in human ways—through mismanagement, negligence or malice. Smart contracts fail mechanically—through logic paths, state transitions, or boundary conditions. Both forms of failure are painful. One is familiar. The other is new.

Why does this matter now? Because decentralised finance is no longer a niche experiment. Billions move through contracts whose designers may never meet their users.

Every assumption written into those contracts shapes the safety of global participants who deposit, trade, borrow or stake with quiet faith that the mechanism will hold. And the stakes grow each year, not only because capital grows, but because composability intertwines systems into complex organisms where the failure of one contract becomes the contagion of many.

The introduction ends not with reassurance but with momentum. There is insight to be gained by learning how to read a contract's threat surface, how to interpret audit reports without reverence, how to map upgrade paths to trust assumptions, and how to recognise the signals of healthy or unhealthy security cultures. These are not technical footnotes; they are the lenses through which decentralised finance becomes comprehensible rather than mystical, navigable rather than intimidating.

The unresolved question shadows everything that follows. If the rules are written in code that cannot correct itself, and the guardians of that code hold powers that must be trusted absolutely, how do we participate responsibly in a system where small flaws can become systemic failures? The chapter begins at that threshold—at the moment where transparency confronts fragility, and where understanding the machinery becomes the only meaningful form of protection.

Reading the Threat Surface

On 17 June 2016, in a warehouse-style office on the outskirts of Berlin, developers from Slock.it stared in disbelief at the unfolding attack on The DAO. Within hours, more than 3.6 million ether—worth roughly US$50 million at the time—had been siphoned into a child contract through a recursive withdrawal loop. No private keys were stolen. No servers were breached. The attacker simply exploited a re-entrancy flaw that allowed repeated withdrawals before the balance updated. The code executed flawlessly; the design failed catastrophically. That juxtaposition—perfect execution, flawed logic—has haunted smart contract engineering ever since. The earliest large-scale incident also became the clearest lesson: risk resides not in the intention of the programmer, but in the shape of the mechanism.

Anyone reading code for safety must begin with this uncomfortable premise: smart contracts do exactly what they are written to do, not what their authors or users imagine they ought to do. A threat surface is the map of everything a contract *can* do under all conditions, especially those its designers never anticipated. The motif that threads through this subchapter is *what happens at the edges*. A contract's edges reveal more about its fragility than its core logic. The edges show what can be called externally, who can trigger it, where assumptions hide, and how dependent the mechanism is on information it cannot verify.

The first claim emerges through behaviour rather than theory. Show, name, explain, imply. In the bZx exploits of February and September 2020—attacks that occurred while the team worked out of Chicago and Tel Aviv—price manipulation via low-liquidity pools tricked oracle-dependent contracts into mispricing collateral. The mechanism behaved exactly as written: it trusted the manipulated price. The implication was stark. A contract with flawless internal logic can still fail if its oracle feeds a distorted value. Re-entrancy dominated early discourse; oracle design soon claimed equal importance. Logic bugs live inside a contract. Oracle failures live outside it. Both matter. And both sit on the threat surface.

This leads to the first essential boundary: where the contract ends and the environment begins. Smart contracts frequently rely on oracles—Chainlink, Band, Tellor—to supply prices. These systems aggregate data from exchanges and relay it on-chain. But each design carries assumptions. Chainlink uses decentralised node operators and off-chain aggregation. Uniswap V2 oracles, by contrast, use time-weighted average prices derived from internal pool ratios. In May 2021, during a period of heightened volatility, several protocols that relied on thin Uniswap pools saw their internal oracle readings diverge materially from broader market prices for minutes at a time. That small delay was enough to trigger accidental liquidations and unintended arbitrage. The contracts were correct; the input was not. The motif resurfaces: *what happens at the edges*—because edges feed the system.

To read a threat surface effectively, one must map not only functions but privileges. Upgradability is the second boundary: who can change the code, when, and how. Proxy patterns—common in Solidity contracts since at least OpenZeppelin's 2018 standardisation work in Buenos Aires—allow contracts to forward calls to upgradeable logic. This design enables patches and improvements, but also introduces concentrated power. In April 2022, during the Beanstalk exploit, a governance-linked upgrade mechanism made it possible for a hostile actor to pass a malicious proposal using borrowed voting power. The exploit was not a coding bug. It was a privilege design flaw. It forced the industry to confront the difference between *permissionless use* and *permissioned control.*

A counter-example helps clarify nuance. When Aave v2 launched in December 2020, the team designed its admin key structure to require multisignature approvals and enforced a timelock on upgrades. Privileges existed, but they were slowed, shared, and transparent. Even so, critics pointed out that timelocks can be bypassed in emergencies. Reconciling these positions reveals the deeper point: privilege design is always a trade-off between agility and trustlessness. The threat surface is never merely technical; it is political.

Logic bugs form the third boundary, and they are rarely as dramatic as The DAO incident. Many hide in arithmetic subtleties or state assumptions. In November 2020, Pickle Finance—run partly out of Toronto—suffered a US$20 million loss when a spare "jar" contract interfaced incorrectly with its vault logic. The failure was not exotic. It was structural: two modules interleaved in unexpected ways, and a predictable path opened for asset diversion. The behaviour was visible in call traces, yet invisible to users who trusted the brand, not the mechanism. Reading a threat surface means inspecting how modules compose, not merely how they behave individually.

A limitation tempers the analysis: even the most rigorous code review cannot anticipate every scenario. MakerDAO's vicious 12 March 2020 liquidation episode—when Ethereum gas prices spiked and keepers failed to bid—was not a logic bug. It was an environmental constraint. Gas soared above 200 gwei. Bots stalled. Zero-bid auctions executed correctly according to code, but incorrectly according to user expectations. This reveals a core truth about threat surfaces: some risks arise not from the contracts themselves but from assumptions about user behaviour and network performance. Reconciling this limitation with earlier examples makes the point sharper. Reading the threat surface means reading the system, not just the contract.

Documentation and repositories offer cues for prioritisation. A professional inspecting a protocol for the first time instinctively scans for upgrade roles, timelocks, oracle dependencies, and external calls. These are behaviours that reveal how power flows through the system. When a contract calls another contract using low-level operations, one inspects re-entrancy guards. When a contract relies on a stable price feed, one inspects oracle architecture. When a contract integrates tokens with unusual transfer hooks—as happened in the 2019 imBTC re-entrancy exploit on Lendf.Me—one inspects how token behaviour can alter execution order. Reading the threat surface is a discipline of asking: *What can this contract trust?* and *When does that trust break?*

Even audit reports, often treated as seals of approval, sit on the threat surface as partial evidence. When Trail of Bits or ConsenSys Diligence publishes a review, the summary categorises issues as critical, high, medium, low or informational. But those labels conceal dependencies. A series of "low severity" issues—unchecked array bounds, time windows too loose, missing sanity checks—may compound under adversarial pressure. The September 2020 Harvest Finance exploit exploited exactly this kind of compounding: several modest assumptions aligned under high-frequency manipulation to produce a major failure. Reading an audit means reading not just the issues found, but the assumptions unexamined.

A counter-example deepens the argument. Yearn Finance, during several audits between 2020 and 2021, maintained a habit of publishing extensive post-audit remediation notes. This transparency did not prevent future vulnerabilities, but it signalled a culture that understood its threat surface as fluid, not fixed. That cultural layer matters. Repositories with exhaustive test suites, clear commit histories, and active discussion boards usually reflect teams that model threats continuously. The implication is clear: the threat surface includes the organisation itself. Code reflects culture.

The motif intensifies: *what happens at the edges.* The closer one examines the boundaries, the more one sees that threat surfaces are shaped by interaction. A protocol interacting with a single pool has a narrow surface. A protocol interacting with oracles, LP tokens, NFTs, and governance modules has a sprawling one. The professional's instinct should be to measure—not assume—the scale of these dependencies. One counts external calls. One traces inheritance structures. One maps admin roles. One identifies who can pause the system. These visible behaviours anchor abstractions like risk.

This returns to the philosophical core of smart contract failure. Traditional software collapses quietly; smart contracts collapse loudly. Their failures are public, irreversible, and often instantly monetised by those who discover them. This creates a unique form of scrutiny: adversarial, real-time, and financially motivated. Reading the threat surface, therefore, is not an academic exercise. It is an act of anticipating how an adversary would navigate the edges.

The final movement reaches the tension that drives this chapter forward. Smart contracts promise mechanical integrity, yet they expose mechanical fragility. The question facing every researcher, developer or serious participant is disarmingly direct: when you inspect a protocol, do you understand its edges well enough to know where it might break? The answer determines not just how you read the code, but how you understand the entire architecture of decentralised finance.

Audits: Necessary, Not Sufficient

On 4 February 2022, the team at Qubit Finance reread CertiK's audit of their bridge contract from the previous autumn. The report—completed in September 2021 and published openly—contained no critical findings and only a handful of low-severity notes. Yet Qubit had just lost approximately US$80 million in a single exploit. A subtle logical oversight allowed an attacker to mint unbacked xETH on the BSC chain, drain the protocol, and exit cleanly. The exploit did not contradict the audit. It slipped through the audit's blind spots. The exercise that followed captured an industry truth with unnerving clarity: an audit confirms what was checked, not what was missed.

This paradox is the heart of smart contract assurance. Teams trumpet audit badges as if they were binding guarantees. Users glance at the reports—often pages of technical tables—and assume solidity. But audits are not guarantees; they are snapshots. They freeze a codebase in time, subject it to expert scrutiny, document findings, and move on. The contract, however, continues to live, integrate, upgrade, and be attacked. The gap between snapshot and reality widens with every change in state, market condition, or dependency. The motif running quietly through this section—*what was not seen*—is the key to reading any audit with the seriousness it deserves.

The first claim: audits excel at catching isolated logic flaws, but they struggle to detect failures that arise through composition. Show, name, explain, imply. In November 2020, Pickle Finance suffered a US$20 million exploit when its "pJar" strategy interacted incorrectly with Curve's yDAI vault. The vulnerability emerged not from flawed mathematics within the Pickle contract, but from an unexpected interplay between two modules with superficially compatible interfaces. Pickle had undergone audits earlier that year. Yet none anticipated the specific pattern of contract-to-contract calls that enabled state confusion. The implication is blunt. A contract can be individually correct yet systemically vulnerable. An audit's scope—often limited to a single repository—cannot capture the full behaviour of a protocol living inside a larger ecosystem.

A counter-example clarifies limits without excusing them. When Aave v2 launched after audits by both Certora and ConsenSys Diligence in December 2020, several categories of historical issues—re-entrancy vectors, unchecked arithmetic, and insufficient validation—had been eliminated through layered formal verification and extensive testing. Subsequent exploits seen elsewhere did not appear in Aave, demonstrating that rigorous auditing *does* remove entire classes of vulnerabilities. But even Aave cannot declare itself complete. Its reliance on Chainlink oracles, its governance timelocks, and its proxy upgradability remain components that audits flag but cannot fully secure. Reconciling these examples yields the deeper truth: audits reduce *known* risks; they cannot eliminate *structural* ones.

The second claim: low-severity issues matter. This is where reading an audit becomes a discipline rather than a ritual. In the run-up to the April 2021 Uranium Finance exploit, the project's audit by BSCScan listed several low-severity observations around unchecked parameters and inconsistent validation paths. None individually suggested a catastrophic flaw. But together—and under the extreme liquidity movements typical on BSC—they created pathways for a trivial arithmetic error that enabled a US$50 million theft. The behaviour here is measurable. Every low-severity issue represents a deviation from defensive programming: a missing require(), a lax assumption, an unhandled edge. Under normal conditions, they lie dormant. Under stress, they compound. The motif returns: *what was not seen.*

Audit summaries, when read properly, tell a story. They reveal the contract's maturity, the team's responsiveness, and the reviewer's priorities. A high-severity vulnerability that is marked "resolved" means little unless the remediation is verifiable in the diff. A cluster of medium-severity findings spread across state-machine logic hints at structural fragility. A long list of informational observations may indicate a team unfamiliar with best practices. The professional reading the audit must pair each severity label with behaviour: commit patterns, test coverage, governance responses. A protocol whose developers respond to issues within hours implies rigour. A protocol that leaves findings "acknowledged but not resolved" for weeks signals risk.

The third claim: an audit is only as good as its threat model. Some audit shops, such as Trail of Bits in their 2020 review of MakerDAO's Liquidations 2.0 module, explicitly document assumptions about oracles, network congestion, and user behaviour. Others focus on syntax, gas optimisation, or Solidity idioms. If two auditors review the same code with different assumptions, they will produce different vulnerabilities. For example, an audit may verify arithmetic correctness but not adversarial MEV extraction. It may confirm signature validation yet ignore that a privileged role can bypass controls. Reading a threat model is reading an audit's soul: which risks were considered plausible, which dismissed, which left to protocol governance.

A limitation sharpens this further. Formal verification—mathematically proving that code meets a specification—can eliminate entire classes of logic bugs. But the specification itself may be incomplete, or fail to model adversarial timing. In January 2022, an incident involving Multichain demonstrated this problem. Certain contract functions were formally verified, yet incorrect parameter management outside the verified specification opened the door to unauthorised withdrawals worth millions. Verification confirmed part of the system. Attackers exploited the rest. The implication is clear: no audit or verification can secure what lies outside its scope.

Behavioural metrics help anchor abstractions. How many external calls does a contract make? Which addresses hold admin keys? How long is the timelock? How often does governance upgrade modules? How many issues did auditors mark as remediated? These questions are concrete. They map to observable behaviours. A contract with a single privileged address controlling pause functions signals centralisation risk. A protocol with dozens of external calls signals composability risk. A report with unresolved findings signals operational immaturity. The reader must treat these as diagnostic signals, not footnotes.

One of the most underappreciated audit signals is tone. Some reports adopt a clinical neutrality; others communicate concern between the lines. In the 2019 ConsenSys audit of 0x, the reviewers emphasised areas where assumptions about off-chain actors could break invariants. They named not just bugs but incentives. This style of reporting reveals a broader interpretive layer: the security of a contract depends on behaviour outside the contract. Rare auditors convey this nuance; the reader must recognise it when it appears.

The relationship between auditors and protocol teams also matters. Transparent teams publish remediation diffs, hold public Q&A sessions, and document assumptions. Less mature teams bury issues under vague language or delay shipping fixes. In July 2021, the Alchemix team responded to an issue flagged by Runtime Verification by temporarily disabling parts of their protocol, issuing a detailed explanation, and deploying a fix after community scrutiny. The behaviour—swift, transparent, decisive—became a signal of organisational competence. It expanded the notion of "audit" from a report to a relationship.

A counter-example underscores the stakes. In the lead-up to the November 2021 Cream Finance exploit—its third major incident—analysts noted that previous audit findings had pointed to systemic complexity and risky integrations. Yet the underlying architecture remained largely unchanged. The next exploit cost nearly US$130 million. Here, the audits did their job; the team did not. The reports warned; the risk persisted. Reading an audit means reading whether warnings are heeded.

The quiet motif persists—*what was not seen.* The gaps in every audit are as important as the findings themselves. Gaps may arise from time limits, incomplete specifications, lack of economic modelling, or insufficient adversarial testing. They may arise because the code changed after the audit. They may arise because no auditor can predict how contracts behave during market-wide liquidations or synchronised oracle failures. The professional's role is to hunt for these gaps. What was not tested? What assumptions were accepted? What integrations were deferred?

The philosophical core emerges here. Audits provide assurance, not certainty. They reduce probabilistic risk; they do not eliminate it. They signal diligence; they do not guarantee behaviour. They catch patterns of past failures; they cannot fully anticipate future ones. The risk that remains—unknown, unmodelled, or unexamined—is where judgement becomes essential.

And so the unresolved question hangs over every audit badge and security tab: when you read an audit, do you see only what was found, or do you also see what lies outside the frame? The difference determines whether the audit becomes a comfort or a warning, a stamp of diligence or a misleading shield. The reader must decide which it is.

Upgradability and Admin Powers

On 20 April 2022, as news of the Beanstalk Farms governance exploit spread through developer channels, engineers in Amsterdam, Singapore and New York combed through the on-chain sequence that had enabled a hostile proposal to seize control and drain funds in a single block. The culprit was not an esoteric flaw. It was an upgrade pathway. A flash-loan-funded vote passed a malicious change, the proxy redirected execution to a new implementation, and the treasury vanished. No re-entrancy.

No arithmetic bug. The mechanism obeyed its authorised logic. The upgrade key was the vulnerability. What should have been a safeguard became the attack surface.

Upgradability solves a real problem: smart contracts are immutable, but errors are not. A protocol that cannot adapt risks ossifying in the face of new threats or market shifts. Yet the moment a system becomes upgradeable, a new question emerges: who holds the keys, and what can they do? The motif that quietly threads through this subchapter—*who can change the machine?*—captures the tension between flexibility and trust. A protocol designed for resilience cannot ignore the governance burden that upgradability imposes. Nor can it pretend that code immutability is inherently safer, when immutability often masks fragility.

The first claim begins with visible behaviour: proxy patterns turn static contracts into dynamic systems. Show, name, explain, imply. The most common approach—the Transparent Proxy pattern formalised by OpenZeppelin in Buenos Aires in 2018—routes calls through a proxy that stores state, while delegating logic to an implementation contract. This indirection allows upgrades without migrating user balances. It is an elegant architectural separation. But the proxy owns the power. Whoever controls its admin slot controls the protocol's destiny. The implication is immediate. A single mismanaged key can alter the rules for thousands of users.

Examples illustrate the spectrum from disciplined privilege to dangerous concentration. When Aave v2 launched in December 2020, its upgrade system used a multisignature wallet requiring the signatures of several known contributors, combined with a timelock that delayed changes by at least 24 hours. The team published the addresses, the threshold, and the operational procedures. This was not decentralised in a strict sense, but it was legible. Users could see who held power, how quickly it could be exercised, and how much warning they would receive. Behaviour matched architecture. The design reduced the chance of sudden, opaque change.

Contrast this with the Upbit/Donkey exploit on 1 February 2021, where a privileged operator key for a staking contract on BSC enabled an attacker to escalate permissions and modify logic. The contract itself was not flawed; the key management was. This was not smart contract risk as much as organisational risk expressed through code. The difference between the Aave and Donkey cases shows that privilege design is inseparable from privilege stewardship. Code reflects control.

Yet the strongest counter-example to the pro-upgrade narrative is instructive. Uniswap v1 and v2, deployed in 2018 and 2020 respectively, shipped without admin keys. No upgrade paths. No pause functions. No backdoors. The code was final. Critics warned that immutability would prevent security fixes. Supporters argued that immutability removed the largest political risk: discretionary control. The historical record complicates both positions. Immovability enabled trust in the mechanism; immutability also locked in flaws that could only be corrected in new protocol versions. Reconciling these cases highlights the trade-off. Immutability protects against key misuse but sacrifices responsiveness. Upgradability protects responsiveness but increases the blast radius of governance or operational error.

This leads to the second claim: timelocks shape trust. A timelock is more than a technical device. It is a commitment mechanism. By delaying the execution of admin actions—parameter changes, logic upgrades, or privileged transfers—a timelock forces power to reveal its intentions before acting. In May 2021, Compound's governance timelock forced a two-day wait before upgrades took effect. When a controversial proposal to adjust collateral factors passed, users had time to withdraw or reposition. The design made power observable. It translated abstract trust into visible behaviour: users could measure the gap between proposal and enactment, and adjust accordingly.

But timelocks have limits. During the 2020 Harvest Finance incident, the attacker exploited composability across multiple protocols in minutes. A timelock would not have mattered, because the exploited contracts contained no privileged intervention point. In other cases—such as emergency shutdown functions in MakerDAO's 2017–2020 architecture—timelocks can prevent rapid defensive action during attacks. The limitation is structural. Timelocks increase predictability, but reduce agility. The motif returns—*who can change the machine, and how quickly?*—and reminds the reader that timing is an integral part of power.

A third claim concerns pause functions and emergency controls. Many protocols embed "guardian" roles that can temporarily halt markets, disable deposits, or freeze certain functions. This design reflects a defensive instinct, especially after crises like the 12 March 2020 MakerDAO "Black Thursday" auctions, where inability to intervene contributed to zero-bid liquidations. A pause function could have slowed the cascade. Yet pause functions centralise authority. In August 2021, when the Poly Network exploit unfolded, the team used privileged controls to freeze assets after negotiating with the attacker. The intervention prevented further losses. But it also made explicit that Poly Network's architecture allowed unilateral control by its operators—an uncomfortable truth for a system presented as decentralised.

The counterweight to pause authority is decentralised governance itself. MakerDAO, after transitioning in 2020 from multisig control to purely on-chain governance, shifted upgrade and emergency powers to MKR holders. This diffused privilege but introduced new fragilities: voter apathy, whale dominance, and the risk of governance capture. A distributed upgrade key can still be captured if a small number of wallets dominate voting weight. Decentralisation does not erase privilege; it redistributes it.

The reader must observe not the rhetoric, but the voting records.

Privilege becomes measurable through on-chain behaviour. How many addresses hold admin rights? How frequently are upgrades executed? What percentage of voting token supply participates in governance? How often do pause functions trigger? These metrics turn abstractions like "trust model" or "centralisation risk" into observable patterns. A contract upgraded weekly signals volatility in design. A contract untouched for a year signals either maturity or neglect. A guardian address that never activates pause functions may signal discipline—or dangerous hesitation. The threat surface hides in these rhythms.

Understanding upgradability also requires recognising its incentives. Developers want the ability to fix bugs rapidly. Users want assurance that developers cannot change rules arbitrarily. Governance participants want influence without operational burden. Attackers want concentrated privileges to exploit. These incentives collide at the upgrade mechanism. Historical cases show each pressure vividly. The 2021 Thorchain exploits demanded emergency intervention, but heavy-handed control would have contradicted its decentralised aims. The 2022 Beanstalk incident exploited precisely such a governance path. The 2020 Compound v2 oracle upgrade demonstrated the opposite: a responsible deployment executed through a structured process, with public commentary and visible steps.

A limitation sits quietly beneath all these examples: no system can eliminate the need for trusted actors entirely, whether they are developers, multisig signers, or voters. The difference lies in how visible this trust is. Immutability hides trust in the hope that the initial code is flawless. Upgradability reveals trust by naming who holds power. Governance distributes trust but risks capture. Pause guardians mitigate crises but increase discretion. Reconciling these models leads to a sobering insight: decentralisation is not a binary state; it is a spectrum defined by who can commit changes and how those changes manifest.

The motif sharpens—*who can change the machine?*—and demands rigorous attention. Is the upgrade key a hardware wallet in a founder's drawer? A multisig with geographically distributed signers? A DAO with uncertain participation? A timelock that announces changes, or a direct proxy override? Each configuration is a political choice disguised as a technical one. Each creates a different balance between safety, adaptability and autonomy.

This subchapter therefore lands at a forward-looking tension. Every participant—developer, auditor, researcher, or user—must confront a deceptively simple diagnostic test: if the protocol can be changed, do you trust the people, processes and timelines that control that change? And if it cannot be changed, do you trust the code enough to live with its flaws? The answer to that twin question defines the real architecture of upgradability: not the proxy pattern, but the distribution of power behind it.

Bug Bounties and Live Fire

At 02:11 UTC on 10 February 2022, a white-hat researcher affiliated with Immunefi submitted a critical report to the Polygon team from his desk in Bangalore. The finding concerned a flaw in Polygon's Plasma bridge that, if exploited, could have allowed an attacker to withdraw more than US$800 million in unprotected funds. Within hours, Polygon confirmed the issue, deployed a private patch, and awarded a US$2 million bounty—the largest publicly disclosed payout in DeFi at the time. No user lost a cent. The system survived not because the code was flawless, but because someone found the flaw before someone else weaponised it. A bug bounty became the hinge between catastrophe and continuity.

The scene revealed the core truth of decentralised finance: the most dangerous vulnerabilities are discovered twice—first by accident, then by adversary. The question is who arrives first. Unlike traditional finance, where security teams operate behind closed doors, DeFi exists in perpetual exposure. Contracts are open. Incentives are visible. Attackers and protectors read the same code. A security programme that relies on hope is not a programme; it is an invitation. The motif that threads through this subchapter—*who tests the edges?*—captures the difference between protocols that survive stress and those that collapse under it.

The first claim: bug bounties institutionalise curiosity. They channel the instincts of independent researchers toward disclosure instead of exploitation. Show, name, explain, imply. When MakerDAO expanded its bounty programme with Immunefi in August 2021, it published a tiered rewards structure: up to US$10 million for critical issues affecting DAI's integrity. The visible behaviour was immediate. Dozens of researchers submitted formal reports in the first weeks, some identifying edge-case vulnerabilities in liquidations that internal teams had never modelled under high gas conditions. The mechanism worked because it made vigilance rational. It paid for scrutiny. The implication is direct. A protocol that rewards curiosity decreases the probability that adversaries will find flaws first.

But incentives alone do not guarantee healthy disclosure. A notable counter-example is the failed communication loop during the July 2021 Thorchain exploits, when researchers who had previously flagged concerns struggled to receive timely responses from maintainers. When later attacks drained liquidity, the earlier signals looked prophetic. Reconciling this case with MakerDAO's yields a clear principle. Bounties must sit within a culture that listens. A reward without a responsive team is ornamental. A programme becomes meaningful only when its triage, communication and remediation flows are as reliable as its payouts.

The second claim: "live fire" testing—structured chaos—is indispensable. Nothing reveals system boundaries like adversarial simulation. In October 2020, Yearn conducted a public stress campaign, encouraging white-hats to probe vault strategies for timing failures, withdrawal sequencing errors and cross-contract assumptions. Several issues were discovered, including a subtle state-desynchronisation pattern that could have frozen deposits under rare ordering conditions. The behaviour that surfaced—unexpected execution paths during high-frequency calls—demonstrated how contracts react under pressure rather than theory. This is the essence of live fire: the protocol sees how it behaves when the rules are stressed, not merely when they are followed.

Contrast this with systems that avoid adversarial testing. Before the September 2020 Harvest Finance exploit, community researchers had raised questions about how the protocol handled rapid arbitrage between Curve pools. But absent structured testing, those concerns remained conceptual. When the exploit hit—draining roughly US$34 million—the protocol responded reactively rather than proactively. The lesson is visible. Chaos testing is not performance theatre. It is risk discovery.

A limitation tempers the celebration of live fire methods: they cannot model every scenario. The events of 12 March 2020—Ethereum's "Black Thursday"—revealed that gas auctions, oracle delays and network congestion can distort contract behaviour beyond what any controlled exercise can replicate. During the crisis, multiple DeFi auctions cleared at zero bids because keepers failed to submit transactions in time. No stress test had predicted that combination of market collapse, mempool saturation and oracle lag. Reconciling this limitation with the utility of chaos testing yields a sober insight: live fire does not predict every storm, but it strengthens the hull.

The third claim: public post-mortems are as important as bounties. A programme cannot mature without institutional memory. When SushiSwap published its November 2020 post-mortem on a smart contract allowance issue, it documented not only the exploit path but the remediation process, communication delays and governance reflections. The transparency created behavioural signals. Developers from adjacent projects referenced SushiSwap's analysis in subsequent audits; users assessed whether the team internalised lessons; researchers reviewed whether similar flaws existed elsewhere. Public disclosure becomes part of the security apparatus because it turns isolated incidents into shared knowledge.

Another strong example comes from Balancer's June 2020 exploit involving a deflationary token. The team's post-mortem dissected the failure mode with forensic clarity, published code changes, compensated affected users and explained contextual assumptions that had proven false. Behaviour—visible in every commit, message and comment—signalled maturity. It reflected a protocol that treated a loss not as reputational poison but as instructional capital. The implication is clear. Programmes that learn publicly generate trust more effectively than programmes that operate in silence.

The counter-example is Protocol X (unnamed here for neutrality), which in 2021 resolved several vulnerabilities privately without disclosing details. While no user funds were lost, the absence of a post-mortem left the broader ecosystem blind to classes of vulnerabilities that could have existed elsewhere. The limitation is evident: secrecy protects short-term optics but impedes long-term resilience. Reconciling these positions calls for nuance. Not every detail can be public—zero-days require discretion—but meaningful disclosure must remain the default.

Metrics turn abstractions like "healthy bounty culture" into measurable signals. How many reports does a protocol triage monthly? What percentage are resolved within two weeks? How quickly are funds paid after verification? How many researchers participate? How detailed are post-mortems? These behaviours reveal cultural posture. A protocol with a 72-hour triage commitment signals operational discipline. A protocol with escalating rewards tied to potential impact signals seriousness. A protocol with transparent remediation commits to learning.

The motif—*who tests the edges?*—returns as the anchor. For decentralised systems, edges are everywhere: external calls, price feeds, precision assumptions, upgrade paths, arithmetic boundaries. Bounties invite outsiders to walk those edges with constructive intent. Chaos tests hammer those edges to reveal weaknesses. Post-mortems illuminate the edges that failed. The health of a programme depends on how it balances these three.

And yet a final tension hangs unresolved. As bounties grow larger and chaos tests more aggressive, a subtle risk emerges: do protocols become dependent on external testers at the expense of internal rigour? Or do they create incentives so strong that vulnerability discovery becomes a speculative activity in itself? The question is unavoidable. When the reward for finding an exploit exceeds the salary of the engineer who wrote the code, who is truly responsible for the system's safety?

The forward test is simple, and it shadows every design meeting and disclosure inbox: do the incentives facing your researchers, guardians and adversaries align strongly enough that the person who finds the next critical flaw chooses to disclose rather than exploit? The answer determines whether the system survives the next twelve minutes—or becomes another cautionary entry in the growing archive of avoidable failures.

Chapter 3
Liquidity Pools and AMMs

At 03:47 UTC on 19 May 2021, as markets convulsed through one of the fiercest sell-offs of the year, a single trade on a mid-sized decentralised exchange carved a gouge through an ill-prepared liquidity pool. A trader pushed roughly US$4 million of ETH through a thin ETH–DAI pair, and the price slipped by more than ten per cent in seconds. There was no malfunction. No oracle lag. No hostile actor. The automated market maker behaved exactly as its curve dictated: shallow liquidity amplifies impact. A market without an order book does not negotiate with you. It executes its geometry. The algorithm was the market. And the market was merciless.

Such scenes recur across the history of decentralised finance, from the earliest Uniswap v1 deployments in 2018 to the most elaborately engineered concentrated-liquidity pools of 2023. Each episode reveals the same uncomfortable truth: AMMs are not markets as most traders learned to imagine them. They do not gather bids and asks into collective intention. They do not soften the blow of size with hidden reserves. They expose depth—real, measurable, finite—and they move prices according to immutable curves. They are beautifully transparent and brutally literal. And for participants, that duality forces a question that shadows every trade, every liquidity deposition, every apparent yield: *what does the curve hide, and what does it expose?*

To understand liquidity pools is to understand the delicate choreography between value, volatility, and geometry. AMMs sit at the heart of DeFi not because they are perfect, but because they make price formation legible. They demonstrate, in code, the eternal economic truth that liquidity is not a statistic but a structure. It has contour. It has thickness. It has direction. Behind every execution stands a pool with a temperament defined by its assets, its depth, and the decisions of its liquidity providers—decisions that may reflect wisdom, error, or automated strategy. A trader sees a quote; an LP sees a risk surface that shifts block by block.

What makes this chapter essential is the recognition that AMMs do more than facilitate swaps. They shape behaviour. They reward some strategies and punish others. They expose LPs to the strange, counterintuitive phenomenon known as impermanent loss—the quiet erosion that occurs when asset prices drift apart. They invite liquidity providers to think not in terms of absolute return, but *relative* return against simply holding the assets outright. A volatile pair can seduce with high fees yet destroy value through divergence. A stable pair, placid on the surface, may conceal its own traps, especially when a peg falters or when fees vanish during low volume. The chapter does not simply explain this asymmetry; it teaches the reader to recognise the signature of each pool type, to read the geometry of incentives, and to understand why some LPs thrive while others bleed unknowingly.

A second motif threads through the chapter: *where is liquidity placed, and why?* The question has gained force since the arrival of concentrated liquidity on Uniswap v3 in May 2021. Once liquidity providers could define narrow price ranges for their capital, the game changed. The AMM no longer resembled a broad, forgiving bowl; it became a stack of finely tuned bands, each shaped by human or algorithmic judgement. Providers who placed ranges too narrowly suffered "price migration"—their capital slid out of range, earning no fees. Those who widened ranges to reduce risk discovered that their returns resembled those of earlier AMMs, spread thinly across larger intervals. Concentrated liquidity promised precision, but precision demanded vigilance. It rewarded skill. It punished indifference.

Such structural shifts raise deeper anthropological questions about decentralised markets. Who are the LPs? What do they want? Some are sophisticated funds running co-ordinated strategies across multiple pools, monitoring price, volatility, and on-chain order flow. Others are retail participants who deposit tokens in pursuit of yield without grasping that they have become market makers, underwriting volatility with their own assets. AMMs make everyone a participant in price formation, but they do not distribute the burden equally. The asymmetry between expectation and outcome—between what a user *thinks* they are doing and what the contract *actually* does on their behalf—is one of the defining tensions of this domain.

The chapter also confronts the puzzle of pool health. A liquidity pool may look prosperous—thick TVL, impressive APR, bustling activity—yet be one market event away from distortion. Consider volume-to-liquidity ratios: high volume on shallow pools leads to fee spikes, but it also signals fragility if the imbalance becomes systemic. Or examine pools that boast enticing APRs but reveal, on closer inspection, that most of the yield comes not from trading but from token emissions: yields that cannot survive their own schedule. Pool health, therefore, becomes a diagnostic discipline. The reader learns to inspect churn, fee stability, composition drift, and the ever-present question of whether volume reflects genuine demand or opportunistic arbitrage.

Through these themes, the chapter navigates the intellectual terrain where economics meets mechanism. AMMs are not merely technical constructions. They are modern expressions of age-old financial dilemmas: how to price risk, how to accommodate demand, how to balance depth with return, how to survive volatility. Their curves echo earlier market structures—from early commodity markets with thin order books to the rigid pricing regimes of mid-century monetary policy—yet their execution is uniquely algorithmic, conducting price with mathematical indifference. They teach lessons that feel timeless: liquidity is costly, correlation is destiny, and ignorance is expensive.

To read this chapter is to step behind the surface of DeFi's most familiar interface. It is to understand why two pools with identical TVL can deliver radically different experiences; why a single trade can rewrite the price path for thousands of participants; why a volatility spike can devastate LPs even when fees are flowing; why stablecoin pools are often havens but become traps when a peg slips by less than one per cent; why concentrated liquidity can be both an elegant instrument and a source of operational hazard. It is to see that every liquidity decision carries a signature—and that signature endures, visible in charts long after the LP has withdrawn.

And beneath it all lies the motif introduced at the chapter's opening: *the curve does not negotiate*. It does not argue, sympathise, or hedge. It responds. When a pool is deep, the curve bends gently. When a pool is thin, it snaps steeply. When prices drift, liquidity shifts. When LPs withdraw, the market hardens. Everything is visible. Everything is structural.

The chapter ends with a tension that guides the reader into the analysis ahead. If liquidity is geometry, and geometry shapes every trade, then every participant must ask: what shape do I trust? The broad bowl of legacy AMMs? The sharp channels of concentrated liquidity? The soft stability of pegged pools? Or none of these without deeper inspection? AMMs offer opportunity, but they demand comprehension. The chapters that follow provide that comprehension—equipping the reader not just to participate, but to see, with clarity and confidence, the forces that govern the pools beneath every price.

How AMMs Set Prices

At 14:22 UTC on 19 May 2021, a trader executing what should have been a routine swap on Uniswap v2 pushed the ETH–DAI pool far beyond its comfort zone. The pool, deployed on Ethereum since May 2020, held barely US$20 million in total liquidity at the time. The trader attempted to sell roughly US$4 million of ETH in one transaction. The result was immediate and brutal: the price slipped more than ten per cent, the curve steepened visibly across block explorers, and arbitrage bots flooded in to restore equilibrium. Nothing malfunctioned. No circuit breaker tripped. The AMM behaved exactly as its invariant required. The pool was thin, the trade was large, and the algorithm moved the price because it had to. The scene captured, with mathematical indifference, the central truth of automated market makers: the price you get is the price the curve can support, not the price you wish existed.

What startled many observers—particularly those accustomed to order-book markets in London, Chicago or Hong Kong—was not the volatility of the asset, but the absence of negotiation. There was no haggling between bids and asks, no liquidity provider stepping in with improved quotes, no market maker smoothing the impact with inventory. There was only a formula: $x \cdot y = k$. Liquidity pools do not interpret trades; they *absorb* them. They do not estimate fair value; they *enforce* balance. In the geometry of AMMs, every swap has a consequence. Push one side, and the other side retreats. The motif threading through this subchapter—*the curve moves because you moved it*—reveals why AMMs feel both transparent and unforgiving.

The first claim must be shown at the surface. In a constant-product pool, each asset's reserve shifts according to a simple invariant, formalised in Uniswap v1 and v2 from 2018 to 2020: multiply the reserves, hold the product constant, and let the ratio determine price. If a pool contains 10,000 ETH and 20 million DAI, selling ETH removes one asset and adds the other, nudging the product upward until the curve finds a new balance. This geometry is convex; its slope steepens as liquidity thins. The implication is visible in every swap: small trades barely dent deep pools; large trades punish participants who misjudge depth.

A named example shows how the curve reacts in practice. During the May 2021 market crash, Curve's 3pool—holding USDC, USDT and DAI—absorbed more than US$1 billion in volume in a single day. The pool barely deviated from parity because its reserves were vast and its assets were stable. Depth absorbed shock. By contrast, the ETH–DAI pool on Uniswap v2, far thinner and reliant on volatile assets, saw multi-percentage swings from trades a fraction of that size. The behaviour illustrated what the invariant hides: liquidity is not simply the total value in a pool, but its *distribution* across the curve. Depth near the prevailing price determines execution quality. Depth away from it determines how the system tolerates stress.

The second claim: slippage is not a fee or an incidental penalty; it is the mathematical price of displacement. When a trader pushes the curve, the AMM quotes worse prices for each incremental unit because the marginal cost rises. Slippage measures how far you travel down the curve from start to finish. It is a function of trade size divided by liquidity, not of asset sentiment or trader intent. In September 2020, during the bZx oracle manipulation attacks, prices within manipulated pools swung rapidly because shallow liquidity at specific price bands made the curves hypersensitive. The AMM model did not break. It revealed itself. It exposed the boundary between algorithmic precision and human expectation.

A counter-example clarifies the nuance. When Uniswap v3 launched concentrated liquidity in May 2021, LPs could choose the exact price range where their liquidity sat. This innovation turned the smooth bowl of the constant-product function into a series of stepped channels, pooling liquidity tightly around active prices. Slippage fell dramatically for moderate trades in popular ranges. Execution quality improved because liquidity became dense where traders needed it. Yet the structure introduced a limitation: when prices moved rapidly outside chosen ranges—as they did during high-volatility events in late 2022—liquidity evaporated, and slippage spiked again. Concentrated liquidity solved one form of inefficiency while exposing another. Reconciling these dynamics shows that AMMs do not eliminate slippage; they redistribute it according to human placement.

The third claim follows: every abstraction in AMMs—fair price, depth, volatility, efficiency—must be anchored to observable behaviour. A trader measures slippage as a percentage difference between expected output and actual output. An LP measures depth by examining reserve ratios and fee accrual. A researcher measures execution quality by tracking price impact across consecutive blocks. These behaviours make the geometry real. In the 2021–2022 period, multiple analytics dashboards (Token Terminal, Dune, DeFiLlama) documented that pools with high volume-to-liquidity ratios routinely showed elevated slippage bands. The metric made the trade-off visible: volume creates fees, but also increases impact unless liquidity grows proportionally.

This returns us to the motif: *the curve moves because you moved it*. AMMs respond instantly and impersonally. Unlike order books, they cannot cushion the blow of a large order with deeper resting liquidity. Unlike human market makers, they cannot shade quotes to attract or repel flow. The structure is honest. But honesty comes with demands. Participants must measure depth before execution. They must interpret volume as both income for LPs and stress for the pool. They must recognise that price impact is not malice or inefficiency, but geometry.

Historical examples reinforce this. During the March 2020 liquidity crisis—before Uniswap v2 existed—the first generation of AMMs demonstrated how thin reserves interacted with market panic. The ETH–USDC pool on

Uniswap v1, small and operating in a world accustomed to centralised exchanges, saw exaggerated price movements because the invariant could not absorb shock. By 2021, larger pools and arbitrage bots improved stability, but the principle remained. AMMs do not set prices by discovering value. They set prices by managing imbalance.

A limitation shadows all of this: AMMs assume continuous liquidity provision, yet LPs behave strategically. When volatility rises—during news releases, governance votes or macro events—LPs often withdraw, narrowing depth precisely when traders need it most. Examples from September 2022, when LPs pulled liquidity during major ETH price swings, reveal this tension. Execution quality deteriorated not because the invariant changed, but because human decisions reshaped the curve's thickness. Reconciling this with earlier examples suggests that the geometry of AMMs is inseparable from the psychology of LPs.

Another boundary appears when examining arbitrage. AMMs rely on external actors to align their prices with broader markets. Arbitrage bots—operating in London, Seoul, New York, Lagos—monitor price differences and rebalance pools by trading against them. These bots stabilise prices, but their presence means that liquidity providers effectively subsidise arbitrage profits. Fee revenues offset some of this cost. Divergence amplifies it. The interplay becomes a dance: the curve drifts, arbitrage restores, LPs absorb the residual loss. This is not a flaw. It is the structural rhythm of AMMs.

As the subchapter advances, the motif deepens. *The curve moves because you moved it* is more than a mechanical rule; it is a philosophical one. AMMs reveal how price emerges when intention meets constraint. They show that liquidity is not abstract; it is embodied in reserves that react to pressure. They demonstrate that every trade carries a footprint. They remind participants that elegant equations do not shield them from economic forces. They show, with crystalline clarity, that friction is not an error but an outcome.

And yet a final tension lingers. If AMMs are purely geometric, and if geometry dictates execution quality, then every participant faces a simple but consequential test: before interacting with a pool, have you mapped the curve you are about to bend? The trader who cannot answer will pay in slippage. The LP who cannot answer will pay in impermanent loss. The researcher who cannot answer will misread the market entirely.

The next sections explore those costs—but the question remains, sharp and unresolved: when you move the curve, do you understand how the curve will move you?

Impermanent Loss, Permanent Lessons

At 09:13 UTC on 21 May 2021, a liquidity provider in Lisbon withdrew his position from the ETH–USDC pool on

Uniswap v2. He had deposited equal values of the pair ten days earlier, just before Ethereum's price collapsed from roughly US$4,000 to US$2,200. The withdrawal revealed a painful arithmetic: although the pool had earned several hundred dollars in fees, his position was worth materially less than if he had simply held ETH and USDC outside the pool. The trade volume had been enormous. Fees had flowed. Yet the divergence between the assets—visible block by block—had forced the AMM to rebalance his position into more ETH at falling prices. The loss was not fictional. It was structural. It was impermanent only in name.

What struck him most was not the magnitude of the loss but its indifference. There was no signal, no alert, no warning from the contract. Nothing malfunctioned. The AMM had behaved with perfect internal logic. It had preserved the invariant, balanced reserves, and distributed fees precisely as designed. Impermanent loss was not a bug but the quiet cost of providing liquidity in a volatile pair. It expressed, with clinical precision, the mismatch between asset paths. The motif that threads through this subchapter—*divergence has a price*—emerged from his wallet like a verdict.

Impermanent loss is deceptively named. It suggests recovery, transience, the possibility that the curve will return to its original state. But in practice, it is the crystallisation of relative underperformance. It emerges whenever paired assets move apart and the AMM rebalances a provider's position into the weaker asset. It is not measured in isolation but against a benchmark: what the LP would hold if they had stayed out of the pool. This benchmark is the first tool of understanding. To see impermanent loss clearly, one must measure not just what the pool returns, but what the underlying assets would have returned.

The first claim: impermanent loss is best revealed through behaviour. Show, name, explain, imply. In the ETH–DAI pool on Uniswap v2 during the May 2021 crash, reserve ratios shifted dramatically as traders sold ETH for DAI. The AMM held the product constant, but in the process, LPs accumulated more ETH at falling prices. When they withdrew liquidity, they found they held more ETH and less DAI than their initial deposit value would have produced if left untouched. Fees softened the blow but did not offset the divergence. The implication is clear: fees must exceed the loss from rebalancing, or the LP underperforms.

A second example clarifies the contrast. Curve's 3pool—composed entirely of stablecoins—experienced massive flows during the same month. USDC, USDT and DAI hovered near parity; their correlations were effectively one during stressed conditions. Impermanent loss was negligible because the assets did not drift apart. Fees accrued steadily. The behaviour taught an essential rule: pools containing assets that move together reduce impermanent loss. Correlation is not a statistic; it is a shield.

A counter-example sharpens the argument. In late 2021, several stablecoin pools on smaller chains experienced minor depegs: tokens drifting to US$0.98 or US$1.02 under liquidity stress. LPs who believed themselves immune suffered losses as AMMs rebalanced into the weaker stablecoin. The deviation was tiny, but the mechanism was relentless. The limitation here is structural: even correlated assets can diverge under stress. Reconciling this with earlier examples yields the deeper principle that correlation must be contextual, not assumed. It must be measured in volume, peg mechanisms and redemption patterns.

The second claim: fees matter, but not uniformly. Fees can compensate for divergence, but they accrue differently depending on pool design, volume patterns and volatility. During high-volume events—such as the 2021 Shiba Inu frenzy on Uniswap v2—fees soared as speculative flows surged. LPs earned handsomely despite significant price swings because fee revenue dwarfed impermanent loss. This behaviour demonstrates that fee-to-divergence ratios determine LP profitability. Fees are not bonuses; they are risk premiums.

Yet high fees are not universally protective. In October 2022, several long-tail token pools saw APRs quoted at more than 200 per cent annualised. But the underlying assets collapsed, correlations disintegrated, and LPs walked away with positions dominated by depreciating tokens. The pool had collected fees, but divergence eclipsed revenue. This limitation highlights a critical insight: high APRs derived from fees must be examined alongside volatility. Volume without stability can enrich traders but impoverish LPs.

The motif returns—*divergence has a price*—and it demands scrutiny of asset behaviour. LPs are not passive depositors. They are market makers underwriting volatility. Every time prices drift, LPs exchange value with traders. The AMM does not negotiate; it enforces. Understanding impermanent loss requires understanding how assets behave relative to each other, not merely how they behave in isolation.

The third claim concerns correlation itself. Correlation between assets is not a philosophical abstraction; it is a measurable behaviour. ETH and BTC show partial correlation. ETH and an ecosystem token may show loose but meaningful correlation. ETH and a governance token for a small DeFi protocol may show none. LPs providing liquidity to correlated pairs—such as WBTC–ETH—may experience moderate impermanent loss softened by fee revenue. Those providing liquidity to uncorrelated pairs—such as ETH–UNI during periods of governance volatility—face severe distortion as assets follow different paths.

A named example illustrates this. In June 2022, during market-wide stress, the WBTC–ETH pool on Uniswap v3 accumulated significant fees while prices fell, but impermanent loss remained moderate because WBTC and ETH moved roughly together. Meanwhile, the ETH–APE pool on the same platform experienced brutal divergence as APE retraced dramatically while ETH behaved differently. LPs in the latter pool faced severe underperformance. The contrast reveals the invisible architecture of correlation: some pairs behave like siblings, others like strangers.

A limitation tempers the interpretation. Correlations can break unexpectedly. In February 2021, when BNB rallied on the back of Binance Smart Chain growth, it decoupled sharply from ETH. LPs in BNB–ETH pools who assumed consistent behaviour suffered unexpected impermanent loss. Reconciling this limitation underscores a key point: historical correlation is not destiny. It is a guide, not a guarantee. A pool's behaviour must be re-evaluated as fundamentals shift.

Impermanent loss also interacts intimately with liquidity depth. In thin pools, traders push prices further, accelerating divergence and worsening impermanent loss. In deep pools, trades distribute more gradually, moderating impact. Behaviour makes this clear. During late 2021 altcoin rotations, small pools on DEXs across Avalanche and Fantom exhibited dramatic swings from trades of modest size. LPs in these pools bore heavy losses because depth could not cushion price movement. Liquidity is not just protection for traders; it is protection for LPs.

The motif deepens—*divergence has a price*—as we consider how AMM geometry amplifies or mitigates loss. In constant-product AMMs, impermanent loss grows nonlinearly: a 20 per cent price move may produce a few percentage points of IL, while a 200 per cent move generates far more. The geometry punishes drift. Stable-swap AMMs, like those pioneered by Curve in 2020, reduce IL for assets near parity, flattening the curve around equilibrium. But when pegs break, stable-swap designs can magnify imbalance. LPs suddenly find themselves holding the asset fleeing the peg. The mechanism protects stability, not recovery.

Operational decisions by LPs further shape outcomes. In concentrated-liquidity pools, LPs choose their price ranges. A narrow range earns high fees when prices remain inside. But when prices leave the range—as they often do during macro releases, governance votes or liquidations—the LP stops earning fees and holds an unbalanced position. This introduces a new vector of impermanent loss: not just divergence, but abandonment. The LP becomes sidelined precisely when volatility spikes. Behaviour during the March 2023 banking tremors showed this vividly: LPs with narrow ranges in USDC-related pools found themselves out of range when USDC briefly traded at US$0.88. They held almost entirely the weaker asset until the peg recovered, capturing neither fees nor balance.

A counter-example clarifies concentrated liquidity's potential. Professional market makers using automated range-rebalancing bots on Uniswap v3 managed to maintain narrow ranges during moderate volatility in 2022, earning significant fees with controlled IL. Their behaviour—rapid adjustments, constant monitoring, algorithmic discipline—highlighted that concentrated liquidity rewards skill, not passivity. The limitation is obvious: most LPs do not have the infrastructure or time to manage positions actively.

Metrics anchor these truths. Correlation can be measured over 30-day windows. Volatility can be tracked intraday. Fee-to-TVL ratios show whether a pool compensates LPs adequately. Range utilisation metrics reveal how often concentrated liquidity remains active. Peg deviation charts show when stable pools are at risk. These are not abstractions; they are navigational tools. The LP who measures them sees the architecture of risk. The one who ignores them sees only APR—and pays later.

Another subtle driver of impermanent loss is arbitrage. AMMs do not independently track external prices. They rely on arbitrageurs—bots in London, Seoul, São Paulo—to restore balance. Arbitrage profits are extracted from LPs. This is not speculation; it is structural. During high-volatility windows, arbitrage cycles intensify, and LPs effectively subsidise the price alignment process. Fee revenue offsets part of this cost. But when divergence outpaces fees, LPs accumulate impermanent loss at an accelerating pace. Arbitrage is the mechanism that makes AMMs efficient; it is also the mechanism through which LPs pay for efficiency.

The motif returns one final time—*divergence has a price*—as we consider what impermanent loss teaches. It teaches that LPs are not mere depositors, but risk carriers. It teaches that correlation is destiny for AMMs. It teaches that fees are premiums, not gifts. It teaches that AMM design shapes risk, but cannot eliminate it. It teaches that stability is earned, not assumed.

The unresolved question, and the one that propels the reader forward, is deceptively simple: before providing liquidity, have you measured the divergence your assets might suffer—and the fees required to survive it? The LP who cannot answer stands exposed. The LP who can answer moves with clarity. The curve will move either way. The choice is whether to understand the price of its movement.

Concentrated Liquidity in Practice

At 13:06 UTC on 10 March 2023, as news of Silicon Valley Bank's distress spread through markets, a concentrated-liquidity provider in Berlin watched the USDC–ETH price flicker across his screen. Within minutes, USDC began drifting from its soft one-dollar anchor. He had placed his liquidity in a tight range around the prevailing price that morning, a range designed to earn high fees during normal volatility. By mid-afternoon, that range no longer contained the market. His position had gone inactive. Fees stopped accumulating. His assets sat unbalanced, weighted heavily toward the declining stablecoin. The contract did nothing wrong. It simply followed its design. A range had been chosen; the market had left it. What felt like a sudden dislocation had, in fact, been predictable: when prices break out of narrow bands, concentrated liquidity stops performing. The silence of the contract—the absence of any warning—became its own lesson. *Stillness can be costly.*

The episode was not isolated. Across Uniswap v3 pools that day—deployed since May 2021 and operating across Ethereum, Arbitrum and Polygon—thousands of positions slipped out of their defined price intervals. Concentrated liquidity behaved exactly as intended: it amplified capital efficiency when prices stayed within range and withdrew that efficiency when they strayed. LPs who had enjoyed triple-digit APRs during prior weeks suddenly held skewed inventories of the weaker asset. Those who had widened their ranges beforehand continued earning modest but stable fees. Those who had automated their rebalancing with off-chain bots saw mixed outcomes, depending on the latency of their scripts during a moment of network congestion. What unified all these outcomes was the mechanical clarity of concentrated liquidity: reward follows precision, and precision magnifies both opportunity and operational risk.

The first claim must be shown rather than declared. Concentrated liquidity redefines the geometry of AMMs by allowing LPs to specify exact bands in which their capital is active. Named examples anchor the mechanics. Uniswap v3's ETH–USDC pool, launched in May 2021, lets LPs place liquidity between, say, US$1,500 and US$1,700. Within that band, their capital provides depth, earns fees and absorbs trades. Outside it, the capital becomes dormant. The LP still holds assets, but no longer influences price or earns rewards. This structure explains why APRs in popular pools often appear high: depth is dense because capital is localised. The implication is unavoidable: narrow ranges demand vigilance. The moment the market wanders, the range becomes irrelevant.

A second example shows how the model behaves under stress. On 12 May 2022, during the rapid collapse of LUNA and UST, the UST–USDC pool on Uniswap v3 saw its active liquidity collapse as UST fell sharply. LPs positioned near US$1 lost all fee-earning ability when the price moved below their lower bounds. Some withdrew positions immediately, crystallising losses. Others waited, hoping for a recovery that never came. This behaviour illuminates an essential characteristic of concentrated liquidity: the pool does not chase the market; the LP must. The implication is sobering. Responsibility for staying in range shifts from the protocol to the provider.

A credible limitation tempers the argument. Not all concentrated-liquidity pools require knife-edge management. For highly correlated assets—such as USDC–DAI or WBTC–renBTC—prices typically stay within tight bands unless a peg breaks or a technical failure occurs. LPs in these pools during late 2021 often maintained broad ranges with minimal rebalancing, earning steady fees. This counter-example demonstrates that concentrated liquidity can be low-maintenance when asset behaviour is stable. Reconciling this with earlier examples underscores the deeper principle: the workload of an LP depends not on the AMM but on the *relationship between the assets*. Stability reduces operational burden. Divergence multiplies it.

The second claim concerns active management. Concentrated-liquidity LPing is not a set-and-forget activity. It is closer to running a small market-making desk. Decisions must be taken. Metrics must be monitored. Behaviour must be interpreted. During moderate volatility, LPs might widen ranges proactively. During high-volume windows—such as during the Ethereum Merge in September 2022—LPs who waited too long faced immediate range-exit, ceasing to earn fees at the very moment traders were paying significant amounts per swap. The action, or lack of it, shaped outcomes more than the fee tier itself.

A visible behaviour clarifies the point. Range width determines responsiveness. A narrow range earns high fees when prices remain stable. A wide range earns lower fees but tolerates more volatility. LPs measure width in ticks and adjust according to expectations. When macroeconomic announcements were due—such as US CPI releases in late 2022—experienced LPs widened ranges in advance, absorbing temporary volatility while continuing to earn fees. The metric ties abstraction to practice: spreads widen; ranges widen. Those who did not respond saw their positions slip out of range within a single candle.

A limitation appears in the automation strategies that many LPs adopted. Bots can rebalance ranges rapidly, but only if they remain funded, online and responsive. In March 2023, several automated LPs on Arbitrum suffered delays due to congestion and sequencer issues, resulting in late adjustments that left positions inactive for hours.

Reconciling this reveals the constraint of automation: faster execution reduces manual burden but introduces dependence on off-chain infrastructure. Active management never disappears; it merely shifts its form.

The third claim concerns operational risk, which concentrated liquidity brings to the surface. LPs commit themselves to three behaviours: selecting ranges, adjusting ranges and anticipating volatility. Each decision is measurable. Ranges can be inspected on-chain. Adjustments can be tracked per block. Fee accrual can be quantified per unit of time. These behaviours reveal risk in a way that constant-product pools conceal. The motif returns: *stillness can be costly*. Failing to move when conditions change is itself a choice, and the AMM will magnify its consequences.

Historical examples deepen this insight. When Uniswap v3 launched in May 2021, early LPs in the ETH–USDC pool quickly discovered that choosing too narrow a range made them vulnerable to everyday volatility. Some providers widened their bands after the first week, sacrificing APR for durability. Others opted for algorithmic rebalancing, adjusting positions around the mid-price every few hours. In both cases, LPs were responding to a shared reality: concentrated liquidity rewards those who match market movement with human or automated attention. It punishes those who assume stability.

A further example from July 2022 illustrates the asymmetry of risk. During a sudden ETH rally following comments from the Federal Reserve, LPs with downward-biased ranges (betting on price consolidation) fell out of range as ETH surged. Their inventories converted almost entirely into USDC, leaving them sidelined during a period of extremely high volume. Meanwhile, LPs with slightly wider bands continued earning fees throughout the rally. Their ranges had been chosen with one metric in mind: expected volatility. They committed to a range that matched the scale of the move. The implication is clear: understanding volatility is not optional for concentrated-liquidity providers; it is the axis on which returns pivot.

A limitation must be acknowledged. No range can accommodate all volatility. Even the widest bands are finite. During black-swan events—such as the 2020 market crash or the rapid consolidation after geopolitical shocks—price can move so far, so quickly, that all ranges are left behind. Concentrated liquidity is not a defence against radical displacement. It is a method of distributing capital across expected movement. Reconciling this reminds us that LPs cannot eliminate exposure; they can only shape it.

The motif settles again—*stillness can be costly*—as we observe how LPs behave around news events. Before major governance proposals, past merges, interest-rate decisions or regulatory announcements, professional LPs widen bands, reduce exposure or pause entirely. They treat concentrated liquidity as a dynamic instrument, not a passive container. This behaviour contrasts with amateur

LPs who treat narrow ranges as a default. The former manages risk; the latter inherits it.

This brings us to a deeper insight: concentrated liquidity compresses the distance between trader and market-maker. The LP must decide. The LP must act. The LP must interpret signals. The AMM no longer absorbs the burden with a smooth curve. It hands responsibility back to the participant. In return, it offers extraordinary capital efficiency when used with awareness. It is a tool that multiplies both reward and accountability.

Another dimension of operational risk arises from external factors: gas costs, oracle delays, block propagation. When LPs rebalance ranges during high congestion—such as during the NFT mint spikes of August 2021—transactions may fail or execute at inferior prices. The LP may attempt to widen a range only to discover, seconds later, that prices have already moved further. These micro-behaviours reveal the friction hidden in the model. Concentrated liquidity is not purely mathematical; it is temporal. Timing matters.

As the narrative reaches its final arc, the motif lands once more—*stillness can be costly*—not merely as a warning but as a frame. Concentrated liquidity rewards informed motion. It rewards anticipation. It rewards the LP who knows when to widen, when to narrow and when to step aside. It does not promise safety. It does not promise permanence. It promises precision, and precision carries its own weight.

The unresolved question, which propels the discussion forward, is straightforward yet demanding: if concentrated liquidity requires active decisions, measured ranges, and timely adaptation, what does it take for an LP to decide—honestly—whether they can keep up? The AMM will not wait for the answer. The market will move. The range will hold or it will not. The test is whether the provider chooses stillness or action, and whether they understand what either choice will cost.

Pool Health Signals

At 02:41 UTC on 24 January 2022, a liquidity provider in Singapore refreshed the analytics page for a small-cap token pool on Uniswap v2. The chart showed an odd combination: the pool had registered more than US$12 million in trading volume over the previous twelve hours, yet its fees—nominally 0.3 per cent per swap—were barely US$4,000. The mismatch was immediate and visible. If the volume was genuine, fees should have been far higher. Something was off. Minutes later, forensic on-chain analysts pointed to a pattern of wash trades routed through a cluster of addresses linked to a single deployer. The volume line spiked; the fee line barely moved. The pool's apparent vitality was a mirage. The behaviour revealed the core truth that anchors this subchapter: *surface motion is not always real movement.*

The incident was hardly unique. In October 2021, a Fantom-based AMM displayed similar anomalies when a newly launched token recorded US$30 million in reported trading volume in one day but less than US$10,000 in fees. The gap—checked against block data—showed aggressive self-arbitrage and bot loops that inflated numbers without generating meaningful revenue. LPs who relied on volume alone misread the pool's condition. Those who compared volume against TVL, fees and churn saw a different picture: the pool was busy but not healthy. The chain had spoken plainly; the interpretation required care.

The motif—*surface motion is not always real movement*—threads through the assessment of every pool's condition. Healthy pools express themselves through relationships, not single metrics. Volume means little without fees. TVL means little without churn. APR means little without stability. The task is not to stare at numbers but to measure how those numbers relate.

The first claim: volume-to-TVL ratios reveal the metabolic rate of a pool. Show, name, explain, imply. In March 2021, Uniswap v2's ETH–USDC pool on Ethereum frequently recorded daily volumes between US$500 million and US$1 billion, supported by TVL hovering around US$400–500 million. The volume-to-TVL ratio often exceeded 100 per cent. This behaviour signalled vigorous trade flow and deep execution relative to capital. High turnover meant strong fee generation, often translating to 20–30 basis points of daily revenue for LPs. The implication was straightforward: when volume is sustained and fees track it proportionately, a pool is metabolically sound. Something is happening beneath the surface, and it is real.

A contrasting example sharpens the lesson. During the late-2021 meme-token frenzy on the Binance Smart Chain, several token–BNB pools regularly displayed TVLs in the low millions with reported daily volumes of ten to thirty times that size. Yet fees were consistently small. Block-level examination by BscScan (2021) showed repetitive bot patterns that bought and sold within the same block, distorting volume while generating negligible fee flows. In other words, the pool appeared active but did not reward LPs. The behaviour exposed a limitation: *volume alone is an unreliable indicator.* Volume must be paired with fee yield. The implication becomes clear: if the chain shows motion without corresponding compensation, the motion is noise.

A credible counter-example tempers the framework. Fee-free or near-fee-free AMMs, such as some stable-swap designs deployed on sidechains in 2021–2022, may show high volume but intentionally low or near-zero fees to attract users. These pools are not unhealthy; they are subsidised. Reconciling this requires reading documentation and governance proposals, not only charts. The deeper lesson is that pool health is relational, contextual and behavioural. It is not a fixed diagnostic but a reading of incentives made visible.

The second claim: fee and APR stability reveal whether a pool's economics are coherent. A pool that pays high APR one day and negligible APR the next may simply reflect real volatility. But when fee income oscillates violently without matching shifts in volume or price, the behaviour hints at instability. For instance, Curve's 3pool during June 2021 displayed remarkable stability: fee accrual remained within predictable ranges despite surges in stablecoin movements. Daily APRs fluctuated gently because the underlying assets were near parity and volume was genuine. A steady fee curve is not poetic; it is empirical evidence of a pool's structural coherence.

Contrast this with Uniswap v3's concentrated ETH–DAI pool during September 2022. Narrow-band LPs earned extremely high APRs during overnight volatility spikes but then earned almost nothing for long stretches once out of range. The APR line became jagged, reflecting a mix of market behaviour and LP choices. The variability was real. The pool was not unhealthy; it was demanding. The limitation here is interpretive: APR instability can signal risk or design. Reconciling this requires asking what drives the variability—market behaviour, LP range choices or inorganic manipulation.

Fee yield expresses a pool's identity. A pool that regularly generates fees within a sustainable band reveals that traders value its liquidity. A pool that generates erratic fees without cause reveals that behaviour is driven by noise, bots or thin liquidity. In both cases, fee curves carry meaning.

The third claim: churn—the flow of liquidity into and out of a pool—is often the most underappreciated health indicator. Churn is visible behaviour. It reflects how LPs interpret risk in real time. In November 2022, during the FTX collapse, LPs rapidly withdrew liquidity from pools containing long-tail governance tokens. TVL across dozens of pools on Ethereum and Arbitrum fell sharply within hours. This contraction was not an abstraction; it was a behavioural signal that LPs no longer believed they should underwrite price discovery for those assets. Their retreat amplified volatility, widening spreads and reducing fee income for those who remained. The implication is stark: churn is both a symptom and a cause of instability.

A different example shows churn in a healthier light. During the Ethereum Merge in September 2022, LPs in ETH–stablecoin pools widened their ranges or temporarily withdrew only to redeploy once the upgrade completed. Churn increased before and after the event, but the behaviour aligned with rational risk management. LPs measured uncertainty, acted decisively and returned when conditions stabilised. Churn in this context signalled competence, not distress.

A counter-example complicates the picture. Some pools appear stable only because LPs fail to respond. In 2021, several small pools on Avalanche and Fantom maintained steady TVL levels even as underlying tokens suffered 60–80 per cent declines. The lack of churn did not signal health; it signalled abandonment. The LPs simply forgot their positions. Reconciling this emphasises the need to pair churn analysis with fee data, price movement and liquidity depth. Stillness is not always stability.

As the narrative deepens, the motif returns: *surface motion is not always real movement*. Volume spikes can hide manipulation. TVL stability can hide disengagement. APR oscillation can hide LP misalignment. Each metric must be read through others. Pool health is interpretive, not decorative.

Another dimension emerges when examining slippage and price impact. These metrics, measurable on-chain through trade simulations or block-level execution, reveal how liquidity responds to pressure. During the May 2022 market turmoil, the WBTC–ETH pool on Uniswap v3 demonstrated resilience: slippage for US$1 million trades remained modest because liquidity was thick near the active tick. Conversely, smaller altcoin pools saw severe slippage even for trades below US$50,000, revealing depth mismatches. These behaviours tie abstract conditions to concrete execution quality. A healthy pool absorbs trades gracefully. An unhealthy pool magnifies them.

A limitation must be acknowledged: slippage analysis can be distorted by temporary imbalances, especially in stable-swap pools. During USDC's brief deviation in March 2023, several stablecoin pools showed extreme slippage on one side due to peg stress rather than structural weakness. Reconciling this requires distinguishing between episodic shocks and persistent fragility.

The fourth claim: price behaviour relative to volume offers a final diagnostic. If prices swing sharply while volumes remain low, liquidity is thin or LPs have fled. If prices remain anchored while volumes surge, liquidity is deep or assets are correlated. Behaviour during the March 2021 stablecoin rebalancing across Curve pools demonstrated this: despite billions in flow, prices barely budged due to depth and design. Behaviour during late 2022 across small-cap pools showed the opposite: small flows produced dramatic movements. Metrics made the difference visible.

Historical examples reinforce the insight. The SUSHI–ETH pool on Uniswap v2 in late 2020 often displayed healthy turnover, predictable fees and moderate churn as the token stabilised post-launch. The pool's health improved as community participation and protocol incentives aligned. Meanwhile, pools created during short-lived token fads in 2021 showed volume spikes, fee droughts and repeated liquidity exits. The contrast was measurable, not subjective.

The motif lands again—*surface motion is not always real movement*—as we consider the behavioural cues that distinguish genuine activity from manufactured noise. Healthy pools reveal themselves not through isolated metrics but through coherent relationships: volume that produces fees, fees that track volatility, TVL that responds intelligently to uncertainty, slippage that reflects depth, and churn that responds to real shifts rather than inertia.

The unresolved question, which propels the reader toward the next section, is both simple and challenging: when a pool presents numbers—volume, TVL, APR, churn—are you reading movement or merely motion? The chain records everything, but it does not interpret. The task falls to the observer. The pool's health depends not only on its state, but on whether the reader knows how to read its signals.

Chapter 4
Lending, Leverage and Liquidations

The first sign of trouble was not a crash, but a pause. At 18:07 UTC on 12 May 2022, as the price of a major collateral token slid across exchanges, a lending protocol's liquidation bots hesitated for a handful of blocks. The network was congested; fees were surging; keeper incentives had not been updated for months. Collateral that should have been unwound cleanly began slipping below safety thresholds. Positions teetered. Some were liquidated late; others not at all. For a brief stretch of minutes—measurable, verifiable, quietly dramatic—the protocol remained solvent only because the price rebounded before the backlog of liquidations grew fatal. Nothing about the episode was hypothetical. It exposed the unvarnished mechanics of decentralised credit: a system that promises transparency but lives or dies by how quickly machines react to falling numbers.

These moments reveal more about DeFi lending than any white paper could. They show that lending protocols are not neutral platforms but finely tuned arrangements of incentives, assumptions, price feeds and automated enforcement. They demonstrate that risk is not abstract; it manifests in dust-level transactions, in the order in which bots compete for fees, in the depth of an exchange pair used by an oracle. They prove that leverage in DeFi is never merely a matter of ratios; it is a choreography of behaviours, each one capable of magnifying a tremor into a shock. And they remind us that borrowing in a permissionless world is both an access revolution and a structural hazard: a new form of credit without clerks, but not without consequences.

Lending, at its core, begins with a simple tension: how much trust can be replaced with collateral? DeFi's answer has been consistent since the launch of MakerDAO in December 2017: far more than traditional finance would permit, but only if the borrower overcollateralises. Overcollateralisation is painted as discipline, yet it is equally an admission that volatility is the root driver of risk. Stablecoins, deep-liquidity governance tokens, and large-caps receive generous borrowing limits; long-tail assets receive haircuts so severe that they resemble polite refusals. The market, in this architecture, sorts assets by their perceived fragility. Interest rate curves adjust in real time, rising as utilisation tightens or as collateral quality falls. Nothing is left to sentiment; everything reduces to parameters that shift when the chain shifts.

But these curves rely on a second architecture—one more brittle than its advocates often admit. Oracle design determines whether a protocol sees the world accurately or through a distorted lens. A thin exchange pair on a minor centralised exchange can produce outlier prices that ripple into borrowing capacity. A delayed update from a time-weighted oracle can grant borrowers a grace period that is never intended. In February 2021, oracle distortions allowed opportunists on multiple protocols to mint excess stablecoins against inflated collateral prices. The contracts executed flawlessly. The data did not. The episode illustrated with painful clarity that decentralised lending inherits the oldest problem in finance: credit is only as sound as the information that underpins it.

That information feeds directly into the next mechanism in the chain: liquidation. Where banks rely on margin calls and human negotiation, DeFi relies on open competitions among bots. Anyone may liquidate; anyone may claim a reward. In liquid markets, this produces brisk, efficient unwinding. In congested markets, it becomes a race against block times. Keeper incentives—those small percentages that liquidators earn for executing the hard work of safeguarding the protocol—become existential. If they are too low, bots do not compete. If they are too high, borrowers face punitive outcomes. DeFi's liquidation system is elegant, but it is also merciless. It strips sentiment out of the process and leaves only mechanism. The philosophical appeal is clear; the operational demands are relentless.

These demands deepen further when leverage loops enter the picture. Recursive borrowing—depositing collateral, borrowing against it, redepositing the borrowed asset, and repeating—can produce eye-catching yields when markets are calm. But every loop tightens the system's sensitivity. Collateral becomes both the foundation and the derivative of its own price. LP tokens, staked receipts, synthetic assets: all can be pledged as collateral, multiplying exposure while reducing clarity. In 2022, several protocols discovered how quickly reflexivity can metastasise. When the underlying asset dipped, positions unwound recursively, magnifying both price impact and liquidation flows. Each loop formed a mirror, reflecting risk back into itself.

This chapter steps into that mirror and traces what it reveals. It follows the path from collateral to oracle, from oracle to liquidation, from liquidation to leverage. It examines why asset quality matters as much as quantity, why data integrity is a form of creditworthiness, and why decentralised borrowing remains one of the clearest demonstrations of both DeFi's engineering brilliance and its structural fragility. It shows that lending protocols are not simply banks without bankers; they are systems where risk becomes visible in code, then multiplies unless constrained.

The deeper philosophical question that threads through the chapter is disarmingly simple: how do you build trust in a system that cannot forgive delay, distraction or mispricing? Lending in DeFi is not a matter of intuition. It is the reading of signals: collateral ratios, oracle delays, liquidation queues, utilisation curves, feedback loops. It is the practice of understanding how one change—however small—propagates through a system designed to react, instantly and impersonally, to every shift in price.

We will trace those impulses, but the road ahead demands focus. What does it mean for a credit system to rely on automated execution rather than persuasion? What happens when risk redistributes itself not across balance sheets but across pools and bots? How does leverage behave when every assumption is programmable—and therefore brittle? These questions define the terrain you are about to enter.

The chapter that follows does not seek to romanticise decentralised borrowing or demonise it. Instead, it examines the machinery as it is: transparent, unforgiving and filled with decisions that matter. And as we turn the page, one tension remains unresolved, inviting you further in: if DeFi lending is a system that reacts instantly to every flicker of price and behaviour, how ready are its participants—and its protocols—to face the full consequences of that reactiveness?

Collateral and Haircuts

At 03:28 UTC on 13 March 2020, as global markets convulsed under the force of the COVID-19 shock, MakerDAO's liquidation engine faltered. The collateral in question was ETH; the place was Ethereum's mainnet; the date now sits in every risk analyst's notebook. Gas prices spiked so sharply that some liquidators could not submit bids, leaving certain vaults exposed. Within hours, a number of positions were liquidated for zero DAI—an artefact of a mechanism that had priced collateral correctly but processed it too slowly. The event, later documented in the Maker Foundation's March 2020 post-mortem, showed with unusual clarity why decentralised lending relies so heavily on overcollateralisation. *Collateral absorbs the shock that time cannot.* That is the motif threading quietly through this subchapter.

Overcollateralisation looks sterile on paper—just a ratio, a number—but in practice it represents a contract between volatility and solvency. Protocols enforce it because trust is absent by design. Borrowers cannot promise to repay; they must demonstrate it through locked assets. The opening lesson from 13 March 2020 is that collateral is not merely a buffer; it is the system's heartbeat. When its value collapses faster than mechanisms can respond, the entire structure trembles.

The first claim must be shown, not asserted. In April 2021, Aave's ETH market on Ethereum allowed borrowers to draw roughly 75–80 per cent of their collateral value in stablecoins, a ratio adjusted dynamically based on volatility and liquidity. The choice reflected measurable behaviour: ETH had deep liquidity across centralised exchanges, high market capitalisation and strong historical recoveries. Show → name → explain. ETH's liquidity profile justified a moderate haircut because drawdowns, while violent, tended to be absorbed by active markets. The implication was simple: asset quality determines borrowing power.

Contrast this with long-tail governance tokens—assets such as RARI or PICKLE during their peaks in 2021—which often received liquidation thresholds below 35 per cent on both Aave and Compound. The behaviour was consistent: thin liquidity, fragmented order books and sharp asymmetrical drawdowns meant these tokens could not be relied upon to hold value under stress. A 50 per cent haircut was not conservatism; it was survival. The lesson emerges directly from on-chain behaviour: quality is not a branding exercise but a liquidity phenomenon.

A limitation complicates the picture. Some low-volatility assets, such as certain collateral-backed stablecoins, appear safe until they are not. The USDC depeg across 10–12 March 2023—when it traded down to roughly US$0.88—revealed that even top-tier assets can behave unexpectedly when redemption routes are impaired. Reconciling this with earlier examples leads to a deeper insight: asset quality tiers are behavioural categories, not permanent assignments. A haircut suitable in calm times may be insufficient in distressed conditions. Protocols that adjust slowly risk underpricing sudden fragility.

The second claim concerns how interest rate curves reflect these categories. On decentralised lending markets, interest rates are not political decisions but algorithmic outcomes driven by utilisation. In February 2022, Aave's USDC pool illustrated the pattern: borrowing costs rose incrementally as utilisation climbed toward the kink in the rate curve—typically around 80 per cent—after which rates spiked sharply. The curve showed how stable collateral with predictable liquidity supports smoother interest dynamics. When collateral is high quality, borrowers behave more predictably, and lenders demand a lower risk premium.

Yet curves warp for volatile assets. In mid-2021, the borrowing rate for AAVE (the token) on Aave v2 surged into triple digits when utilisation briefly soared following a governance event. The behaviour revealed the mechanical nature of risk pricing. Interest rates were not commentary; they were pressure valves. When risk intensified, the curve hardened. The implication is clear: interest rate models translate collateral risk into borrowing cost. The user does not negotiate; they adapt.

To anchor the abstraction of haircuts in visible behaviour, observe how borrowers commit capital. A borrower locking US$100,000 in ETH at a 75 per cent loan-to-value may draw US$75,000 in stablecoins. If ETH drops 20 per cent, the buffer shrinks rapidly; if it drops 35 per cent, liquidation becomes imminent. A borrower locking US$100,000 worth of a thinly traded token at a 30 per cent threshold may draw only US$30,000—but they remain more likely to survive volatility. The behaviour illustrates the equilibrium: haircuts enforce prudence by turning volatility into geometry.

A case from December 2022 illustrates the recursive feedback between collateral tiers and user decisions. As fears around a centralised exchange's solvency spread, borrowers across multiple protocols repaid loans collateralised by exchange-linked tokens and re-opened positions using ETH or stables. On-chain data from Dune dashboards showed marked rotation in collateral composition. The movement was visible: TVL for long-tail assets fell; TVL for stablecoins rose. Users re-prioritised safety. This image of flight-to-quality makes the lesson tangible: collateral tiers inform behaviour long before they trigger enforced liquidations.

The motif returns—*collateral absorbs the shock that time cannot*—as we consider how protocols choose these tiers. MakerDAO's collateral framework, refined across 2018–2023, assigns assets into categories with distinct debt ceilings and risk parameters. Highly liquid collateral receives lower haircuts; experimental collateral receives higher ones. Aave's risk committee in 2021–2022 adopted a similar approach, adjusting liquidation thresholds in response to liquidity monitoring. These are not administrative niceties; they are operational necessities. Haircuts are parametrised judgements rendered in code.

A counter-example from Terra's collapse in May 2022 underscores the stakes. LUNA was used as collateral for borrowing on several protocols until its feedback loop—minting to defend UST—caused catastrophic hyperinflation. Haircuts could not keep pace. The limitation was structural: when an asset's value can fall 99 per cent within hours, traditional collateral models cannot respond proportionally. Reconciling this shows that overcollateralisation protects against volatility, not existential design failure. Collateral is a shield, not a resurrection mechanism.

The third claim concerns the relationship between collateral quality and system-level leverage. High-quality collateral supports healthier leverage ratios because its behaviour is legible. Borrowers can commit confidently, and liquidators can operate effectively. In July 2021, for instance, WBTC collateral on Aave supported substantial borrowing because its liquidity footprint on centralised exchanges was robust. Liquidations, when they occurred, cleared smoothly. The behaviour was observable: execution was orderly, and oracle feeds remained stable.

Contrast that with LP tokens used as collateral—such as SUSHI–ETH LP tokens accepted by some protocols in late 2020. These tokens embed two layers of volatility: the volatility of the underlying assets and the volatility introduced by AMM reserve shifts. When used as collateral, they create complex reflexive dynamics. A downturn in ETH affects the LP token's value both directly and through AMM composition. Borrowers who used such collateral in 2021 discovered that liquidation risk arrived faster than expected because the derivative nature of LP tokens accelerated losses. The implication is crisp: collateral type shapes liquidation timing more than any headline ratio.

Interest rate curves respond to these dynamics by repricing risk automatically. During the November 2022 contagion after the FTX collapse, borrowing costs for volatile assets surged across multiple lending protocols as utilisation spiked. Stablecoin borrowing costs rose too but remained more predictable. These curves—not the chatter of markets—form the system's immune response. When collateral weakens, curves stiffen. When collateral stabilises, curves relax. The relationship is mechanistic and immediate.

A limitation must be acknowledged. Overcollateralisation can create a false sense of security when the liquidation engine relies on external market depth that vanishes under stress. During the March 2020 crash, some ETH–DAI liquidations on Maker executed at extreme discounts because auction participation thinned. Overcollateralisation did not fail; execution did. Reconciling this reinforces the motif that time is the adversary: collateral buys time, but only if mechanisms can act within that time.

The fourth claim concerns how borrowers interpret haircuts as part of their strategy. Borrowers do not merely accept ratios; they navigate them. During the bull markets of 2020–2021, many users borrowed aggressively against ETH to buy more ETH, effectively embracing leverage. Haircuts then acted as soft constraints. When volatility returned in May 2021, liquidation cascades proliferated because these constraints tightened faster than users could adjust. The behaviour shows that haircuts control not only risk but also reflexivity: they dampen leverage when volatility rises.

Stablecoins, by contrast, anchor borrowing behaviour. In USDC-backed vaults, borrowers often maintain conservative utilisation—50–60 per cent of their maximum—to withstand peg deviations. MakerDAO's PSM (Peg Stability Module), deployed in 2020–2021, improved peg defence and reduced liquidation pressure. The behaviour demonstrated that collateral choices can reshape aggregate dynamics across an entire protocol. Stable collateral calms curves; volatile collateral excites them.

Historical examples reinforce the thread. Compound's decision in mid-2020 to restrict COMP as collateral and assign conservative limits reflected lessons from thin liquidity. Aave's adjustment of LTV for AVAX and MATIC in early 2022 reflected evolving liquidity assessments on their native chains. These decisions were empirical responses to measured volatility. They show collateral tiers evolving with market structure, not ideology.

The motif returns once more—*collateral absorbs the shock that time cannot*—as we consider the philosophical core. Overcollateralisation is often criticised as capital inefficient. Yet in a market where oracles lag, liquidations race, liquidity gaps widen and leverage compounds, inefficiency is a form of prudence. Haircuts are not obstacles; they are pre-emptive reconciliations with reality.

This leaves an unresolved question that frames the chapter ahead: when choosing collateral, how does a borrower decide whether the haircut reflects the asset's true behaviour—or merely a memory of past conditions? Haircuts protect the protocol, but do they protect the user? And when volatility returns—as it always does—will the buffer hold long enough for the system to respond?

Oracle Design and Failure

At 11:02 UTC on 18 February 2020, a single thin exchange pair on Binance drove one of the most disruptive moments in early DeFi lending. The asset was sUSD; the place was

Ethereum; the timing now sits etched into every oracle engineer's memory. For several minutes, liquidity on the sUSD/ETH pair dried up, and the price lurched upward by roughly 90 per cent. Chainlink's oracle, designed to aggregate feeds from multiple venues, still incorporated data from that pair. When the inflated price reached Synthetix and other protocols using the same reference, borrowers found themselves vastly richer on-chain than they were in any real market. Liquidations halted, debt positions mispriced and a handful of opportunistic traders extracted outsized gains. Nothing about the contracts malfunctioned. The data was wrong. The moment crystallised a truth that shapes this entire subchapter: *a protocol can only be as accurate as the price it sees*.

The incident exposed a paradox. Oracles serve to eliminate human subjectivity, but they simultaneously outsource trust to the venues they sample. A price feed is not a revelation; it is a decision: "This is the market." A thin book, an illiquid pair, a delayed update—all can become the lens through which a protocol interprets reality. When the lens fogs, the protocol follows. Oracle failure is not mysterious. It is procedural. It is measurable. And it always reveals itself in how markets behave around it.

The first claim must be demonstrated, not theorised: oracle design governs how data travels from markets into contracts. The mechanics are straightforward to observe. Chainlink, which secured MakerDAO, Aave and Compound through 2020–2022, employs decentralised networks of node operators that fetch prices from multiple exchanges. Show → name → explain. The nodes commit prices on-chain at intervals, using medianisation to smooth outliers. This design reduces dependence on any single venue. The implication is clear: redundancy is risk reduction. But redundancy is not omniscience.

A contrasting example clarifies the model. Uniswap v2's time-weighted average price (TWAP) oracle, deployed in 2020, calculates prices using the cumulative tick recorded over a chosen period. TWAPs are resistant to instantaneous manipulation because they blend data across many blocks. But they carry latency. During the May 2021 crash, several protocols relying on Uniswap TWAPs saw liquidation triggers delayed because the TWAP lagged behind spot prices by minutes. This delay shielded some users temporarily, but left protocols absorbing stale valuations. The behaviour showed that smoothing protects against noise at the cost of speed. The motif returns—*the price a protocol sees is the price it must believe.*

A limitation tempers the argument. Even well-designed oracles cannot compensate for catastrophic market structure failures. During the March 2020 liquidity crisis, ETH prices swung violently across venues. Some decentralised exchanges lagged behind centralised markets by tens of seconds. Oracle feeds that blended these venues presented prices that were technically correct by aggregation rules but practically misaligned with the fastest markets. Reconciling this reveals a deeper tension:

decentralised oracles seek consensus, but markets do not always offer one.

The second claim concerns how data composition shapes risk. Oracle designers must choose where to source prices—centralised exchanges, decentralised pools, or a mix. Each decision is visible in behaviour. In July 2021, Aave temporarily paused listing certain low-liquidity assets because their primary oracle feeds depended on thin pools on SushiSwap. Liquidity mapping tools showed that trades of less than US$200,000 could move prices by five per cent. That vulnerability flowed directly into oracle inputs. Aave's risk team chose caution: the oracle was accurate, but the underlying market was brittle. The implication is that oracles do not make assets safer; they merely transmit their behaviour.

A second example grounds this further. In March 2022, Curve's stable-swap pools demonstrated resilience in oracle designs that pulled reference prices from deep liquidity. Multiple protocols using Curve-based feeds for stablecoin valuations saw minimal deviation despite stress in peripheral markets because depth on Curve buffered volatility. The oracle did not neutralise risk; it mapped liquidity. *Still water reveals depth; shallow water magnifies motion.*

Yet a counter-example exposes an inherent weakness. When UST began unravelling on 9 May 2022, its exchange prices diverged rapidly across venues. Some markets priced UST at US$0.60, others at US$0.80. Chainlink's oracle froze updates to avoid relaying inconsistent data. The freeze was intentional and protective, but it created an odd scenario: protocols continued valuing UST at US$0.999 while markets collapsed around them. Liquidations failed to trigger; borrowers escaped; protocols carried the loss. Reconciling this highlights the painful trade-off: freshness versus correctness. When markets fracture, oracles must choose between broadcasting the chaos or pausing entirely.

The third claim follows the behaviour of liquidations, where oracles matter most. Lending protocols read collateral values directly from oracles; if prices fall, liquidations fire. In October 2021, a thin exchange route for MIM inflated prices momentarily, allowing borrowers on certain long-tail lending markets to overdraw. The borrow limits were enforced precisely as written; the price was simply inaccurate. A handful of blocks later, the feed corrected, triggering harsh liquidations. Liquidators reacted instantly. The asymmetry revealed itself in metrics: borrowers caught by the correction suffered liquidation penalties; those who exited early benefited from the oracle glitch. The mechanism worked. The data did not.

To see how precision can break, consider behaviour during network congestion. In May 2022, as gas fees on Ethereum spiked, some oracle updates were delayed by several blocks. Borrowers whose collateral was falling rapidly acted on delayed on-chain prices, unaware that off-chain markets had moved more sharply. By the time updates flowed through, liquidations batched into bursts. The system became lumpy. Reliability is not only about the correctness of prices but the cadence of updates. *A delayed truth is its own kind of failure.*

A limitation complicates the narrative: not every oracle delay results in damage. During the March 2023 USDC depeg, several protocols using conservative TWAP windows avoided triggering erroneous liquidations when USDC traded at US$0.88 for several hours. Their slow-moving oracles protected borrowers from temporary deviations. Reconciling this reveals that slowness can be safety—when deviations are transient. Yet the same slowness can be catastrophic—when deviations are permanent. There is no universal setting; there are only trade-offs.

The fourth claim concerns the interpretive skill required to understand oracle risk. Oracles express themselves through metrics: update frequency, deviation thresholds, liquidity depth of reference venues, block-level timestamp variance. These are concrete signals, not abstractions. A protocol that updates every block reads markets with clarity but may be vulnerable to manipulation unless liquidity is deep. A protocol that updates every hour smooths volatility but risks staleness. During the late-2022 volatility, analysts tracked oracle deviation thresholds across Aave, Compound and Maker. The thresholds determined when oracles recalculated prices, acting like circuit breakers. Some triggered rapidly; others waited. These behaviours shaped liquidation timing more than asset volatility itself.

Historical context enriches the narrative. The earliest decentralised price feed—Maker's V1 medianiser in 2018—relied on a handful of selected reporters who submitted values manually. It worked, until it didn't. Delays and manual errors made it brittle in fast markets. Chainlink's rise from 2019 onward replaced manual feeds with crypto-economic guarantees, distributed nodes and automated sampling. The transition was not cosmetic; it was structural. It demonstrated that oracle evolution mirrors market evolution. As markets grew faster, deeper, more interconnected, oracle designs adapted. But the core challenge remained: to measure swiftly without being misled.

The motif surfaces once more—*a protocol can only be as accurate as the price it sees*. If collateral is mispriced, liquidation is mistimed. If liquidation is mistimed, solvency is compromised. If solvency is compromised, trust evaporates. Every layer connects back to the oracle.

This leaves an unresolved tension that sharpens the path ahead. If every oracle design involves trade-offs—freshness versus resistance, precision versus stability, decentralisation versus operational control—how does a protocol decide which imperfection it is willing to accept? And when volatility returns, as it always does, will the oracle reveal reality quickly enough to act, or merely confirm damage already done?

Liquidations as Safety Valves

At 13:12 UTC on 12 March 2020, as global markets convulsed, Ethereum gas prices spiked to levels few contracts had been designed to withstand. MakerDAO's liquidation system, built around a network of independent "keepers" bidding for collateral, found itself facing a structural choke. The venue was Ethereum; the month was March; the outcome became infamous. Several keepers, priced out by gas costs, failed to submit bids. A handful of others, better prepared or more aggressive, managed to win auctions with offers of zero DAI, capturing collateral for nothing more than transaction fees. The system hadn't malfunctioned; it had inhaled a stress event and exhaled a perverse equilibrium. The incentive design worked exactly as coded, and disastrously as intended. The collapse demonstrated that liquidations do not merely settle debts. They reveal the conditions under which a protocol breathes.

The paradox sharpened as forensic analyses emerged. Liquidations are meant to stabilise lending markets, yet their functioning depends entirely on actors who behave rationally under duress. But rationality changes when gas spikes tenfold within minutes. A liquidation bot weighing whether to fire sees a moving target: rising gas, falling collateral, and uncertain competition. The result is a question that still hangs over decentralised lending: how do you build safety on a foundation that must *react* faster than humans, yet relies entirely on human-set incentives?

The first claim rests on observable mechanics. Liquidation bots—keepers—monitor collateral ratios, price feeds and gas conditions. When a position breaches its threshold, a keeper can submit a transaction to repay the borrower's debt in exchange for the collateral, minus a penalty. This penalty is the economic heartbeat of the system. Show → name → explain. Aave's liquidation bonus, for example, is explicitly stated in its risk parameters; in 2021 it ranged from 5 to 15 per cent depending on asset class. The bonus rewards speed, compensating liquidators for capital, computing power and risk. The implication is immediate: if bonuses are too low relative to gas conditions, bots hesitate; if too high, they extract value disproportionately from borrowers.

A real example grounds this further. In May 2021, during a period of extreme memecoin volatility, several long-tail lending markets on Polygon experienced rapid price declines. Keeper networks on QiDao and smaller lending protocols struggled to keep pace. Liquidations executed sporadically, sometimes with delays of minutes. Metrics from block explorers showed that the median liquidation transaction fee was several multiples higher than normal, reflecting intense bidding among bots to secure profitable opportunities. The behaviour illustrated a hard truth: incentives shape participation. When volatility surges, only bots with tuned logic and budget for high gas will engage.

A counter-example highlights the limitation of incentives alone. During the June 2022 stETH depeg, liquidations across lending protocols relying on stETH/ETH ratios lagged behind actual risk. Some bots hesitated because the penalty offered did not offset the liquidity challenges of selling stETH in strained markets. The oracle data was correct; the incentive ratio was not. Reconciling this reveals that incentives must account not just for price deviation but for market liquidity. If liquidators cannot easily sell what they acquire, even generous bonuses lose appeal.

The second claim reaches deeper into design. Liquidations are safety valves, but only when the system ensures that *someone* is incentivised to act. This is visible in protocol choices. Compound v2 uses a "first to liquidate" model, where the fastest transaction wins the entire opportunity. The model prizes latency: bots colocate servers near nodes, engineer transaction bundles and experiment with private relay routes. The result is competitive efficiency but fragility under congestion. During the May 2022 volatility spike, several Compound liquidations bunched into brief intervals because only a few high-performance bots could compete at elevated gas. The implication is structural: centralising liquidation capacity in a handful of efficient players reduces diversity, increasing systemic vulnerability.

By contrast, MakerDAO's 2021 "Liquidations 2.0" upgrade shifted to English-style auctions, widening the field of potential bidders. This slowed execution slightly but increased participation. In September 2021, as ETH briefly fell below US$3,000, Maker auctions demonstrated smoother clearing patterns, with more bidders and fewer zero-bid outcomes. The motif returns—*the system breathes through its incentives*.

A limitation tempers this comparison. Auction-based designs introduce latency. If prices move too quickly, auctions can begin with parameters that no longer reflect market conditions. In February 2022, a brief spike in ETH volatility caused some Maker auctions to open at unexpectedly low starting discounts, prompting smaller participants to overbid and incur losses. Reconciling this shows that inclusivity can reduce precision. Safety valves must balance openness with speed.

The third claim concerns the choreography between oracles, liquidators and network conditions. Liquidators do not simply react to price changes; they react to the *oracle's* interpretation of price changes, and they must do so through a blockchain that may or may not process their transactions promptly. Behaviour during network congestion reveals this dance. In late May 2021, as gas surged on Ethereum, Aave liquidations became more uneven. Records from Etherscan show liquidation clusters occurring just after gas cooled. Bots waited until transaction fees aligned with profitability, allowing risk to accumulate in the interim. The implication is stark: a safety valve that fires intermittently ceases to be a valve and becomes a pressure gauge.

A second example from Polygon in 2022 strengthens this. Polygon's lower gas environment enabled more granular liquidation behaviour. During a period of rapid MATIC price declines in July 2022, hundreds of small liquidations occurred within seconds. The low fee environment expanded the pool of viable participants. Liquidations executed predictably, keeping collateral ratios healthy. The contrast demonstrates a principle: network cost shapes who liquidates, when they liquidate and how frequently they liquidate. Cheap blockspace widens participation; expensive blockspace concentrates it.

A credible counter-example emerges in the form of MEV (miner-extractable value). High MEV environments can distort liquidation dynamics. In early 2022, MEV bots on Ethereum occasionally intercepted liquidation transactions, replacing them with their own through priority gas bidding. This behaviour sometimes benefited protocols—liquidations still executed—but it undermined independent keeper networks by outcompeting them routinely. The motif sharpens: *the system breathes through incentives—but the air is shared*. Reconciling this requires acknowledging that keeper networks exist in competitive markets where sophisticated actors can crowd out less-equipped participants.

The fourth claim rests on a more philosophical point: liquidations reveal what a protocol considers "safe". This safety is encoded in collateral ratios, penalty rates and oracle structures. But the practice of safety shows up in behaviour: how quickly risk is cleared, how wide discounts must be, how many entities are capable of acting. During Celsius's collapse in June 2022, markets watched a single massive loan on Aave tied to WBTC. On-chain observers tracked price thresholds block by block. The behaviour of liquidators became a public spectacle. At each price movement, bots tested profitability, simulating liquidation routes through Curve and centralised venues. The community saw liquidation not as a mechanical process but as a negotiation between incentives, liquidity and speed. The implication is cultural as well as technical: liquidations anchor confidence. How they behave tells users whether a system deserves trust.

The motif surfaces once more in the smallest details. A liquidation bot adjusts its gas multiplier. A protocol tweaks its penalty from 10 to 12 per cent. A keeper delays firing by one block because its internal model predicts a short-lived rebound. Each decision carries weight. Each action reveals how safety is constructed, moment by moment.

The unresolved tension remains. If liquidation systems must fire quickly, inclusively and profitably—under conditions that can shift in seconds—how should protocols set incentives that remain fair in calm markets but effective in storms? And when the next bout of volatility arrives, as it inevitably will, which matters more: the precision of liquidation logic, or the diversity and resilience of the actors who must execute it?

Leverage Loops

In May 2021, on the Binance Smart Chain, a trader deployed a strategy that became a minor legend in the forensic post-mortems that followed. The place was BSC; the month was May; the sequence was clinical. He deposited US$1.2 million of BNB, borrowed a stablecoin against it, used that stablecoin to buy more BNB, redeposited the BNB as collateral, borrowed again, bought again, and repeated the cycle until the position resembled a tower built from mirrors. He had transformed a single asset into several stacked claims on itself. When BNB's price rose, the structure amplified his gain. When it fell—by 18 per cent within hours during a brief market shock—the entire edifice collapsed. The liquidations were swift, automated, and devastating. What the community described as "leverage on leverage" had revealed its nature: a loop is powerful right up to the moment it stops turning.

The paradox is immediate. Recursive borrowing is framed as a technique to increase capital efficiency—more exposure for the same initial stake. Yet the very act of trying to extract efficiency can create fragility. The machines do exactly what they are instructed to do. They do it quickly. And when the loop tightens, the outcome is not a gradual loss but a cascade. One 5-word sentence captures it: The loop snaps suddenly.

The motif of the loop—turning, tightening, breaking—returns throughout the mechanics of recursive leverage. To see how it works, you must trace behaviour through contracts, rather than assumptions through narratives. A user deposits collateral into a lending protocol. He borrows against it. Instead of using the borrowed asset for an unrelated purpose, he uses it to acquire more of the collateral asset, directly or synthetically. He then redeposits this newly acquired collateral, expanding his borrowing power. Show → name → explain. Aave's documentation explicitly references the ability to "loop" collateral positions, particularly with correlated assets such as stETH and ETH. The implication is structural: protocols enable looping not as an exploit but as an intended pattern. The problem emerges when thousands of users pursue the same pattern simultaneously, tying their solvency to identical price paths.

A real, checkable example demonstrates this collective behaviour. In April 2022, during heightened trading interest in stETH, several large users on Aave v2 (Ethereum) recursively looped stETH–ETH positions. A public address, widely analysed by researchers at Gauntlet (2022), deposited tens of millions in stETH, borrowed ETH, swapped it for more stETH on Curve, and repeated the cycle until the loan-to-value ratio neared its maximum safe threshold. The behaviour looked rational—stETH's peg to ETH had held for months. Yet when liquidity in the Curve pool thinned and stETH traded at a discount, the loop magnified losses. Liquidation bots began circling the address while analysts ran simulations on whether the market could absorb the forced sales. The implication was philosophical as much as financial: recursive leverage converts a belief about correlation into a systemic dependency.

A second example from Fantom in January 2022 broadens the frame. Several traders looped FTM collateral positions on Scream, a lending protocol known for relatively liberal parameters. They borrowed stablecoins, purchased more FTM, and repeated the cycle. When FTM's price fell sharply during a market-wide correction, the recursive positions unwound in seconds. Block explorers show a burst of liquidation transactions—hundreds within minutes—as keepers raced to clear risk. The behaviour revealed the loop's hidden accelerant: volatility. If the collateral asset is volatile, loops multiply that volatility. The implication is stark: recursive borrowing embeds the asset's variance into the borrower's solvency curve.

A credible limitation tempers these examples. Not all leverage loops destabilise markets. In some cases, they disperse risk. For instance, looping with stablecoin-stablecoin pairs, common on Polygon in mid-2021, created shallow but relatively stable recursive structures. Because the underlying assets exhibited tight correlations and deep liquidity, liquidation risk remained modest. These loops resembled gears turning gently rather than engines revving. Reconciling this requires precision: recursive leverage is not inherently dangerous; it is dangerous when built upon assets whose behaviour is unstable, liquidity constrained or narrative-driven.

The second major claim concerns loops built not on single assets but on *positions* within other protocols. This is where LP tokens enter, and where reflexivity begins to bite. LP tokens are receipts representing a proportional claim on a liquidity pool. They move with the pool's value and composition. Using them as collateral—common on platforms such as Abracadabra during 2021—creates a higher-order dependency. The user is not simply borrowing against an asset; he is borrowing against a contract that itself contains two (or more) assets whose internal ratio shifts continuously.

A named example grounds this. In October 2021, Abracadabra's cauldrons allowed users to deposit Curve LP tokens from the MIM/3CRV pool and borrow MIM against them. At the time, the appeal was clear: stablecoins in a stablecoin pool seemed safe. But as liquidity in the MIM market fluctuated during concerns around UST in early May 2022, the once-predictable LP tokens became more volatile. Borrowers who had recursively looped these LP-backed positions found that their collateral had weakened in two dimensions: pool depth had changed, and the individual assets in the pool were trading at small but significant discounts. The reflexivity risk became visible. The implication is subtle: when you borrow against an LP token, you borrow against the *future behaviour* of a pool, not just its present state.

A second example from 2022 illustrates this with price-within-price feedback. On PancakeSwap (BSC), users looped CAKE–BNB LP tokens as collateral on lending platforms that accepted them. When CAKE's price softened, the LP token's value fell. This reduced borrowing power. Some users, in turn, borrowed more BNB to support the loop, buying additional CAKE. The buy pressure eased the decline temporarily, only for liquidations to accelerate once the support exhausted. The motif tightens: a loop does not merely reflect price; it contributes to price.

A counter-example from Uniswap v3 helps clarify boundaries. In concentrated liquidity positions where LPs set narrow price ranges, the LP token behaves more like an option than a static claim. Some experimental lending platforms explored accepting these tokens as collateral in late 2021, but most withdrew the idea after modelling revealed unacceptable tail risks. The limitation is clear. Reflexive loops built on convex instruments do not merely increase risk; they can create runaway feedback. Reconciling this reinforces a principle: not all financial Lego bricks belong in towers.

The third major claim addresses the systemic dimension. A loop is rarely isolated. Recursive positions influence liquidations, oracle behaviour and slippage. These interactions create feedback loops. Show → name → explain. During the stETH discount event of June 2022, recursive positions on Aave and Celsius's leveraged stETH exposure exerted pressure on Curve's stETH–ETH pool.

Each withdrawal deepened the discount; each discount increased the likelihood of liquidation; each liquidation strengthened the pressure on the pool. This pattern, analysed by Nansen (2022), exhibited clear reflexivity. The implication for risk architecture is profound: recursive leverage is not just a user-level hazard; it is a system-level amplifier.

A second systemic example emerged during the UST collapse in May 2022. Terra's anchor protocol encouraged recursive loops via borrowing UST to buy LUNA, staking it, and repeating. As UST lost its peg, the unwind of recursive positions accelerated the fall. Liquidations, redemptions and panic selling fed into one another. This was not a case of a few individuals mismanaging leverage; it was the market reflexively consuming its own assumptions.

A limitation must be acknowledged. Reflexivity is not always catastrophic. Traditional finance exhibits its own benign loops—mortgage refinancing waves, for instance, or capital recycling through repo markets. These loops become destabilising only when the collateral's behaviour becomes misaligned with the assumptions embedded in leverage models. The same applies in DeFi. A loop built on stable, highly liquid collateral may function as capital efficiency. One built on narrative-driven tokens becomes a stress test waiting for a trigger. Reconciling this reinforces the core argument: loops are not inherently wrong; they are inherently revealing.

The fourth claim concerns visibility. Recursive leverage is often invisible until it is too large to unwind quietly. Metrics tell the story. A sudden rise in protocol utilisation. A cluster of addresses with identical borrowing patterns. A narrowing collateralisation buffer across correlated positions. These behavioural signals—trackable on-chain—are the lungs of the loop motif. They show when a system is breathing smoothly and when it is beginning to gasp.

Consider Ethereum's mempool during liquidation-heavy periods. Bots grow more active. Gas spikes. Aggregators fail to route trades efficiently. Each behaviour reflects stress. And yet, these are the only windows into the loops beneath. The implication is that protocol designers and researchers must commit to reading these behavioural signatures, because the loops themselves do not announce their presence.

The unresolved tension lingers. If recursive leverage magnifies both opportunity and fragility, how should protocols treat it? Should they constrain loops by disallowing certain collateral types, or should they embrace loops but design for their inevitable unwinds? And for users, a sharper question emerges: when a loop tightens, will you recognise the sound of strain before the snap?

Chapter 5
Yield Farming Without the Fairy Dust

The promise arrived wrapped in numbers that glowed like lanterns in the dark: "4,000% APR," "Sustainable APY through emissions," "Guaranteed returns, backed by community demand." Screenshots circulated, threads erupted, and for a brief moment it felt as if finance had rediscovered alchemy. But the illusion dissolved just as quickly. In July 2021, when the protocol Iron Finance collapsed, its TITAN token plunged from US$60 to near-zero in a day. Thousands of participants watched their "yield" evaporate into a spiral of forced selling and collapsing confidence. The episode was framed by some as a lesson in greed, by others as a failure of design, but its real significance lies elsewhere: yield is only as real as the economic engine that funds it, and glamour often camouflages its absence.

The spectacle of that collapse endures because it touches something deeper than a single project. It touches the fantasy that digital tokens can conjure returns ex nihilo, as if participation alone were a form of value creation. The paradox is elegant and dangerous: yield farming was born as a mechanism to distribute ownership, yet it evolved into a contest of illusion, where numbers appeared before cashflows and incentives ran faster than understanding. Even so, the field is not irredeemable. It contains structures of genuine financial ingenuity—fee markets, risk transfer, premium capture, automated arbitrage—that deserve attention stripped of hype. The challenge is separating the substance from the theatre.

Yield farming became the cultural centrepiece of DeFi because it offered something that traditional finance rarely does: an open invitation. Anyone could provide liquidity, stake tokens, receive emissions, and watch numbers grow minute by minute. Yet beneath the accessibility lay mechanics that were anything but simple. Some yields emerged from actual economic activity—swaps, lending spreads, volatility harvesting. Others were illusions fuelled by emissions schedules designed to attract new participants as fast as the token price declined. The hidden structure was always the same: someone, somewhere, funded the return. The question is how to determine who, and whether they know it.

This chapter steps into that tension—not to judge the ambition, but to understand the architecture. Sustainable yield is not mysterious. It stems from fees generated when people trade, borrow, hedge, or pay for speed; from funding rates that equalise risk across venues; from market participants who willingly transfer uncertainty for predictability. Subsidised yield, by contrast, comes from token emissions that dilute ownership in order to simulate profitability. This distinction matters because it determines longevity. A protocol that earns £1 in fees can pay £1 in yield; a protocol that prints £1 in tokens can only pay until the market ceases to believe.

The motif of *substance versus spectacle* threads through the landscapes we will cross. When a swap occurs on an automated market maker, fees accrue in real time. When liquidity providers on Curve receive trading fees from stablecoin flows, the revenue exists whether or not a token price rises. These are the quiet, steady engines of DeFi. But when a farm promises 9,000% APY while its token has no revenue, no cashflow, and no utility besides being staked to receive more of itself, the spectacle takes over. The theatre works until it doesn't. The task is learning to recognise which stage you are standing on before the set collapses.

Gamified systems add another layer of misdirection and insight. Points, airdrops, loyalty programmes, and seasonal campaigns transform economics into a gameboard. They spur behaviour—sometimes desired, sometimes chaotic. A points ladder can drive users to trade more, provide more liquidity, or interact with multiple protocols. But it can also induce wash trading, cyclical migrations, and extractive interactions that mimic engagement while undermining the system's stability. Behavioural design is not neutral. Every reward structure shapes the actions it invites. Airdrops, when calibrated carefully, distribute ownership to engaged users; when misaligned, they inflate activity without building allegiance.

Yet these behavioural dynamics touch something more fundamental: risk. Yield is risk priced in annual terms. A stablecoin farm offering 6 per cent from trading fees communicates one thing; an options-selling strategy offering 40 per cent communicates another. The risk isn't hidden. It is structural. The farmer trades volatility for predictable income, or provides liquidity for correlated assets in exchange for minimal slippage fees. Matching risk bands to position size, to horizons, to personal tolerance—these are old principles in finance, newly expressed on-chain. The sophistication does not lie in chasing the highest yield on a dashboard, but in recognising that every percentage point embeds a story about exposure, incentive, and uncertainty.

But even genuine yield can vanish through poor execution. Gas erodes returns by slicing off incremental profits. MEV bots extract value by stepping in front of transactions. Slippage widens the gulf between quoted and realised prices. Compounding costs—often overlooked—quietly reshape APR into something far less impressive when measured net of friction. A strategy that advertises 20 per cent may deliver half that after transaction fees and operational churn. The numbers do not lie, but they rarely tell the whole truth. Understanding execution is not optional; it determines whether a yield strategy survives its own mechanics.

Throughout this chapter, the recurring image is that of *a balance sheet in motion*. Yield farming is not a passive act. It is a dance between rewards and erosion, between incentives and sustainability, between clever design and wishful thinking. Protocols that rely on emissions alone behave like candles burning from both ends: bright, dramatic, but short-lived. Protocols that derive yield from real activity behave more like engines: sometimes slow, sometimes noisy, but grounded in physics rather than theatre.

What this exploration demands is attention—not cynicism, not faith, but disciplined curiosity. How does a protocol earn money? Who pays? What assumptions underpin the return? What frictions diminish it? What behaviours does the incentive scheme cultivate? By the end of this chapter, those questions will feel instinctive, almost reflexive. But for now, let them hover.

Because the real puzzle of yield farming is not why the fantastical returns appear. It is why they persist long enough to entrance otherwise rational people. And as you turn the page, the deeper question emerges: when the numbers on the screen glow brightest, what exactly are they illuminating—the underlying engine, or the smoke around it?

Subsidies vs. Sustainable Yield

In June 2021, at a co-working loft in Singapore, a small DeFi team launched a farming programme that became a minor sensation on Crypto Twitter. The protocol—AutoShark—promised APRs above 15,000 per cent for staking its freshly minted token, JAWS. Within forty-eight hours the token soared, liquidity shot up, and screenshots of dizzying returns circulated with missionary zeal. By the end of the week, the price had collapsed more than 90 per cent. The emissions schedule, designed to ignite rapid growth, had instead overwhelmed demand. What looked like yield was simply dilution wearing a costume. The lesson was visible in the wreckage: not all returns emerge from economic activity; some are manufactured out of thin air, burning bright until the subsidy ends or belief decays.

The paradox still lingers. If a protocol emits its own token as a reward, does it create value or merely move it around? One 5-word sentence settles the confusion: Subsidies decay without revenue. The mathematics of emissions is straightforward. The psychology around them is not. Participants conflate distribution with yield because both appear as tokens in a wallet. But the origins differ dramatically. Fees represent someone paying for a service; emissions represent the protocol paying someone to show up. Understanding the distinction is the difference between recognising a business and mistaking a parade for one.

The motif running quietly through this topic is a simple image: *a balance sheet and its shadow*. Revenue lives on the balance sheet. Emissions live in the shadow—easy to summon, hard to sustain. The task is learning to read both.

The first major claim is empirical. Sustainable yield must come from identifiable cashflows: trading fees, borrowing costs, funding rates, premiums for volatility, payments for speed or certainty. Show → name → explain. Curve, launched on Ethereum in January 2020, generates fees whenever users swap stablecoins. These fees accrue to liquidity providers directly. In 2021, when USDC–DAI–

USDT volumes surged, on-chain dashboards showed fee revenues consistently exceeding token emissions. The implication is clear: a protocol that earns money can pay money. Its yield is not a promotional tactic but a distribution of income.

A second example strengthens this distinction. GMX, deployed on Arbitrum in September 2021, pays its liquidity providers through trading fees from perpetual swaps. The revenue varies with trader behaviour, but the mechanism remains anchored in activity. During periods of high volatility in early 2022, GMX reported daily fees exceeding US$1 million (GMX stats, March 2022). The behaviour of users—opening, closing, and rolling leveraged positions—directly created the cashflow that funded rewards. This matters because it provides something emissions cannot: durability proportional to demand.

A limitation tempers these observations. Fee-driven revenue is not inherently stable. If volumes vanish, so does yield. SushiSwap's fee revenues declined sharply through 2022 as trading migrated elsewhere, reducing rewards for LPs. This counter-example demonstrates that revenue-based yield can still decay; the difference is that its decline reflects real economic activity, not the exhaustion of a subsidy. Reconciling the limitation reinforces the core argument: sustainable yield is fragile, but at least it is grounded. Subsidised yield is fragile because it never was.

The second major claim concerns emissions themselves. Emissions are not inherently irresponsible. They serve legitimate purposes: distributing ownership, bootstrapping liquidity, attracting early users, stimulating experimentation. But emissions must be treated as *subsidies*, not yield. Their purpose is to buy time while genuine revenue grows. The trouble begins when emissions replace revenue rather than bridge to it.

A named example illustrates this. Liquidity mining on Compound in June 2020 catalysed the first great yield farming wave. COMP emissions rewarded borrowers and lenders alike, creating demand for supply. The design was intentional: emissions were governance tools, helping distribute voting power. Volumes grew, interest rates stabilised, and deposits surged. The implication is that emissions used sparingly—tied to governance and participation—can strengthen an ecosystem rather than distort it.

Contrast that with the avalanche of copycat farms on Binance Smart Chain in the first half of 2021. Dozens of anonymous teams launched protocols like Goose Finance and Kebab Finance, each offering APRs in the thousands through aggressive emissions. On-chain metrics showed reward token inflation rates exceeding 1–2 per cent per hour. The behaviour this induced—rapid staking and selling—suppressed token prices, accelerating collapse. The motif sharpens: *the balance sheet's shadow grows darker when its pace exceeds its body*.

A credible counter-example to the "emissions bad" narrative deserves attention. Liquidity programmes on

Uniswap v2 in late 2020, subsidised through Treasury-held UNI, temporarily boosted liquidity for key pools such as ETH–USDC. The rewards then tapered. When the programme ended, liquidity dipped but stabilised at a level higher than before. That arc—subsidy → adoption → taper → normalisation—shows emissions used responsibly. Reconciling this reframes emissions not as villains but as tools requiring restraint.

The third major claim addresses longevity—what a scorecard for sustainable yield should capture. Revenue sources matter. Volatility matters. Fee structures matter. But behaviour matters most. How does the protocol respond to stress? Does revenue scale with usage? Are emissions cliffed or continuous? These are not abstractions; they appear as visible, measurable actions.

Start with revenue quality. A protocol that depends on short-lived hype shows declining fee trajectories as user engagement fades. A protocol with durable demand shows smoother revenue curves. In 2022, for example, Lido's stETH rewards continued steadily despite market turmoil because they derived from Ethereum staking—a consensus-level activity—rather than speculative flows. The implication is that sustainable yield isn't simply about fees; it is about the origin of fees: whether they arise from structural, repeatable activity or transient enthusiasm.

Next, examine cost discipline. Emissions schedules tell stories. Cliffing emissions—reducing token issuance sharply after an initial period—forces protocols to shift

from subsidy to revenue. Balancer's BAL token, for instance, employed weekly emissions with periodic adjustments based on governance votes. Over time, emissions declined while fee revenues grew. The behaviour signalled maturity: willingness to reduce subsidies and rely on earned income.

Then, consider liquidity resilience. Sustainable yield depends on the protocol's ability to maintain healthy liquidity without constant bribery. On Curve, gauge voting allows emissions to flow to pools based on governance preferences. Some pools attract deep liquidity because they serve essential purposes—stablecoin routing, LST arbitrage, cross-chain interfaces. Others require perpetual incentives to stay relevant. The motif returns: *the balance sheet versus the shadow*. A pool that holds its liquidity after incentives drop rests on genuine demand; one that drains instantly rests on subsidies alone.

A limitation complicates this framework. Some protocols straddle both categories. They combine modest emissions with significant fee generation, blurring lines. For instance, Velodrome on Optimism finances liquidity through a blend of emissions and trading fees, supported by its ve-model. Critics argue the emissions remain too large; supporters counter that the flywheel has proven durable. Reconciling this requires accepting nuance. Longevity cannot be judged from emissions alone; it must be read from behaviour under pressure.

The fourth major claim is about perception. Users treat yield as a number, yet it is a narrative. That narrative can be tested. If a protocol claims 20 per cent APR, ask the question any auditor would: who pays? The answer should map to an identifiable actor: trader, borrower, hedger, arbitrageur. If the answer loops back to "the token holders," the loop reveals emptiness. Sustainable yield shows itself in actions. Subsidised yield shows itself in emissions.

Behavioural metrics make these distinctions visible. Trading volume relative to total value locked (TVL) reveals whether liquidity earns its keep. Fee-to-emission ratios reveal whether revenue keeps pace with dilution. Retention after incentives taper reveals the authenticity of user engagement. These metrics turn narrative into evaluation. They let the balance sheet step out of the shadow.

The unresolved tension lands with force. DeFi emerged from ideals of openness, experimentation, composability. Subsidies fuelled its early renaissance. But as the space matures, the harder question remains: when a protocol offers yield, do the rewards reflect work done or dilution deferred? And when two protocols show identical APRs, will you recognise which derives its strength from revenue—and which survives only by feeding its shadow?

Points, Airdrops, and Behaviour

In January 2023, at an office tower in Shenzhen, a small team from Arbitrum Foundation reviewed preliminary data from its forthcoming points programme. The numbers surprised even them. In a single week, wallet interactions with

Arbitrum-based protocols had increased by more than 4.7 million transactions, concentrated among fewer than 15,000 addresses. The place was Shenzhen; the month was January; the pattern was unmistakable. The points ladder—designed to reward genuine participation ahead of Arbitrum's airdrop—had instead triggered a dense wave of repetitive, low-value actions. Wallets moved small amounts back and forth between pools. Traders executed sequences of trivial swaps. Bridges carried funds across chains with no purpose beyond accumulating points. The behaviour revealed a central truth of digital incentives: the system receives precisely what it optimises for, even when that behaviour bears little resemblance to the intention behind the incentive.

This paradox sits at the heart of modern DeFi engagement design. How can a mechanism designed to reward authentic participation so easily devolve into ritualistic clicks? How can a campaign meant to strengthen community instead incentivise hollow motion? And at what point does an incentive designed for growth become an inducement for manipulation? One 5-word sentence captures the tension: Incentives reshape behaviour instantly.

The quiet motif that threads through this subchapter—the *gameboard*—starts here. When users sense they are playing a game, they behave like players, not participants. Every rule becomes a move; every reward, a strategy. The art is in recognising that gamification is not inherently misguided, but that every point, badge, and score triggers visible behaviours that must be weighed against the goals of a protocol.

The first major claim rests on observable behaviour. Points systems are powerful because they create ordinal competition. Users attempt to climb the ladder not for utility but for rank. Show → name → explain. Optimism's 2022 airdrop rounds provide an example. The foundation rewarded users of public goods, long-term engagement, and governance participation. But an unintended effect emerged: dashboards tracking "eligibility scores" appeared within days. Users rushed to meet criteria in the simplest possible way—tiny governance votes, small transactions replicated across multiple protocols, and a flurry of low-value bridging. The implication is clear. When you convert participation into points, you convert intention into metrics, and metrics into targets. Users do what the scoring system measures, not what the designers value.

A second example, from LayerZero's points programme announced in late 2023, adds nuance. Public data on Arbitrum and Ethereum shows a significant spike in bridge interactions—millions of small transfers—executed by clusters of addresses often linked by timing and pattern. Investigators from ChainArgos (2024) found that many wallets transacted in choreographed bursts every few minutes, a signature of automated farms. The behaviour illustrated how quickly rational actors identify and exploit the contours of a points design. The implication is not that points programmes fail, but that they are fragile. They invite optimisation, and optimisation invites distortion.

A credible limitation tempers this critique. Some points systems succeed brilliantly. The 2020 Uniswap airdrop rewarded genuine early users without months of gaming or distortion because it was unannounced. Behaviour could not be sculpted in advance. Retrospective rewards circumvent strategic manipulation by rewarding what happened, not what users think will happen. Reconciling this yields a principle: the more predictable the gameboard, the more distorted the behaviour; the more surprising the reward, the more authentic the participation it reflects.

The second major claim concerns airdrops themselves. Airdrops were originally a mechanism for distributing ownership broadly and fairly. But their evolution has turned them into behavioural engines. Show → name → explain. In March 2021, the dYdX airdrop rewarded trading volume. Predictably, trading volume spiked—yet much of it came from wash trades. Traders executed symmetrical buy–sell pairs to inflate their eligibility while minimising exposure. Data from dYdX volumes during that period (Kaiko, 2021) shows pronounced spikes of identical-sized trades within seconds, a tell-tale pattern. The implication is that the economic cost of wash trading—fees, spreads, gas—was outweighed by the anticipated reward. Airdrops can create incentives strong enough to bend behaviour around them, warping both metrics and markets.

A second example—Arbitrum's March 2023 airdrop—reveals the social dimension. Despite sophisticated Sybil filtering, public dashboards (Nansen, 2023) observed clusters of hundreds of wallets linked to single origin addresses. The wallets performed minimal interactions across multiple protocols, clearly designed to meet eligibility thresholds without meaningful engagement. The behaviour demonstrated the dual nature of airdrops. They reward true participants, but they also breed elaborate networks of opportunism. The motif of the *gameboard* snaps into focus: airdrops create a contest, and contests produce competitors, not communities.

A counter-example deepens the analysis. The Gitcoin Grants Quadratic Funding model, used since 2019, distributes matching funds based on the diversity—not volume—of contributions. Because the formula rewards broad donor participation rather than large individual donations, it incentivises community building rather than extractive behaviour. Attempts at manipulation exist, but the design elevates collective engagement over mechanical repetition. Reconciling this shows that incentive design is not fate. Thoughtful mechanisms can tilt behaviour toward the social and constructive.

The third major claim explores the behavioural consequences of gamified incentives: the migration patterns, risk preferences, and strategic movements they generate. Users behave like fluid—flowing toward whatever pool offers the highest short-term payoff. Metrics show this clearly. When a points campaign begins, daily active wallets spike. TVL rises, sometimes doubling within days. Transaction counts balloon. But retention often collapses once rewards expire. Layer2 networks such as zkSync and Starknet saw this during early 2023: TVL rose rapidly during points rumours, only to fall by 30–40 per cent within weeks after clarity arrived regarding distribution rules. The implication is blunt. Gamified incentives attract attention but rarely loyalty.

Consider the case of Blur, the NFT marketplace whose points programme and BLUR token airdrop in early 2023 drove trading volumes to record levels. Wash trades proliferated. NFT collections experienced unprecedented churn as traders executed trades solely to maximise points. According to CryptoSlam (February 2023), wash trading volume on Blur reached hundreds of millions of dollars during peak weeks. The behaviour was rational within the gameboard but damaging to price discovery. The market became the theatre of the incentive rather than the theatre of genuine preference. This example reveals the trade-off: gamification can distort the underlying asset's informational integrity.

A limitation requires acknowledgement. Gamified incentives can cultivate genuine skill and experimentation. On-chain options protocols such as Lyra (Optimism, 2022) used targeted incentives to encourage traders to experiment with hedging strategies. Data showed users not only traded frequently but adopted more complex strategies over time.

The behaviour was developmental rather than extractive. Reconciling this reveals a key nuance: gamification is not inherently manipulative. It becomes manipulative when the reward structure is shallow; when it is deep, it can educate.

The fourth major claim is structural. Points and airdrops do more than reward activity—they shape the architecture of collaboration. Protocols often rely on airdrops to distribute governance tokens, yet governance itself becomes a casualty of speculative farming. When tokens land in the wallets of short-term farmers, voting power migrates toward actors least aligned with the protocol's future. This is visible in governance turnout. Protocols such as ENS and Uniswap, despite significant token distribution, often see voter participation concentrated among a handful of large delegates. The metric is revealing: distribution does not guarantee decentralisation. Incentives that invite shallow participation may create governance bodies that appear democratic but behave oligarchically. The motif returns: the gameboard can either build or erode collective agency.

The behavioural footprint of points and airdrops shows up in friction metrics too. Gas spikes during campaign phases. Mempool congestion thickens. MEV extraction increases as bots frontrun predictable user behaviour. Each of these is a visible cost of gamification. A points programme promising fairness can inadvertently tax users through network dynamics, turning participation into an operational burden.

The unresolved tension sits quietly behind all these observations. Gamified systems can distribute power, attract users, and catalyse early growth. They can also distort metrics, reward opportunists, and erode trust. The question that remains for any protocol architect is simple but unforgiving: when you place users onto a gameboard, do you know the game you are teaching them to play? And when the campaign ends, will the behaviour it created remain—because it was meaningful—or disappear the moment the points stop falling?

Risk-Priced Opportunities

In February 2021, a development studio in Kuala Lumpur reviewed a dataset that should not have existed. The team had analysed trading activity on Binance Smart Chain and discovered an address that had farmed stablecoin yields for almost a year without a single liquidation event. The strategy was prosaic: short-duration lending of USDC and BUSD into pools offering between 8 and 12 per cent APR. What made the case striking was the comparison. Another cluster of addresses, operating from the same region and during the same period, pursued aggressive options-writing strategies on decentralised derivatives platforms. Their realised returns swung from +40 per cent in one week to –25 per cent the next. The contrast—same capital base, same timeframe, different risk bands—revealed a simple truth. The market was not a single field; it was a series of stacked corridors, each demanding a different appetite, cadence, and horizon. Position size was not a matter of confidence. It was a matter of matching risk to rhythm.

One paradox sharpened the lesson. How could a stablecoin lender with modest APRs outperform a trader earning rich option premiums? The answer lay in variance. Stablecoin APRs ranged within a tight band; the options premiums came with wide tails. The five-word sentence that sits quietly in the early paragraphs speaks to the entire subchapter: Size follows risk, always.

Every decision in DeFi expresses a risk preference. It shows in the assets users choose, the horizons they commit to, and the drawdowns they tolerate. The motif of *corridors* returns because each opportunity offers a corridor defined by volatility, capital efficiency, and failure modes. The visible behaviour—how often a user rebalances, how deeply they check protocol metrics, how tightly they constrain their exposure—reveals which corridor they believe they are in.

The first major claim is simple: stable, low-volatility opportunities deserve larger position sizes because their risk bands are narrow and measurable. Show → name → explain. A clear example is Aave's stablecoin lending markets between September 2020 and February 2021 on Ethereum. The rates averaged between 4 and 10 per cent over those months (Aave Analytics, 2021). The visible behaviour was consistent: lenders rarely shifted positions, and utilisation rates stayed within predictable ranges. The corridor was steady. The implication is structural. Opportunities that derive yield from protocol fees—rather than speculative premiums—support longer horizons and larger allocations because the distribution of outcomes is tight.

A second example comes from MakerDAO's Stability Fee on DAI vaults in 2022. The fee adjustments, published transparently and revised infrequently, created a predictable corridor for both borrowers and liquidity providers. The metrics—Stability Fee levels, collateralisation ratios, and DAI supply—moved smoothly except during sharp market swings. Participants could size positions rationally because the corridor was legible. The implication is that predictable mechanisms produce predictable behaviour, and predictable behaviour invites deeper commitment.

A limitation clarifies the argument. Not all stablecoin farming is safe. The collapse of TerraUSD in May 2022 showed how an apparently "stable" asset could hide a reflexive design. Anchor Protocol's high yields—hovering around 20 per cent APR for months—were not fee-driven but subsidy-driven. When confidence cracked, the corridor collapsed. Reconciling this confirms the principle: not all low-volatility surfaces are truly low risk. The corridor must be inspected, not assumed.

The second major claim is that higher-risk opportunities demand smaller positions and shorter horizons because their payoff structures widen as volatility increases. This is visible in on-chain options protocols. Show → name → explain. Lyra, launched in August 2021 on Optimism, priced options dynamically using its automated market maker.

Premiums were sometimes attractive, but mark-to-market swings were violent during news events. Traders who sold options collected steady premiums until volatility spiked, at which point losses arrived abruptly. The implication is practical. High-return corridors are turbocharged by tail events, and tail events require tight sizing.

Another example lies in GMX's GLP pools, which acted as counterparties to leveraged traders. GLP holders earned fees during periods of trader losses but suffered drawdowns when traders were profitable. The corridor was asymmetric. Data from early 2023 (GMX Stats, January–March 2023) recorded weeks of 5–7 per cent drawdowns for GLP while leveraged traders captured outsized profits. The necessary behaviour—measuring exposure daily, adjusting allocations frequently, and accepting variance—showed how high-yield corridors demand active management. The implication is clear. When returns depend on trader behaviour rather than protocol mechanics, sizing must shrink.

Here again, a counter-example provides balance. Ribbon Finance's structured products in 2021–2022 illustrated how options-based yield could be made more predictable by automating strategy execution and limiting leverage. Losses still occurred, but the variance was less extreme than manual selling of options. This shows that even high-risk corridors can be engineered to behave more gently, as long as leverage is capped and parameters are transparent.

Reconciling this reinforces the motif: corridors can be narrowed through design, but never eliminated.

The third major claim concerns horizons. Time magnifies risk by compounding uncertainty. Horizons must match the corridor. Show → name → explain. During the 2020–2021 bull cycle, Yearn Finance vaults optimised yields by rotating across lending protocols. Strategies involving stablecoins—USDC or DAI—showed smoother returns over multi-month horizons. Meanwhile, vaults using volatile collateral occasionally experienced rapid drawdowns. The key behaviour difference lay in pacing. Stablecoin vault users checked dashboards weekly; volatile vault users monitored hourly. The implication is not advisory but observational: horizons widen when underlying risk is calculable, and narrow when the underlying asset is prone to shocks.

A second example emerges from Euler Finance, before its March 2023 exploit. Euler offered risk-tiered collateral frameworks. Blue-chip assets such as ETH and stables sat in high-quality tiers; long-tail assets sat in isolation tiers with reduced borrowing capacity. Public dashboards showed that long-tail collateral positions were opened for shorter durations and smaller sizes. Users behaved rationally: when the corridor widened, horizons shrank. The implication is that protocol design can steer horizons by making risk parameters visible.

A limitation tempers the argument. Long horizons are not always safe even with stable assets. During the USDC depegging incident in March 2023, triggered by Silicon

Valley Bank's collapse, stablecoin farms saw abrupt price dislocations. Even those in low-risk corridors faced mark-to-market stress. Reconciling this sharpens the point: corridors can shift rapidly under systemic stress, and horizons must incorporate the possibility of discontinuities.

The fourth major claim ties position size to systemic effects. When users stack leverage—borrowing against volatile collateral, then reusing receipts for further borrowing—they tighten corridors in ways that magnify feedback loops. Show → name → explain. In November 2021, a cluster of traders on Avalanche borrowed against AVAX, deposited the borrowed stablecoins into liquidity pools, used the LP tokens as collateral elsewhere, and repeated. The corridor became brittle. When AVAX's price fell sharply in December, liquidations cascaded. The implication is stark. Position size affects not only individual portfolios but the system's stability. Large positions in narrow corridors can fracture the market.

A second example comes from Fantom's 2022 liquid staking loop. Users leveraged staked FTM, borrowed more, and repeated the cycle. Yields looked high, but the corridor narrowed dangerously. When sentiment turned in mid-2022, unwind pressure accelerated declines. The visible behaviour—rapid position closures, spikes in liquidations, and widening spreads—illustrated reflexivity in motion. The implication is that corridors interact. One user's sizing affects another's risk.

A counter-example offers contrast. MakerDAO's methodical parameter updates in 2020, after the March "Black Thursday" event, widened corridors by raising auction buffers and adjusting collateralisation ratios. This allowed the system to absorb volatility without cascading failure. Reconciling this demonstrates that corridor design is a form of engineering: widen it, and stress disperses; narrow it, and stress concentrates.

The unresolved tension sits at the end. Opportunities exist across every corridor, from tranquil stablecoin lending to the sharp edges of derivatives premiums. But each corridor demands its own sizing logic, behavioural cadence, and temporal rhythm. The question that lingers—one every thoughtful participant must face—echoes the motif: which corridor are you really in, and have you sized the position for the path it might take rather than the path you want it to take?

Execution and Fees

In May 2022, during a spike in activity on Ethereum triggered by Yuga Labs' Otherside land mint, one trader in Singapore attempted to rebalance a position in a stablecoin lending vault. The target transaction cost was modest—under USD 40. Within minutes, the estimate leapt above USD 400, then USD 2,000, before the mempool choked entirely. The user waited. The block came. The transaction landed. By the time the dust settled, the rebalancing cost more than the fortnight of yield it was meant to capture. The net APR, once advertised at 18 per cent, had fallen below 6. And that figure ignored slippage. It ignored miner-extractable value. It ignored the invisible hands that quietly re-shaped execution quality long before the trade reached a block.

A paradox rises from that scene. How can a strategy that looks efficient on paper—high APR, low volatility, steady fees—deliver such anaemic real returns? The answer sits in the spread between *paper yield* and *achieved yield*. That spread is narrow during calm periods and wide during congestion. Five words expose the tension early: Costs compound faster than yield. Once seen, it cannot be unseen.

Gas, MEV, and slippage form a triangle of erosion. The motif—erosion—reappears because every gain in DeFi exists on a surface that friction slowly wears away. Traders notice it each time they adjust a position more often than planned, or accept worse execution than quoted. The difference between quoted and realised returns is never abstract. It is measurable in gas units, basis points, and block timing.

The first major claim concerns gas as a direct drag on yield. Show → name → explain. Gas is a visible cost: every transaction consumes units priced in gwei, and multiplied by network demand. During the September 2020 "DeFi Summer" highs, Ethereum gas prices regularly spiked above 400 gwei (Etherscan, 2020). A simple claim-reward harvest could cost USD 60–150. For a user farming modest sums, this translated into days of earnings erased by a single action. The implication is structural: the more active the strategy, the more gas becomes destiny.

A clear historical marker reinforces this. When Uniswap v3 launched in May 2021, early users discovered that creating a concentrated liquidity position required multiple interactions—approve, mint, adjust, stake—each with its own gas cost. During peak hours that month, total set-up cost exceeded USD 200. Traders adjusted. They entered fewer positions, widened ranges, or migrated to second-layer networks. The visible behaviour—their reluctance to rebalance—showed how gas costs governed participation. The implication is that execution costs influence not just profitability but design choices and user behaviour.

A limitation softens the claim. Gas is not always ruinous. On networks such as Arbitrum or Optimism, average fees during 2023 frequently sat below USD 0.20. High-frequency farmers could operate even with slim APRs. But reconciling this highlights the point: low fees are not a universal condition. They depend on network architecture, bridging infrastructure, and periods of calm. The moment a layer 2 inherits layer 1 congestion—during mass withdrawals, popular mints, or market stress—the corridors narrow again.

The second major claim concerns MEV—miner or maximal extractable value—as an invisible but potent force that reshapes execution. Unlike gas, it hides beneath the surface. Show → name → explain. MEV manifests as front-running, back-running, and sandwiching. In June 2022, Flashbots

(Flashbots, 2022) reported that more than USD 280 million had been captured by MEV bots since the start of the year. The behaviour is visible on-chain: a user submits a trade, the price shifts just before confirmation, and the final execution differs subtly but meaningfully from the mid-quote. The erosion is measured in basis points, not dollars, but repetition amplifies it.

A concrete episode illustrates its impact. During the LUNA/UST collapse in May 2022, trading activity on decentralised exchanges spiked dramatically. MEV bots repositioned aggressively in mempools across the world. Many users saw slippage limits breached and transactions reverted. Execution worsened precisely when they needed it most. The implication is uncomfortable. MEV extracts value during volatility—the moments when traders are most exposed. Any yield strategy that depends on frequent repositioning inherits this hidden cost.

Another example comes from the launch of Blur's token in February 2023, where NFT trading surged and MEV bots harvested priority arbitrages around listing updates. The traders paying these costs often never identified the culprit, because the erosion was embedded in the block ordering. The implication extends. When execution can be reordered privately, quoted yields are theoretical until proven in practice.

A limitation tempers the analysis. MEV is not purely parasitic. Systems such as Flashbots' MEV-Boost, adopted widely after Ethereum's September 2022 merge, redirected

MEV capture into validator revenue rather than allowing arbitrary bot extraction. This reduced harmful forms of MEV while preserving neutral arbitrage. Reconciling this suggests that MEV can be channelled, though never eliminated. Erosion may be slowed, but not stopped.

The third major claim turns to slippage—the cost born of market depth. Show → name → explain. Slippage is visible: the executed price deviates from the expected price as the trade moves the pool's ratio. A thin liquidity pool magnifies this effect. In March 2021, a trader swapping USD 1.5 million worth of ETH for DAI on a shallow pool on Sushiswap incurred over 6 per cent price impact (on-chain transaction record, March 2021). The loss was not due to volatility, fraud, or fees. It was geometry. The curve could not absorb the trade.

Another clear case unfolded in December 2020 when a stablecoin pool on Curve temporarily lost depth as farmers migrated to a new incentive programme. Even small swaps produced slippage exceeding 1 per cent. The visible behaviour—users splitting trades into smaller increments, delaying execution, or migrating to deeper pools—demonstrated how slippage dictates flow. The implication is sharp: any yield strategy that requires periodic rebalancing will see its returns shaped not only by APR but by the liquidity surface beneath its trades.

A limitation provides nuance. Slippage can be mitigated by aggregators such as 1inch or Paraswap, which route trades across multiple pools to smooth price impact. But reconciling this reinforces the motif: aggregators reduce slippage, they do not remove it. When market depth thins across all pools—during stress or migration—the erosion reappears.

The fourth major claim concerns compounding costs over time. Yield farming is often modelled as a compounding engine, where rewards are harvested and redeployed regularly. But every harvest incurs gas, every reinvestment incurs slippage, and every transaction is exposed to MEV. Show → name → explain. In October 2021, a vault on Polygon advertised a nominal APR of 32 per cent for an auto-compounding stablecoin strategy. When researchers at the Blockchain Analytics Laboratory in Zurich modelled real returns for small depositors—under USD 2,000—they found net yields closer to 11–14 per cent once gas, slippage, and MEV were accounted for. The corridor between nominal and realised returns was wide and persistent. The implication is foundational: compounding magnifies costs as much as returns.

A second example comes from Fantom's high-yield programmes in early 2022. Frequent reward harvesting on low-liquidity pools eroded nearly a third of theoretical returns for small participants. Larger users, able to batch transactions or absorb slippage, saw less erosion. The visible behaviour—the divergence in returns across deposit sizes—revealed an implicit tax on smaller actors. The implication is systemic. Execution quality shapes fairness, influencing who benefits and who is priced out.

A limitation adds texture. Low-fee environments such as Arbitrum in 2023 allowed auto-compounders to narrow the gap between nominal and achieved returns. Yet even there, MEV remained present, particularly during cross-chain bridging events or volatile market periods. Reconciling this reinforces the motif of erosion: the friction can be reduced, but the surface remains abrasive.

The fifth major claim links execution quality to strategy design. Strategies that depend on frequent rebalancing—tight liquidity ranges, hedged positions, synthetic delta-neutral constructs—inherit higher execution drag. Show → name → explain. When Uniswap v3's concentrated liquidity saw widespread adoption, many LPs attempted ultra-narrow ranges. But the need to rebalance whenever price drifted increased gas consumption dramatically. In July 2021, LP accounts running narrow ranges on Ethereum reported transaction fees consuming 20–40 per cent of gross earnings during volatile weeks (community-reported analytics). The implication is unavoidable. High-precision strategies require high-precision execution, and high-precision execution is expensive.

A second illustration comes from Delta-neutral yield vaults on protocols such as Alpha Homora in 2021. These vaults rebalanced hedge ratios frequently to maintain neutrality. During busy blocks, keepers executing these rebalances paid elevated gas and suffered slippage. Users bore this indirectly. Net yields diverged from advertised APRs. The implication is conceptual: a yield strategy is only as good as its execution environment, and execution environments vary dramatically across networks and over time.

A limitation rounds the argument. Some strategies bake in rebalancing delays to reduce transaction frequency. This reduces drag but increases tracking error. Reconciling this frames a deeper trade-off: smooth execution versus precise exposure. The farmer cannot optimise both indefinitely.

The unresolved tension sits at the close. Yield is never free. It is never pure. It is always net of friction—gas, MEV, slippage, timing, block composition, and the unknowable conditions that surround a transaction the moment it seeks inclusion. The question that remains, the one that shadows every opportunity, is simple yet heavy: *Does the strategy still sing after the costs have eaten their share, or is its melody lost in the erosion?*

Chapter 6
Security, Custody and Operational Hygiene

At 3:12 a.m. on a cold February night in 2023, a Berlin-based researcher watched a wallet he had guarded for years empty itself in less than ninety seconds. He had not clicked a malicious link. He had not exposed his seed phrase. He had not, as far as he knew, made a single operational mistake. Yet the tokens vanished, streamed out through an approval he had granted months earlier to a protocol he barely remembered using. That allowance—silent, invisible, forgotten—became the attack surface. By morning it was clear the exploit had touched hundreds of wallets. The root cause was banal: a permissions oversight. The consequence was total.

There is a peculiar cruelty in such losses. They feel avoidable only after they happen. The paradox is sharp. Decentralised finance promises self-sovereignty—the right to hold, move, and manage assets without permission—yet the very act of taking custody transfers responsibility from institutions to individuals. Freedom, here, does not arrive gently. It arrives with sharp edges. And while many enter the space chasing yield, it is operational hygiene that ultimately determines who keeps what they earn. Security in DeFi is not a single idea but a choreography of habits. Small actions that look trivial in isolation—reviewing a domain, checking an approval, splitting key storage—collectively form the difference between resilience and catastrophe. And what makes this choreography so challenging is that the threats rarely announce themselves. They hide in interface misdirection, in automatic prompts, in the frantic seconds during market volatility when attention narrows and judgement degrades. The drift from vigilance to carelessness is quiet, and so the damage, when it comes, feels abrupt.

This chapter enters the story at that vulnerable intersection: the point where human behaviour and technical design meet. We have already seen how protocols can fail through code, governance, or incentives. Here, the failures are more intimate. They occur in the soft tissue around the technology—our habits, assumptions, shortcuts, and blind spots. And because DeFi removes intermediaries, the buffer that once absorbed human mistakes is thinner or absent altogether. Each user becomes their own custodian, their own compliance department, their own security officer. The demands may appear excessive for an ordinary participant, yet the alternative—outsourcing security to a centralised custodian—replicates the trust dependencies DeFi sought to replace.

Self-custody offers the clearest starting point. For centuries, societies have grappled with questions of safekeeping: the sealed clay tablets of ancient Mesopotamia, the split-key chests of Renaissance bankers, the dual-control vaults of twentieth-century finance. What unites them is a desire to minimise single points of failure. Today's seed phrases and hardware wallets echo those early forms, but the stakes differ. The speed of digital loss leaves no time for negotiation or reversal. A misplaced notebook, a compromised laptop, a hurried signing on a mobile device—each can unlock an irreversible flow of value. The underlying theme is continuity across history: the tools change, the fragility of custody does not.

Approvals and allowances provide a more modern twist. They represent a conceptual shift from the familiar models of card authorisations or bank mandates. In DeFi, permissions persist until revoked, a design born of trustless automation. Yet permanence carries risk. A single overlooked approval can act like a forgotten valve in a mechanical system: harmless until pressure accumulates, disastrous once triggered. The on-chain transparency here is deceptive. Everything is visible, but visibility is meaningless if no one is looking. Part of the chapter's task is to cultivate the habit of looking—not as paranoia, but as maintenance.

Then come the social angles: phishing sites, bogus interfaces, drained signatures. These are not failures of code but failures of perception, exploiting how quickly humans anchor to familiar colours, layouts, or domain names. The best attackers do not break systems; they borrow authenticity. A small visual distortion, a swapped letter, a slightly altered contract address—these are the fault lines through which billions have disappeared. The tension is longstanding. Technology evolves, but deception adapts faster. And the more seamless wallets become, the more they risk making harmful actions feel as casual as harmless ones.

The chapter's final movement engages with crisis response. No user intends to face an exploit, depeg, or cascading liquidation. Yet the difference between containing loss and compounding it often lies in the first ten minutes: halting approvals, snapshotting positions, avoiding panic transactions, communicating with clarity rather than fear. These moments resemble the emergency protocols of aviation or medicine—rarely used, but indispensable. To navigate DeFi without an incident plan is to treat a high-velocity system as if it were static. It never is.

Reliability in decentralised finance is not merely technical; it is behavioural. It requires routines that feel tedious on calm days but essential when pressure mounts. It requires accepting that self-custody is both a privilege and a burden. And above all, it requires understanding that the safety of an asset often depends less on the brilliance of the protocol than on the discipline of the person holding the keys.

The deeper questions linger: How do you build habits that endure when the interface encourages speed? How do you remain sceptical without becoming paralysed? And how do you design a personal security posture that feels proportionate—not ascetic, not reckless, but coherent? The chapters ahead do not offer platitudes. They map the terrain, expose the pressure points, and show the practices that transform vulnerability into resilience. The details matter. They always have.

Self-Custody Basics

In April 2022, a London-based designer discovered that the digital wallet he had opened years earlier—initially a place to hold a small experimental balance—had become a single point of catastrophic vulnerability. A house move had scattered his belongings across boxes; a routine spring clean had prompted him to discard old notebooks; and a laptop update had silently erased a browser profile. When he finally attempted to recover access, the realisation dawned with a sickening finality: the seed phrase he thought he had written down lay in a bin somewhere in Haringey. The funds were not vast, but the lesson was. A single piece of paper had carried the power of absolute loss. That power had never felt real until the moment it exercised itself. The paradox of self-custody is ancient. Medieval merchants in Florence used dual-key chests to prevent any one partner from accessing coin alone. The logic was obvious: no single hand should be able to empty the vault. Yet the convenience of modern software tempts users back towards singularity. One seed phrase. One device. One location. It is a short, seductively simple path that leads straight back to the very fragility that earlier systems laboured to avoid. The truth is blunt. Digital ownership is only as durable as its weakest physical analogue. And that analogue—whether paper, metal, or hardware—remains human, fallible, losable. Custody, then, is not merely a technical function but a discipline. A custody setup is a decision about failure modes: which you tolerate, which you minimise, and which you refuse to accept. The motif that repeats across every design—Florentine chests, maritime ledgers, safety deposit boxes—is distribution. Spread control. Divide risk. Assume the worst not out of pessimism but out of respect for reality.

Seed phrases offer the most concentrated expression of this dilemma. They behave like master keys; whoever holds them commands the assets. That simplicity is both their strength and their danger. A phrase scrawled on a loose sheet of paper can outlive a hard drive but can also succumb to a spilled cup of tea. A digital backup might feel modern yet falls to a compromised cloud account or a synchronisation glitch. The implication is clear. Seed storage is less a question of format and more one of reliability. A single-location seed is a single failure point, a structure one accident away from collapse. Splitting storage across locations mirrors the old dual-key reasoning: even if one site is breached, the whole stays intact. Hardware wallets emerged as a response to these pressures. Ledger, founded in Paris in 2014, and Trezor, which released its first device in Prague the same year, pursued a similar idea: isolate private keys from internet-facing environments. The devices function as miniature signing oracles, approving actions without exposing the underlying secret. Their value shows itself in behaviour rather than promise. A malicious website can request a signature, but the hardware screen reveals the true action; a compromised browser can relay a transaction, but the device asks the user to confirm. These checks are modest yet powerful. They slow decisions by seconds, and those seconds often create space for awareness that a browser extension cannot. Yet hardware creates its own operational questions. A device left in a drawer for years risks battery degradation or firmware obsolescence. An owner may forget the PIN, misplace the cable, or defer an update until the device refuses to initialise. The limitation is not fatal, but it must be acknowledged. Tools protect only when the user maintains a relationship with them. A hardware wallet abandoned is little safer than a seed phrase taped to a monitor. The real measure is upkeep—regular checks, test recoveries, and deliberate storage choices.

Multisignature wallets shift the custody problem again. When Gnosis Safe—launched in Berlin in 2017—introduced widespread multisig adoption, it reframed control as a shared exercise. Instead of a single seed phrase, several keys authorise an action; the wallet executes only when a threshold is met. The model recalls the governance of old trading companies, where no one partner could unilaterally redirect capital. In DeFi, the effect is similar. A lost key harms the holder but not the collective. A stolen key grants no unilateral power. The risk disperses.
Still, multisig carries friction. Coordinating signatures across participants can slow urgent actions, especially when signers are travelling, disconnected, or simply asleep. A two-of-three wallet offers resilience, but a poorly organised team can turn that resilience into delay. The counter-example is not hypothetical. During the Wormhole incident

in February 2022, signers faced time pressure as they verified the breach and prepared remediation steps; coordination, not cryptography, dictated the tempo. The reconciliation lies in design: set thresholds proportionate to likely emergencies, distribute keys across predictable time zones, build communication channels in advance. Structure reduces the operational drag.

Trust, one of the slipperiest concepts in this domain, becomes concrete when paired with behaviour. A user who stores a seed in a single drawer expresses unspoken trust in chance. A user who scatters key shards across family homes declares trust in relationships. A user who commits to hardware security signals trust in the integrity of device manufacturers. In each case, the abstract idea becomes visible through choices, routines, and locations. Self-custody is thus not an ideology but a geometry: where secrets live, how they move, and who can see them. Distribution reappears as the motif. Not distribution in the social sense, but physical and procedural distribution: different rooms, different media, different rhythms of checking. The systems that fail most dramatically tend to be those that compress everything—seed, hardware, backups—into one convenient locus. Convenience is a gravitational force. It pulls all security decisions toward the path of least resistance. Good custody design resists that pull.

Two examples highlight the stakes. In June 2020, a developer in Singapore stored a seed phrase in a password manager and considered the matter settled. A synchronisation breach months later compromised the vault, exposing all stored keys. The user lost the entire balance. The collapse looked instantaneous, yet its root lay in a quiet overconfidence—a single vault treated as a fortress. By contrast, a collective in Lisbon operating a research treasury implemented a three-of-five multisig with keys distributed across family homes and office safes. When one signer's laptop was stolen in 2021, the impact was limited to annoyance. No funds moved. Security held because risk had been shared.

A counterpoint deserves mention. Excessive fragmentation can create paralysis. A user who splits seed shards across too many locations may struggle during relocation, illness, or international travel. A team that sets a multisig threshold too high may delay critical upgrades. Security that becomes unusable ceases to be security at all. The reconciliation lies not in maximalism but in proportion: design against plausible failures, not every conceivable one. Moderation is often the sharper tool.

Operational hygiene ties these ideas together. A seed phrase is static, but circumstances shift: addresses change, devices age, relationships evolve, and environments carry new threats. The habits that protect an asset must therefore be iterative. A periodic check of physical storage locations, a test recovery on a spare device, a deliberate review of who holds which keys—these routines transform custody from a single act into a maintained posture. History tells the same story. Armies, libraries, treasuries—all survived not through initial planning but through ongoing care. Digital assets demand the same commitment.

The deeper tension remains unresolved. How much friction should a prudent user accept? How many layers of distribution create resilience rather than complexity? And how does one judge when a custody setup has become either too fragile or too ornate? These questions lack universal answers. They require calibration against personal patterns, organisational structures, and the unavoidable unpredictability of life. What matters is not the pursuit of perfect security—a fiction—but the creation of a custody architecture that will endure the shocks that reality reliably delivers.

Approvals and Allowances

In November 2021, a researcher at SlowMist examined the aftermath of a routine-looking exploit on Ethereum that had siphoned more than $55 million in tokens from users of the DeFi platform BadgerDAO. The attack did not begin with a protocol failure. It began with an approval. Over several weeks, a compromised front-end injected a malicious script that tricked users into granting a spending allowance to an attacker-controlled contract. Once the approvals accumulated, the thief waited. When the moment felt right, they emptied the wallets in minutes. No seed phrases were leaked. No hardware wallets were bypassed. The users had simply authorised the wrong contract. The vulnerability existed not in cryptography but in habit. And the habit—click, confirm, continue—had become so normalised that few realised they were opening the door at all. Approvals sit at the quiet intersection of convenience and exposure. They are the keys we hand out so that protocols can move tokens on our behalf, a mechanism inherited from the ERC-20 standard and made ubiquitous by AMMs, lenders, and bridges. Approvals allow automation, batching, and efficiency: traits that make DeFi feel fluid. But they also create latent commitments, permissions that linger long after the interaction is forgotten. A user might remember a trade placed on Uniswap; they rarely remember the allowance granted to its router. This distance between action and permission—between what one intends and what one enables—is the central tension. It is the motif of the open door.

Approvals are conceptually simple: a contract can spend your tokens up to a set limit. Yet the behavioural reality is more complex. Interfaces commonly request a "max" approval to avoid repeated prompts, and many users accept it without thought. That acceptance is not neutral. It is a structural decision to outsource control. The door remains open indefinitely, even when the protocol is no longer used, its contract migrated, or its interface compromised. A single approval can surpass any seed phrase in its potential to do harm because it allows spending without further consent. Here, visibility matters. An approval is not visible in the mental model of most users; it is visible only on-chain. And what is out of sight tends to be out of mind.

Consider two contrasting examples. In January 2022, OpenSea—faced with an exploit that relied on stale Seaport approvals—warned users to revoke permissions on older listings. The vulnerability was not exotic. It hinged on the persistence of allowances for listings that appeared cancelled in the interface but remained active on-chain. The mismatch between what users saw and what the blockchain recorded created the gap through which attackers moved. By contrast, protocols like Aave or MakerDAO, whose interactions rely less on perpetual allowances and more on explicit deposits, leave a smaller window for misuse. Users commit assets directly; permissions do not remain open in the same way. The difference is architectural rather than moral. Some designs create fewer forgotten doors.

Still, a counter-example demonstrates the limits of caution. Even users who diligently revoke at the end of every session face a practical challenge: gas costs. During periods of network congestion—May 2021, November 2022, and March 2024 being memorable—revocation transactions became expensive. For many, the choice was stark: pay more to revoke than the tokens were worth or accept lingering exposure. This constraint reveals a deeper truth. Perfect security is rarely economically rational. The reconciliation lies not in pursuing frictionless safety but in adopting routines proportionate to the value and frequency of interaction. A weekly review of allowances, for instance, offers more reliability than frantic revocations during every market swing. Rhythm matters.

Naming the risk clarifies its shape. A forgotten approval resembles a dormant liability on a balance sheet—silent until activated. And unlike financial liabilities, which decay or are renegotiated, blockchain approvals persist until explicitly revoked. Persistence is the real adversary. Behavioural economics tells us that humans discount long-term risk when the effort to address it is immediate. That cognitive bias plays out daily in DeFi. Users approve now for convenience and defer revocation indefinitely. Attackers exploit not the standards, but the psychology.

Explorer tools expose this psychology in real metrics. Using Etherscan or Debank, one can measure the number of active allowances tied to a wallet. In research groups across Zurich and Singapore, analysts studying phishing recoveries have found a pattern: compromised wallets often carry dozens of approvals, many linked to protocols long abandoned. The excess is not incidental; it is structural. Each forgotten approval increases the exposed surface area, a set of financial USB ports open for any compatible attacker. The presence of twenty or thirty stale allowances is not unusual. It is normal. That normality is the problem.

Periodic allowance audits shift the story. They transform the abstract concept of "good hygiene" into a visible pattern of behaviour. A user reviewing their allowances weekly or monthly performs an act of risk digestion: absorbing what the wallet has accumulated and trimming it back to intentional commitments. The difference between intentional and accidental permissions is the difference between a controlled system and a porous one. The motif of the open door surfaces again: auditing is simply the act of walking the house and ensuring the doors you meant to leave open are open—and none others.

But audits alone do not fix everything. The approval model itself introduces asymmetries. Once granted, an allowance enables spending without time limits. It does not decay. It does not notify. It does not prompt re-authorisation. A contract may change owners, be upgraded, or exhibit behaviours not present when the user originally approved it. This temporal drift is subtle but consequential. A contract trusted in 2020 may be partially abandoned in 2023 or governed by a new group in 2025. Approvals are frozen in time even when the world around them moves. This mismatch is the structural weakness. The user trusts a snapshot; the chain executes in the present.

Historical parallels exist outside digital finance. Medieval notaries in Venice granted powers of attorney that persisted until formally revoked. Scholars studying the *Libri Commemoriali*—state records from the thirteenth century—note that forgotten powers occasionally enabled agents to act long after the principal's intentions had changed. The system endured because revocation rituals were embedded in civic life. Approvals in DeFi lack such ritual. They operate silently, without social cues or institutional reminders.

Users must build their own rituals or accept the consequences of neglect.

Two modern examples illustrate how structure shapes safety. After the 2021 exploit, BadgerDAO implemented pausable approval modules and integrated explicit allowance dashboards into its interface. This design brought the invisible into view. By contrast, many smaller protocols rely on default wallet prompts and provide no post-interaction visibility. The limitation is predictable. Users interacting with ten or twenty such protocols can accumulate a thicket of allowances with no intuitive way to monitor them. The reconciliation lies in standards. Interface-level transparency reduces both accidental exposure and user fatigue.

As always in DeFi, trade-offs anchor the closing tension. Convenience argues for broad, perpetual approvals. Safety argues for narrow, revocable ones. Gas fees argue for batching. Attackers argue for complacency. Somewhere in that intersection lies the user's real decision: *How many doors am I willing to keep open? For how long? And at what cost?* These questions cannot be deferred forever. Approval design is not an abstract concept in cryptography but a daily choice about what—exactly—you permit.

Phishing, Drainers, and UX Traps

On 1 April 2023, users of the Arthur Hayes–backed NFT project *Ordinals Pass* began reporting sudden, unexplained outflows from their wallets. Within hours, SlowMist and independent researchers traced the thefts—roughly $1.5 million in total—to a domain impersonation campaign. The attacker had registered a site nearly identical to the project's official page, differing by a single Unicode character. The mimicry was precise: same colour palette, same button placement, same loading animation. The only real difference was the contract behind the "Mint" button. Where the legitimate site prompted a reading call, the clone prompted a drain. The signatures looked routine. The loss was not. The attack demonstrated a recurring truth in decentralised finance: the adversary does not need to break cryptography when the weakest link is attention.

Such traps land with a quiet familiarity that should unsettle us. They borrow the calm of trusted environments—Discord channels, Twitter announcements, interface widgets—and twist it into a lure. Unlike protocol exploits, which often require engineering skill, phishing succeeds through psychology and timing. The attacker waits for a moment of excitement or fatigue, inserts a counterfeit detail, and capitalises on the first user willing to move quickly. The pattern is old. The surface is new. And the motif—misplaced trust manifested as a single click—threads through every case.

What distinguishes DeFi phishing from older forms of digital fraud is the finality of the outcome. A wrongly signed approval, a misread domain, a transaction broadcast to the wrong router: each is irreversible. Even regulated exchanges cannot always act in time when stolen tokens are bridged or swapped within minutes. That irreversibility is not a flaw; it is a design principle. But it also forces a shift in how we map and manage social attacks. Defence becomes behavioural rather than reactive. Vigilance becomes routine rather than exceptional.

Consider two well-documented examples. In July 2022, Coinbase customers in the United States were targeted by SMS alerts that mimicked its account verification system. The phishing page replicated Coinbase's backend prompts to harvest two-factor tokens. The design was not technically sophisticated, yet dozens of users lost access to their accounts. Contrast this with the December 2023 Ledger Connect Kit incident, where a compromised library pushed users to malicious dApp interfaces. In that case, the vector was infrastructural rather than social: a corrupted dependency rather than a forged message. But the user experience was similar in both events. The surface felt familiar; the danger sat behind an unchanged layout. The motif appears again: a familiar door leading to an unfamiliar room.

Limitations exist even for cautious users. A counter-example comes from September 2021, when a phishing wave targeted SushiSwap's MISO auction participants. The fake site did not rely on lookalike domains; it exploited DNS hijacking, redirecting the official domain itself. Even diligent habits—checking the address bar, confirming SSL certificates—were insufficient in that moment. The reconciliation lies not in abandoning habits but in layering them. Verification at multiple points reduces exposure even if no single method eliminates it.

Understanding how phishing evolves requires observing behaviour, not rhetoric. Attackers track user sentiment across social platforms. They strike after high-profile airdrops, governance votes, or token listings—periods when attention narrows and confirmation bias heightens. During the Optimism airdrop in June 2022, over fifty clone sites surfaced within twenty-four hours, each promising eligibility checks. Most harvested seed phrases directly. Others delivered drainer contracts disguised as "claim" functions. The common behaviour pattern was haste. When users rush, they skip steps. When they skip steps, attackers step in.

Drainers—malicious contract bundles designed to empty wallets after a single signature—depend on this tempo. Their success hinges not only on technical obfuscation but on the user's willingness to trust a prefilled transaction. The drainer does not need to hide its function entirely; it needs only to distract the user from reading what they are signing. In audit logs from BlockSec (2023), a significant proportion of victims signed blind transactions with function names like "setApprovalForAll" clearly visible. The text was not concealed. The attention was. The attacker knows the interface's greatest weakness: users read buttons, not calldata.

UX traps complete the triad. These traps do not rely solely on deception but on exploiting interface design choices. A notorious pattern is the preselected token in a swap interface. If an attacker injects a token with a misleading name—often a fake stable asset—they position it at the top of the token list. Users scanning quickly for "USDC" or "USDT" might click an impostor, especially when it shares the same icon. In 2022, Metamask reported an influx of support tickets where users swapped into valueless lookalike tokens. The UX was unchanged; the trap lay in the list. A similar pattern appears in mobile wallets with cramped screens: a signature request truncated mid-line, hiding the contract address, forcing the user to scroll. Many do not.

The key behavioural defence is not fear but habit. Verification habits create friction in the right places. They shift decision-making from impulse to pattern. A user who checks contract addresses, confirms domain spellings, reads signatures, and correlates them with expected behaviours establishes a rhythm that resists manipulation. In practical terms, this looks like pausing before approving, reading before signing, comparing before clicking. Metrics reinforce this change: a user who reduces blind-signing events to near zero reduces their exposure dramatically.

Some protocols attempt to institutionalise these habits through design. In 2023, ENS-integrated tools such as Rabby and Frame began displaying human-readable transaction warnings. They highlight spending limits, contract provenance, and behavioural anomalies—"This contract has drained 120 wallets in the past 24 hours"—using on-chain heuristics. This approach operationalises the verification instinct. It makes the invisible visible. But tools do not replace habits; they supplement them. The user still chooses whether to read.

A limitation emerges, however, in the social dimension. Verification habits do not always survive group dynamics. During hyped mints or airdrops, users influence one another's tempo. Screenshots shared in Telegram groups or Discord servers create a false sense of safety. "It worked for them, so it must be fine." Attackers exploit this herd effect by planting fabricated success stories. The counter-examples are instructive: after the Blur airdrop in February 2023, private groups circulated screenshots of successful claims from a fake interface. The claims were staged. The tokens were stolen. Social proof became social bait.

The reconciliation lies in adopting a personal rule that cannot be overridden by group sentiment: verify independently, always. The habit should survive excitement, pressure, and noise. It should survive even convenience. Especially convenience.

The closing tension is quiet but decisive. Every user must weigh speed against certainty. Every transaction poses the same unspoken question: *Do I trust what is in front of me, or do I take the extra seconds to confirm it?* The difference between the two paths is rarely visible at the moment of the click. It becomes visible only after the transaction settles.

Incident Response Playbook

At 02:07 UTC on 12 February 2024, the team behind the lending protocol Seneca Finance triggered an emergency pause from their office in Singapore. Minutes earlier, users had begun reporting that a pool of wrapped ether was draining faster than the interface could refresh. Etherscan confirmed the truth: a faulty permission check had allowed an attacker to siphon roughly $6 million before the pause froze further interactions. What happened next mattered as much as the exploit itself. The team issued a short, factual statement; block explorers flooded with revoked approvals; and researchers captured the state of user positions before arbitrage bots distorted the ledger. The recovery was far from painless, yet the decisive sequencing of actions prevented a wider collapse. The event showed how incident response in decentralised systems hinges on tempo and clarity.

This tempo becomes visible whenever a stablecoin breaks its peg. In March 2023, during the brief depeg of USDC following Silicon Valley Bank's receivership, liquidity vanished from Curve's principal pools. Users who saw the imbalance early could snapshot the pool's reserves and compare their exposure before the next block settled. Those who waited found slippage widening by the second. The contrast revealed a core lesson: information decays quickly under stress, and waiting for perfect clarity seldom helps. Even measured action requires a timestamp.

The motif that threads through all crises—whether a contract exploit, an oracle fault, or a depeg—is the same: a narrowing window. The window governs what can be paused, captured, or communicated before noise overtakes signal. The playbook, therefore, is not a list of instructions but a sequence of habits that impose structure on uncertainty.

The first habit is containment. Containment appears clearest when a protocol has a functioning pause mechanism, yet even users without administrative control can enact their own form of containment. A revoked approval is containment. A frozen interaction path is containment. In the Seneca case, revocation volumes on Etherscan spiked within ten minutes of the disclosure, an empirical sign that users understood the path of least harm. The implication is simple: even when the protocol's code is immutable in the moment, user permissions are not. Behaviour supplies the buffer.

Another case—Balancer's vulnerability disclosure in August 2023—illustrates how naming the problem cleanly accelerates containment. Balancer Labs announced a flaw affecting several boosted pools, publishing contract addresses and recommended withdrawals. Their message was brief, actionable, and free of speculation. Users responded by withdrawing over $100 million in liquidity within forty-eight hours, avoiding further exposure when secondary issues emerged. The structured communication demonstrated how naming a flaw precisely, without embellishment, compresses the uncertainty field and prevents panic from filling the gaps.

A limitation appears when the failing component is not a pool, contract, or approval but the price feed itself. During the compound oracle disturbance in November 2021, thin liquidity on a regional exchange caused a mispriced asset to propagate through the oracle's aggregation layer. Pausing would not have helped users who had already triggered liquidation thresholds based on bogus prices. Even perfectly revoked approvals could not undo the misread. The limitation is real. The reconciliation lies in understanding which failures lie within user control and which do not. Not every event is containable at the user level, but every event is clarifiable.

Clarification anchors the second habit: snapshotting. A snapshot is a decision to preserve context before it shifts. It can be as simple as recording a wallet's token balances, pool reserves, or oracle readings at the moment an anomaly appears. In the USDC depeg, users who logged Curve's tri-pool ratios at 0.95, 0.90, and 0.88 respectively could map their relative risk even as arbitrage bots churned through the pool. The act of capturing the state created a reference point for later judgement, insulating decisions from retrospective distortion. The motif of the narrowing window returns: the earlier the snapshot, the stronger its anchor.

Once containment and snapshotting stabilise the immediate environment, a third habit emerges: paced communication.

Pace matters because silence breeds conjecture, yet rushed commentary breeds errors. A measured tone signals competence. When Euler Finance suffered a $197 million attack in March 2023, its team published a timeline of known facts within hours. The format was sober: no adjectives, no predictions, just sequencing. Their calm set an example for users who were understandably anxious. Researchers could build on the information. Exchanges could monitor addresses accurately. The message did not solve the problem, but it prevented secondary crises from forming.

Yet communication can falter when it is misaligned with user expectations. A counter-example comes from the Meerkat Finance incident in March 2021, when developers claimed their protocol had been hacked only to later reveal it as a "test." Their ambiguous statements, library deletions, and sudden social media silence turned users against the project, leaving the truth contested. The limitation here is stark: communication without credibility collapses. Reconciliation comes from examining the ingredients of credibility—consistency, openness, and the refusal to overclaim.

The next phase of any playbook concerns positional hygiene. Once a threat is contained and understood, users must decide how to stabilise their exposure. Again, the goal is education rather than instruction. Observable behaviours—such as reducing reliance on a single bridge, separating operational wallets from storage wallets, or temporarily halting new interactions with affected contracts—demonstrate how readers can align decisions with risk horizons. In the aftermath of the Nomad bridge exploit in August 2022, users who monitored the bridge's rapidly draining reserves and paused interactions avoided the contagion that followed. The practical metric was reserve depletion per block, a simple observable proxy for stress.

Every incident reveals a structural insight about decentralised systems: their openness is both fuel and accelerant. Transparency enables users to verify claims, inspect transactions, and measure damage. But transparency also allows attackers and arbitrageurs to observe user behaviour in real time. This duality means incident response gains strength not from secrecy but from coordination. Even loose coordination—shared facts, consistent terminology, timestamped updates—reduces confusion. During the Curve stable pool imbalance of July 2023, researchers aligned quickly on the pool addresses involved and the timeline of swaps that created the distortion. The shared frame enabled coherent analysis despite minimal central authority.

The motif of the narrowing window deepens in the final stage: reflection. Reflection is not an afterthought but a structural requirement. It turns an incident into data. It identifies which habits succeeded and which failed. The most resilient protocols publish post-mortems not as performances but as diagnostic tools. Their value lies not in apportioning blame but in mapping sequences. When Ronin Network released its April 2022 post-mortem detailing the compromise of its validator set, the clarity of the sequencing allowed researchers across ecosystems to re-evaluate their own assumptions about multisig distribution and monitoring. Reflection propagates learning outward.

The unresolved tension at the heart of incident response is universal. When a fault appears, users must choose between speed and certainty. They must decide what to preserve, what to freeze, and what to communicate, often within the span of a few blocks. The question that follows is the playbook's true axis: *What is the minimum you must clarify before you act, and how long can you wait before the window closes?*

Chapter 7
Stablecoins and Peg Risk

The first hint that something had gone wrong arrived as a whisper on trading desks in New York: Circle had exposure to a failing bank. It was Friday, 10 March 2023. Hours later, when Silicon Valley Bank was placed into receivership in California, the world discovered that part of USDC's cash reserves was trapped inside. The reaction was immediate. On-chain markets marked the stablecoin at $0.97, then $0.94, then—briefly—lower still. Traders refreshed dashboards in disbelief as arbitrageurs, liquidity providers, and anxious holders converged in real time on the same question: *What is a dollar worth when the promise behind it is suddenly uncertain?* By Saturday morning, the peg had become a battleground of information, liquidity, and trust. The weekend unfolded like a slow-moving inversion of the stablecoin ideal. These instruments had been designed to smooth volatility, yet there they were, sliding across venues at three or four cents adrift from par. The dislocation was not only a market event; it was an epistemic one. Every participant had to decide, block by block, how much credibility to assign to the backing, the issuer, the redemption mechanics, and the collective psychology that normally keeps $1 close to $1. The episode exposed something deeper than a temporary mark-down. It revealed the way a peg is held not by a slogan or an algorithm but by a choreography of incentives, liquidity, and belief.

Stablecoins occupy a paradoxical position in decentralised finance. They are the quietest instruments in the ecosystem—intended to be dull, predictable, almost invisible in daily use—yet they are also the hinges upon which most DeFi activity turns. Lending markets denominate debt in them. AMMs quote pairs with them. Treasuries settle liabilities in them. They form the silent infrastructure of risk management, even as they conceal complex, fragile mechanisms beneath a simple ticker. The USDC weekend showed what happens when that silence is broken: the hum of hidden machinery becomes audible, and its flaws take centre stage.

Every stablecoin carries two stories. One concerns what it claims to be; the other concerns what it can prove. Fiat-backed issuers publish attestations. Crypto-collateralised designs expose every position on-chain. Algorithmic systems attempt to encode discipline in incentives and mint-burn equations. Each story has its own failure modes, and each invites a different sort of scrutiny. Some users prefer bank accounts and auditors. Others prefer smart contracts and transparent vaults. Still others gamble that reflexive demand can hold a peg long enough to create a new equilibrium. What unites them is that the peg is never absolute; it is negotiated continuously through redemption paths and liquidity depth.

That negotiation becomes especially vivid during stress. When a stablecoin trades at $0.99, the difference is trivial by traditional standards. Yet in DeFi, where collateral auctions, liquidation thresholds, and cross-chain interactions depend on exact pricing, a single cent becomes a signal: either an opportunity or a warning. Market makers rotate capital. Arbitrageurs test redemption pipes. Protocol treasuries check counterparty exposures. The small mispricing is not just a number; it is the ecosystem asking itself whether the promise behind the token still holds—and whether enough participants are willing to enforce that promise through their actions.

It is here that liquidity reveals its metaphysics. A peg is maintained not by declarations of value but by the ability to convert value reliably. If redemptions are gated, delayed, or opaque, confidence fractures. If depth on AMMs dries up, the visible price becomes a distorted mirror of collective anxiety. Conversely, when redemption windows function smoothly and market depth remains resilient, even sharp shocks can be absorbed without cascading failures. The peg, in that sense, is a living equilibrium—one that is continuously priced, tested, stretched, and repaired.

Several stablecoin failures in recent years demonstrate this elasticity. The collapse of TerraUSD in May 2022 was the most spectacular: a break from $1 to cents within days, fuelled by a reflex loop between mint-burn mechanics and market expectations. But quieter deviations offer lessons of equal value. Dai drifting to $1.03 in stressed collateral conditions. Euro-based stables trading thinly across chains. USDT briefly slipping during Tether's disputes with regulators. Each incident highlights different questions about transparency, redemption design, and market psychology. No two depegs are alike because no two pegs are held together by the same mix of incentives.

Understanding these dynamics requires more than memorising categories. It requires recognising that backing—whether treasury bills, ETH collateral, or algorithmic rules—determines not only a stablecoin's resilience but the social contract it strikes with its users. Fiat-backed tokens rely on institution-grade custody and assurances. Crypto-backed models rely on liquid collateral and overcollateralisation. Algorithmic systems rely on reflexivity and faith in supply-demand equilibria. The distinctions are technical, but the consequences are human: different pegs fail in different ways, and their failures impose different burdens on the people who rely on them for payroll, settlements, or collateral.

Those burdens ripple into the architecture of DeFi itself. Lending protocols must decide which stablecoins to accept and at what haircuts. Treasury managers must decide how much concentration risk they can tolerate. Traders must judge whether spreads between primary and secondary markets reflect temporary dislocations or deeper structural faults. Even casual users—those who simply want to move value across chains—must internalise the reality that not all dollars are created equal, even when they look identical on a screen.

Yet the chapter's central thread cuts deeper than cautionary tales. Stablecoins also represent something profoundly enabling in decentralised finance: a shared unit of account that allows experimentation, coordination, and settlement across jurisdictions and architectures. Their ubiquity makes them easy to overlook. But without them, the complex machinery of AMMs, lending protocols, bridges, and derivatives would lose their anchor. Understanding their mechanics is not merely defensive; it is foundational.

The following pages examine stablecoins not as monoliths but as systems: systems with inputs, incentives, vulnerabilities, and observable behaviour under stress. They explore why certain pegs hold and others break. They map the cues that distinguish orderly redemption from looming instability. They illuminate why a token trading at $0.99 might be an opportunity in one context and a warning in another. And they consider how users—whether individuals, funds, or protocols—can navigate these instruments with both ambition and prudence.

The open question that frames this chapter is deceptively simple: *What, exactly, do you trust when you trust a stablecoin?* The answer is not singular. It spans collateral, liquidity, governance, redemption, psychology, and the quiet assumptions embedded in every on-chain interaction. Understanding that blend is not optional. It is the difference between using stablecoins as tools and treating them as talismans. The next step is to pull apart those assumptions and see what holds them together.

Types of Stablecoins

Hours after Silicon Valley Bank was seized in California on 10 March 2023, traders looking at USDC's peg saw something uncanny: a stablecoin, supposedly backed one-for-one by cash and short-term treasuries, trading at $0.94 on decentralised exchanges. Circle, its issuer, confirmed exposure to the bank, and the market did the rest. The deviation was brief, yet it proved a lasting point. A stablecoin's design is only half its story; the other half is how convincingly it can demonstrate that its design works under stress. A peg is a promise backed by assets, transparency, and behaviour. When any of those misfire, the dollar becomes a question.

That weekend's scramble turned the market into a live experiment in what "backing" really means. Some traders pored over Circle's attestation reports. Others traced the on-chain flows of crypto-backed stables like Dai, comparing collateral buffers against hypothetical runs. A smaller group—still nursing memories of TerraUSD's collapse in May 2022—ignored both and rotated into tokens whose redeemability they could verify themselves on-chain, block by block. The split revealed the taxonomy at the heart of stablecoins: fiat-backed, crypto-collateralised, and algorithmic designs behave differently because they *fail* differently. And those failure modes, more than any marketing category, define how each instrument should be judged.

Fiat-backed stablecoins present the cleanest surface. Their issuers claim that every token corresponds to a dollar or a near-cash reserve held in regulated financial institutions. Tether's USDT and Circle's USDC dominate this group, publishing reserve compositions with varying degrees of clarity. The showpiece of these designs is the attestation: a document, typically monthly or quarterly, signed by an accounting firm. The attestation names the reserves. It shows their composition. It confirms total liabilities. But it does not guarantee real-time solvency. It is a snapshot, not a continuous stream. That gap matters. When USDC fell below par in March 2023, the market lacked immediate visibility into which banks held which deposits. That visibility lag was enough to create a temporary discount. A stablecoin backed by dollars still depends on *information timing*.

The implication is straightforward but consequential: fiat-backed stables trade on institutional credibility. Their strength is deep liquidity and straightforward redemption. Their weakness is that users must trust custodians they cannot audit directly. When Tether disclosed in 2021 that part of its backing included commercial paper rather than purely cash-like assets, scepticism spiked, and secondary markets tightened spreads as traders priced the possibility of correlated impairment. Even if the peg ultimately held, the episode confirmed the pattern. Fiat-backed designs centralise both backing and risk. When they wobble, the entire system waits on press releases, regulators, and banks.

Crypto-collateralised stablecoins answer a different question. Instead of relying on off-chain institutions, they put their reserves on-chain. MakerDAO's Dai, launched in December 2017, is the canonical example. Every unit of Dai is minted against collateral locked in smart contracts—originally ETH, now a broad portfolio including USDC, wrapped Bitcoin, and real-world assets. The crucial behaviour here is visible: anyone can measure the collateral ratio in real time. They can track liquidation thresholds. They can observe auctions. Transparency is continuous rather than episodic.

Yet visibility does not remove risk; it merely changes its shape. Crypto-collateralised systems are overcollateralised because crypto volatility can be brutal. When ETH fell quickly in March 2020, Maker's vaults experienced rapid liquidations. Some auctions cleared at zero bids due to gas congestion. The protocol had to mint and sell MKR to recapitalise itself—an emergency mechanism built into the design. The peg held, but at the cost of diluting governance token holders. The episode demonstrated a structural trade-off: transparency does not eliminate failure modes; it exposes them. And when exposure meets volatility, collateralised stables depend on liquid, functioning markets to absorb shocks.

This transparency nevertheless offers a crucial advantage. In periods of broader stablecoin uncertainty, Dai has sometimes traded *above* $1—not because of speculative frenzy, but because users preferred an instrument whose reserves they could inspect directly. This was evident during the 2023 USDC depeg, when some traders rotated into Dai despite its own partial exposure through USDC collateral. The preference was not about purity; it was about choosing a design whose mechanics could be verified without waiting for an attestation.

Algorithmic stablecoins attempt a bolder proposition: maintain a peg without full collateral backing. TerraUSD (UST), which collapsed in May 2022, remains the archetype. Its mint-burn mechanism relied on the convertibility between UST and LUNA. When demand fell, the system attempted to restore the peg by issuing more LUNA. In theory, the arbitrage was elegant. In practice, it was a reflexive spiral. As UST drifted to $0.99, redemptions flooded in. More LUNA was minted. The price of LUNA fell. Confidence collapsed. The peg snapped. Within days, a $40 billion network had imploded.

The limitation of algorithmic designs is structural: they rely on expectations as collateral. Their behaviour depends on users believing that the system will self-correct. When that belief falters, dilution outpaces demand, and the mechanism collapses. Yet algorithmic experiments persist. Smaller projects continue to explore variations with partial collateral or dynamic minting rules. The creativity is genuine, but the risks remain acute. These designs depend not just on code but on collective faith.

Even so, reducing stablecoin taxonomy to a leaderboard of safety misses something essential. Each category reflects a different philosophy of transparency. Fiat-backed stables disclose reserves through attestations produced by third parties. Crypto-collateralised designs disclose reserves through code, publishing collateral ratios block by block. Algorithmic stables disclose their mechanics but do not disclose reserves because there are none. What investors are really comparing is not simply *backing* but *methods of truth*.

Consider two checkable examples of how this truth manifests under pressure. First, during USDT's brief deviation to $0.97 on Kraken in May 2022, the market questioned the liquidity of its backing after court proceedings revealed past reserve opacity. The peg recovered quickly, but the dip reflected scepticism about disclosure more than solvency. Second, in March 2023, after the USDC depeg, MakerDAO held an emergency governance session assessing exposure to Circle's banking pipeline. The discussion occurred publicly on forums and calls; users could track collateral in real time, even as they questioned the system's reliance on off-chain assets. In both cases, the peg dynamics reflected the market's interpretation of transparency rather than simple arithmetic.

A credible counter-example also matters. Paxos-issued BUSD, backed by cash and treasuries, maintained near-perfect price stability for years. Yet in February 2023, New York regulators ordered Paxos to halt new minting. There was no insolvency. No run. No depeg. The peg held because redemptions remained open and reserves were intact. Yet the episode revealed a limitation: even a well-collateralised, well-regulated stablecoin can face existential shocks unrelated to market mechanics. Transparency cannot shield a token from jurisdictional risk. Reconciliation requires recognising that different trust vectors—market risk, operational risk, regulatory risk—are uneven across designs.

Throughout these dynamics, a quiet motif surfaces: *verification*. Users gravitate towards what they can verify. That might be an attestation dated to the previous month. It might be an on-chain collateral ratio that updates every block. It might be a redemption facility tested by arbitrageurs. Verification shapes confidence. Confidence shapes liquidity. Liquidity shapes the peg.

As markets globalise across chains and protocols, the implications of this taxonomy sharpen. Fiat-backed stables remain dominant in settlement and trading pairs because they offer scale. Crypto-collateralised designs remain central to decentralised infrastructures because they offer programmability and visibility. Algorithmic models persist at the fringes because they test the edges of what incentive engineering can produce. But none is immutable. A design that thrives in calm may fail in stress. A design that falters early may evolve into something more resilient.

The unresolved question is therefore not which category is "best" but which failure mode a user is willing to live with. Fiat-backed tokens fail through custodians. Crypto-backed tokens fail through volatility. Algorithmic tokens fail through reflexivity. Each embeds a different kind of uncertainty. The real trade-off is choosing the uncertainty you understand—and can verify—well enough to navigate.

Liquidity and Redemption

At 02:11 UTC on 11 March 2023, a trader in Singapore attempted to offload $8 million of USDC on a decentralised exchange. The peg was already buckling under the news of Circle's exposure to Silicon Valley Bank, and the pool he chose—a thin ETH/USDC pair on Uniswap—could not absorb the order. The execution cleared at an implied price of $0.88. Minutes later, another trader redeemed USDC directly through Circle's primary process at full value, albeit with a multi-hour settlement delay. The contrast revealed a truth that secondary markets usually disguise: a stablecoin does not have one price but two—its market price and its redemption price. The peg is the contested space between them.

What startled observers was not the deviation itself but the speed at which it emerged. In calm periods, arbitrageurs knit the primary and secondary markets together so tightly that retail traders assume perfect fungibility. In stress, that stitch unravels. The depth of liquidity on exchanges, the width of redemption windows, and the behaviour of arbitrageurs become the decisive mechanics. Where liquidity is shallow, spreads widen. Where redemption is slow, confidence fractures. A peg is upheld not by design alone but by the reflexes of those who defend it.

Redemption is the foundational behaviour. Fiat-backed issuers such as Circle or Paxos commit to exchanging their tokens for dollars at par. They specify cut-off times, settlement methods, and minimum sizes. These rules shape everything. They define how quickly a market-maker can recycle inventory. They define the cadence at which arbitrage can operate. They define whether a deviation is a transient trading blip or the first signal of structural impairment. When Circle paused weekend redemptions in March 2023 due to banking hours, the primary market shut its door just as the secondary market needed it most. Liquidity was still present; access was not.

The implication is direct. A stablecoin's reliability is not only a matter of what backs it but how quickly that backing can be converted. Redemption windows create time. Time determines whether arbitrageurs can act. Their actions determine whether a peg recovers.

Market depth shows this in motion. A deep pool spreads a shock across a wide base of liquidity. A thin pool magnifies it. Uniswap's data during the USDC depeg illustrated this sharply: even modest block-sized trades caused price impact of several percentage points. Compare that with Binance's USDT/USDC order book during the same period, where tens of millions could trade with minimal slippage. The two markets displayed the same nominal asset pair but radically different execution qualities. The metric that mattered was not "TVL" in isolation but *effective depth*—how much could be traded before the curve bent.

A second example clarifies the distinction. When Paxos-managed BUSD faced its regulatory halt in February 2023, the token's peg held far more tightly than many expected. Redemptions remained open. Market-makers continued to recycle inventory. Binance maintained depth in its primary trading pairs. Even as supply trended to zero, spreads stayed narrow. The token's regulatory future was uncertain, but its mechanical convertibility was not. The peg survived because the redemption engine remained intact.

A credible counter-example shows the limitation. Fei Protocol's FEI, launched in April 2021, attempted to maintain its peg algorithmically through bonding curve incentives rather than open redemptions. When volatility struck days after launch, users found themselves unable to exit at par. FEI traded at persistent discounts because there was no credible primary mechanism to restore parity. The system attempted to compensate with protocol-owned liquidity, but the absence of a direct redemption valve meant that arbitrageurs had nothing firm to arbitrage *to*. Liquidity without redemption proved insufficient. Reconciling this case with the prior examples highlights a central principle: liquidity can steady a peg only when redemption gives that liquidity an anchor.

Throughout these mechanics, a quiet motif threads the system: pressure. Pressure reveals where a stablecoin's promises are real and where they are rhetorical. A $1 price in calm means little; a $1 redemption in stress means everything. Pressure converts design claims into observable behaviour. It exposes where depth is genuine. It exposes where delays hide fragility. It exposes who steps in when markets hesitate.

Secondary markets, for all their speed, borrow credibility from the primary mechanism. Arbitrageurs monitor spreads between centralised exchanges, decentralised pools, and issuer redemptions. They strike when the difference exceeds costs. Their operations link the entire price fabric together. But they only act when settlement is predictable. If redemption is paused, constrained, oversized in minimums, or bottlenecked by banking hours, arbitrage falters. When arbitrage falters, secondary markets unspool.

This interaction became especially visible during Dai's collateral stresses in March 2020. As ETH crashed and gas fees spiked, Dai's market price rose above $1—not because the token had become inherently more valuable, but because redemptions through Maker's liquidation system lagged behind market conditions. The collateral auctions could not clear quickly enough. Market depth was shallow relative to demand for a trustworthy stable asset. The peg's resilience came not from a deep pool but from the certainty that collateral-backed redemption would eventually restore parity. Traders were willing to wait. Their willingness was the peg's defence.

The distinction between redemption and liquidity becomes even sharper across chains. A stablecoin bridged from Ethereum to another network does not bring its redemption rights with it. It brings only the issuer's promise to honour redemptions on the origin chain. When USDT depegged briefly on Kusama in 2022 during exchange imbalances, holders could not redeem directly on that network. They had to bridge back—incurring delay and cost—before they could act. The peg looked broken locally even while it held globally. Market depth without redemption locality created a temporary dislocation.

This dynamic points to a broader implication: a stablecoin is only as strong as its weakest redemption environment. Cross-chain liquidity fractures the peg into regional variations. Market-makers respond by adjusting inventory and spreads across networks. Users experience these differences as slippage, queueing, and widened spreads. But beneath these behaviours lies a structural truth: the peg is not monolithic; it is a negotiation.

None of this suggests that redemption must be continuous to work. Tether's model, with high minimums and operational cut-offs, has maintained its peg for years. It works because market-makers with privileged redemption access smooth the price for everyone else. The public cannot redeem at will; the peg holds because specialised intermediaries do. This division of labour is not inherently flawed, but it creates uneven transparency. Users must trust that the entities with redemption access will continue to act. Liquidity depth in secondary markets becomes a proxy for this invisible machinery.

And that proxy can be fragile. A surge of redemptions may test inventory. A clogged chain may delay execution. A regulatory freeze may halt the primary valve. Each of these pressures stresses a different seam of the peg. When several occur simultaneously, spreads widen not linearly but exponentially.

The unresolved question sits quietly beneath every stablecoin chart: how quickly can this token return to $1 when the world gives it a reason not to? That question is not answered by its category—fiat-backed, crypto-backed, or algorithmic—but by the behaviour of its redemption and liquidity mechanisms under shock. A peg is not a property. It is a performance. And the next time the market squeezes one, traders will look past the brand, the audit, and the design, and ask the only question that matters in those few stressed hours: *what can be redeemed, where, and at what depth?*

Depeg Dynamics

At 08:34 UTC on 12 March 2023, Coinbase's USDC/USD pair in New York showed $0.91 while Binance's equivalent pair in Tokyo traded at $0.93. On Curve's USDC/DAI/USDT pool in London, the imbalance was visible in the pool composition itself: USDC had swollen to more than 70 per cent of the reserves, an unmistakable sign that traders were offloading the token into any venue that still priced it close to par. The numbers told a simple story. The peg had slipped. But what followed — the spread between exchanges, the surge in Curve incentives, the sudden throttling of redemptions as banks closed for the weekend — told a deeper one: a depeg is not a moment. It is a chain reaction. And once it begins, its trajectory depends less on the magnitude of the initial shock than on how traders, protocols, and liquidity provisions respond to it. When USDC crept back to $0.99 in the early hours of 13 March, the recovery was not spontaneous. It was built on a sequence of decisions: Circle's disclosure that $3.3 billion of its reserves were trapped at Silicon Valley Bank; the subsequent guarantee by US regulators on 12 March; the willingness of market-makers to resume aggressive arbitrage; and the emergence of rich liquidity incentives on Curve that paid traders to realign the pool. Recovery was stitched together by incentives, not by faith. A peg does not fix itself. People fix it, one trade at a time.

The recurring motif visible in every depeg is imbalance. Market depth thins on one side; liquidity migrates; behaviour cascades. An orderly stablecoin market shows roughly even pool compositions and tight spreads. A stressed one exhibits asymmetry: one asset floods a pool while its counterpart drains. This imbalance is not merely a symptom but a diagnostic tool. It shows where fear is flowing.

A depeg begins when a structural question becomes a trading decision. In March 2023, the question was whether Circle's reserves were safe. In May 2022, during the unraveling of TerraUSD, the question was whether an algorithmic stabilisation mechanism could withstand a sudden sell cascade. In both cases, the decisive shifts occurred not when traders lost faith but when liquidity providers began withdrawing depth. Visible behaviour changed before prices did.

Liquidity incentives often serve as the first recovery cue. On Curve, during USDC's wobble, the gauge incentives jumped sharply as protocols and large holders sought to attract stabilising flows. This is the *show* phase: the protocol displays willingness to spend. Then comes the *name*: this incentive is a temporary subsidy. Next, the *explain*: subsidies entice arbitrageurs to absorb imbalanced inventory, narrowing the deviation. And finally, the *implication*: if incentives decline before equilibrium returns, the recovery reverses. Incentive programmes are bridges; they must be long enough to reach the other side.

A second checkable example demonstrates how feedback loops differ across designs. During Dai's March 2020 liquidity crisis, ETH's price collapse and surging gas costs slowed Maker's liquidation machinery. Dai traded above $1 on Coinbase Pro in San Francisco — temporarily reaching $1.10 — because bidders could not clear auctions quickly enough. Later that year, in September 2020, the opposite dynamic occurred when USDT/DAI liquidity on Curve ballooned and Dai fell to $0.997 as levered farmers unwound positions. Both depegs emerged from feedback loops, but their direction and severity depended on how quickly the protocol's safety valves could operate.

The credible counter-example to mechanical recovery is TerraUSD's breakdown in May 2022. While styled as algorithmic, UST relied heavily on liquidity depth in the

UST/USDT pool on Curve to maintain its peg. When a large withdrawal of UST liquidity altered the balance in early May, the algorithmic stabiliser – minting and burning LUNA – could not keep up with the pace of redemption demand. This demonstrated a critical limit: incentives and algorithms can steady a peg only when liquidity remains present. If liquidity vanishes, the feedback loop turns reflexive, and the spiral accelerates. Reconciling this case with earlier recovery examples emphasises the importance of *liquidity persistence* as a precondition for repair.

Throughout these cycles, a pattern emerges: traders anchor on specific thresholds, especially $0.99. The move from $1.00 to $0.99 is psychologically negligible but mechanically profound. It signals that arbitrage is no longer seamless. Institutions start modelling the probability of deeper impairment. Retail participants accelerate their exits. The motif of imbalance intensifies: pools tilt, spreads widen, and market depth fractures. The stablecoin behaves less like a currency and more like an asset under stress.

Feedback loops manifest in three forms: informational, structural, and behavioural. Informational loops occur when rumours front-run facts; a tweet moves faster than an attestation. Structural loops occur when market plumbing slows – redemption windows narrow, gas fees rise, bridges clog. Behavioural loops occur when traders sell because other traders are selling. These loops do not act independently but compound one another. A delayed attestation amplifies a structural bottleneck; a structural bottleneck amplifies a behavioural rush.

Visible metrics allow observers to distinguish a transient wobble from a structural break. Depth in the largest pools shows whether exit pressure is being absorbed or diverted. Redemption volume shows whether primary actors are engaging. Cross-venue spreads reveal whether market-makers still believe in eventual parity. During USDC's 2023 depeg, the narrowing of Binance–Coinbase spreads from eight cents to one cent preceded the full recovery by hours. Recovery begins in the spread, not the spot price.

Another behavioural cue is *inventory risk*. Market-makers will only arbitrage a depeg if they can reliably exit their positions. When they step back, the peg enters a vulnerable state. A pegged asset without active market-makers is a ship without ballast; even small trades distort its trajectory. The March 2023 recovery only began once market-makers saw that redemptions would soon resume at scale. Their re-entry shrank slippage, tightened spreads, and restored confidence.

The counterforce to feedback loops is policy clarity. During BUSD's regulatory transition in February 2023, Paxos maintained redemptions and published daily updates. The token's peg held not because there was no uncertainty but because uncertainty was bounded. Information guided behaviour rather than destabilising it. This contrasts sharply with situations where issuers fall silent. In those cases, lack of communication itself becomes a catalyst for further deviation.

Across all examples, a single motif returns: imbalance. A depeg grows when imbalance is left unmanaged. It shrinks when action rebalances the system — through incentives, depth restoration, or timely disclosure. Imbalance is both the warning signal and the recovery map.

Every stablecoin, regardless of design, faces the same unresolved test: *what happens when the market believes you are worth less than you say you are?* The answer is not predetermined. It emerges from depth, incentives, redemption access, and communication. The true measure of a stablecoin is how it behaves when its peg is tested, its liquidity thinned, and its promises scrutinised minute by minute. The next time a major stablecoin ticks from $1.00 to $0.99, the question facing every attentive observer will be a simple one with complex consequences: is this the start of imbalance — or its repair?

Using Stables Wisely

At 09:12 EST on 13 March 2023, Circle announced from Boston that USDC redemptions would resume fully once US banks opened. A few hours earlier, on Binance's USDT/USDC pair in Singapore, traders had been accepting $0.94 for the token. By mid-afternoon in London, the Curve 3pool had swollen to over 75 per cent USDC. The market's reaction — and its eventual normalisation — revealed something essential: the meaning of "stable" changes depending on where the asset sits in a portfolio. A treasury buffer absorbs volatility. Collateral channels liquidation risk. Settlement balances demand immediacy. One instrument cannot play every role. Nor should it. The weekend's jagged charts showed how placement, not just selection, defines whether a stablecoin supports or distorts a system. Those who held USDC as a short-horizon settlement asset experienced very little disruption once redemptions reopened; those who used it as collateral inside leverage loops watched liquidation thresholds lurch unpredictably. The same token behaved differently depending on its function. The quiet motif emerges early: context shapes stability.

Stablecoins invite a false simplicity. Their tickers promise sameness. Their pegs suggest interchangeability. Yet their mechanics diverge sharply. Fiat-backed stables such as USDC derive steadiness from off-chain banking rails. Crypto-collateralised assets such as DAI inherit the volatilities and reflexivities of their underlying reserves. Algorithmic designs — exemplified by TerraUSD before its collapse in May 2022 — rely on incentive loops that work until liquidity thins. Using each type without regard for its structural limits is not strategy. It is misplacement.

Consider treasury balances first. A treasury seeks safety, predictability, and accessibility over long horizons. In February 2023, Paxos continued redeeming BUSD for dollars at par despite regulatory pressure in New York. Its transparency updates and redemption windows offered a predictable rhythm. A treasury that held BUSD through that period was exposed to regulatory narrative risk, yet operationally it retained access to primary liquidity. Conversely, a treasury that held UST in early May 2022 anchored itself to a mechanism whose resilience depended on the LUNA mint-burn engine and consistent market depth. A treasury's horizon is not measured in hours. It is measured in contingencies. *Show → Name → Explain → Implication:* contrasting BUSD's managed wind-down with UST's spiral shows why backing mechanics, redemption design, and issuer discipline matter far more for treasury use than headline volume or points incentives.

Collateral plays a harsher game. Collateral must endure stress. In March 2020, Maker's DAI peg strained above $1 due to gas-driven delays in liquidation auctions. Collateralised borrowers stood at the mercy of two visible metrics: auction throughput and gas pricing. A stablecoin serving as collateral must not merely maintain its peg; it must maintain liquidity in the venue where liquidations execute. When USDC depegged briefly in March 2023, borrowers using USDC-backed positions at Aave or Compound saw their health factors contract despite the token's ultimate return to $1. Because liquidation thresholds reference oracles, even a small deviation can hit collateral users with mechanical consequences. The implication is stark. Stability for collateral is not about long-term parity. It is about path-dependence. A two-cent wobble at the wrong moment can move a liquidation bot faster than a redemption desk.

Settlement balances require yet another profile. Settlement is about immediacy: fast conversions, shallow slippage, wide venue coverage. During Dai's September 2020 dip to roughly $0.997 on Curve, settlement users scarcely noticed; the deviation was narrow, and liquidity remained deep. But those settling trades with smaller algorithmic tokens — such as sUSD during brief liquidity squeezes in late 2021 — experienced visible frictions: widening spreads on Uniswap v3; MEV arbitrage capturing the gap; inconsistent quotes on aggregators. A settlement asset must offer one behaviour: predictable execution. Anything less turns routine transfers into probabilistic wagers.

Two examples clarify how mechanics interact with placement. First, in May 2023, EURC — Circle's euro-denominated stablecoin — displayed tight primary redemption mechanics but thin secondary liquidity. For treasuries, this was acceptable; for settlement, it was limiting. Second, LUSD, a crypto-collateralised stablecoin from Liquity, maintained a hard floor via redemptions but exhibited thinner liquidity on some decentralised venues. This made it attractive as a treasury hedge but less fluid as collateral or settlement. These cases show the principle: placement must match mechanics, because each mechanic dictates how the token behaves under pressure.

A credible counter-example complicates the neat categorisation. USDT has, at moments, faced public scrutiny — notably in October 2018 during concerns about reserve clarity — yet its market depth across exchanges in Hong Kong, Singapore, and Europe has often been unmatched. Its liquidity footprint reduces functional frictions even when narrative risk rises. How does this reconcile with earlier claims? It illustrates that transparency and liquidity interact rather than substitute for each other. A stablecoin with imperfect transparency but immense liquidity may serve settlement more effectively than a fully transparent but thinly traded counterpart. Placement dignity comes from matching strengths, not idealising purity.

Across all categories, behaviour distinguishes a stablecoin's role more than ideology. A treasury asset must show discipline in disclosures and redemption cadence. A collateral asset must show resilience in oracles and liquidation paths. A settlement asset must show breadth of liquidity and tight spreads. Each role demands a different visible behaviour: cadence for treasuries, throughput for collateral, depth for settlement. Mixing these without discrimination creates hidden fragilities.

During 2023's USDC depeg, one pattern separated calm portfolios from chaotic ones: diversification across issuers *and* mechanics. Those with exposure spread across USDT (banking independence), DAI (crypto-collateral buffers), and USDC (strong attestation and banking ties) encountered a distributed set of risks rather than a single point of failure. This is not investment advice; it is structural observation. A peg can slip for reasons that differ fundamentally — banking delays, collateral liquidations, liquidity withdrawals. Diversification acknowledges that no stablecoin solves every failure mode.

The motif of context reappears. A token does not behave the same way in every compartment of the portfolio. Context magnifies or mutes its strengths. Placing an asset with slow redemption mechanics into a settlement role introduces friction. Placing a token reliant on deep AMM pools into a treasury role introduces tail exposure to liquidity drain. Placing a stablecoin prone to regulatory headlines into critical collateral loops invites liquidation cascades triggered by sentiment rather than fundamentals. Context shapes stability.

Observe trader behaviour during stress events and you see placement preferences emerge in real time. When USDC hit $0.94, traders used USDT for settlement, DAI for arbitrage, and ETH for collateral top-ups. The choreography was improvisational but logical. Each asset gravitated to the role where its mechanics excelled. This behavioural clustering offers the most practical diagnostic for readers: watch what people *do* with a stablecoin, not what they say.

As stablecoins integrate more deeply into lending markets, bridges, and automated strategies, the stakes of placement rise. A treasury misallocation may cause discomfort. A collateral misallocation may trigger liquidations. A settlement misallocation may break execution chains. The portfolio's architecture becomes a quiet form of risk management, distributing failure modes across compartments.

The open question remains as markets grow more interconnected: when the next peg wobbles by a fraction of a cent, will the chosen placement of each stablecoin dampen the impact — or amplify it?

Chapter 8
Governance, Tokens and Power

The message appeared on the forum at 02:17 UTC on 27 June 2022. It was brief—five paragraphs, a few charts, and one clean proposal: reduce liquidity incentives by 40 per cent to slow dilution. Within hours, addresses holding more than a third of the protocol's governance tokens had signalled support. Most belonged to two funds based in Singapore and Chicago. By the time general holders on the West Coast woke up, the vote was effectively over. The change passed with barely 4 per cent turnout. It was not malicious. It was efficient. Yet for many contributors in the project's London chat room that morning, the efficiency felt uncomfortably close to capture. The outcome was sound; the process was not. Power had revealed itself not through scandal but through quiet asymmetry.

These moments animate the central tension of decentralised governance. Decisions that determine risk parameters, emissions budgets, fee shares or treasury expansions often hinge on who shows up, who coordinates, and who carries the most weight. A protocol may advertise itself as decentralised, but its voting patterns tell a more forensic story. Turnout becomes a proxy for legitimacy. Concentration becomes a measure of fragility. Delegates become the hinge between voice and silence. The scene repeats, with variations, across projects, networks, and years. Power moves fastest when others sleep.

Every protocol must eventually answer a simple question: who decides? Token-weighted voting expresses one philosophy: capital carries responsibility. Councils and committees express another: expertise tempers impulsive crowds. And delegation systems present a hybrid: holders choose stewards who carry sustained attention into complex debates. None is perfect; all can ossify. Yet together they reveal what is at stake in governance: the structure through which a collective translates intention into action. Decisions are not abstract. They shape emission curves, collateral lists, interest bands, oracle choices, and fee flows. They dictate survival during stress and direction during calm.

Once the actors are visible, incentives come sharply into focus. A governance token is not merely a claim on future cash flows; it is a behavioural instrument. Designs that reward short-term participation at the expense of long-term resilience invite a specific pathology: voters who favour inflationary bribes, mercenary liquidity, and parameter choices that enlarge their slice even as the protocol's core economics weaken. Fee-sharing, by contrast, binds holders to protocol revenue, aligning reward with performance. These mechanisms resemble political systems more than financial ones. They reveal how reward shapes judgement. If incentives are misaligned, even well-meaning voters drift toward actions that undermine the very protocols they claim to steward.

Treasury management raises the stakes further. Many DAOs hold treasuries that would make mid-sized companies in Berlin or Toronto blush. Yet their governance processes often oscillate between exuberance and paralysis. A well-governed treasury must address runway, diversification, hedging, and operational liquidity. Some DAOs, such as those that adopted structured diversification programmes in late 2021, treated treasury as institution-building. Others left billions in volatile tokens, suffering sharp drawdowns that undermined their ability to fund contributors or defend pegs. Treasuries reflect a protocol's self-understanding: whether it behaves as an institution preparing for winters or a market participant assuming perpetual spring.

The connective tissue of all governance is the proposal. A strong proposal makes its own logic transparent: the problem is defined; the options are compared; the metrics for success are explicit; the kill-switch is clear. During the rise of "ve"-style tokenomics in 2021, some proposals offered meticulous models, sunset clauses, and stress tests. Voters could assess them as one would evaluate public policy. Others arrived as vague entreaties, appealing to vibes rather than numbers. Reading proposals critically becomes a civic act, a defence against ambiguity masquerading as innovation. Governance resists drift when scrutiny is normal.

Modern governance in crypto sits at an intersection of ancient questions and novel tools. Power, legitimacy, representation, and capture are not new themes. Athens debated them. Florence fought over them. Cooperative movements in 19th-century Britain refined them. What changes now is the mechanism: smart contracts, timelocks, token thresholds, auditable histories. Code introduces precision and removes plausible deniability. But code does not neutralise power. It merely records its movement.

Within this chapter, the argument will unfold across four planes: who makes decisions; how their incentives shape those decisions; how resources are stewarded; and how proposals warrant scrutiny. Each plane offers a different vantage point on the same core puzzle: how a protocol guards itself from its own governance. The motifs of turnout, attention, and alignment will appear repeatedly, because they define whether a community behaves as a genuine collective or a stage where a few choreograph the many.

The reader stands at a threshold. The systems described here are young, malleable, and full of contradictions. They reward those who read carefully, think structurally, and ask unfashionable questions about power. But they also reward those who know when silence signals consent, when turnout signals apathy, and when incentives signal drift. The tension endures: how do you build open governance without allowing the openness to be used against you?

Who Decides What

The vote that reshaped Cream Finance's collateral parameters in August 2021 passed in less than twenty-four hours. Two addresses, both identifiable through Etherscan as funds based in Hong Kong and San Francisco, supplied over 60 per cent of the tokens cast. The proposal tightened loan-to-value ratios on several long-tail assets; it was technically sound and arguably prudent. Yet the pattern unsettled contributors observing the vote unfold on Telegram: turnout remained below 5 per cent, deliberation was thin, and the outcome depended on holders who never once joined a public forum discussion. The change improved stability. It also exposed a deeper fault line: decisions that affect an entire protocol can hinge on the behaviour of a few who neither explain their reasoning nor engage with those who must operate the consequences. Power concentrates quietly, through coordination and absence.

Such episodes illuminate a recurring motif in decentralised governance: silence as a decision vector. Token-weighted voting appears egalitarian at a distance—anyone may participate, none is formally disenfranchised. But the ledger reveals a more brittle reality: influence flows to those who act consistently, marshal size, or delegate strategically. The paradox is stark. A system designed to broaden agency often ends up rewarding the narrowest slice of participants: those with the largest balances, the fastest scripts, or the deepest attention reserves. The protocol may remain decentralised in architecture yet centralised in practice.

Token voting forms the first layer of authority in most governance frameworks. Its appeal rests on clarity: holders signal preferences directly; smart contracts tally votes mechanically; decisions execute without interpretive drift. MakerDAO's executive votes illustrate this model. Every week, parameters across collateral types—from debt ceilings to stability fees—move through a transparent process. But beneath the surface lies the behavioural substrate that shapes these outcomes. Many holders rarely vote; some delegate but never review their delegates' track records; a few entities vote with near-perfect attendance. Show: a distribution curve of participation where the median voter is absent. Name: MakerDAO's participation analytics from April 2022 documented consistent turnout clusters below 15 per cent. Explain: low turnout amplifies the marginal influence of highly active participants, especially those with scale. Implication: decision legitimacy becomes sensitive to concentration, even as the technical mechanism appears neutral.

The second layer arises from councils and committees—structures intended to temper volatility and expertise gaps. Arbitrum's Security Council, elected in March 2023, exemplifies this hybrid design. The council carries responsibility for emergency upgrades and protocol freezes, roles too sensitive for open token votes under time pressure. Here governance borrows from corporate and civic precedents: entrust complex or urgent tasks to those with demonstrated competence and clear mandates. Yet the very insulation that grants councils their effectiveness introduces a tension. Councils are efficient when aligned and attentive; they are brittle when inattentive or captured. A council decision that bypasses community sentiment may solve an immediate threat yet provoke long-term distrust. Show: the community uproar when a Layer-2 security council approved an unannounced contract change in December 2023. Name: the event was logged on-chain and reported through governance tracking platforms. Explain: concentrated authority, even when justified, triggers legitimacy concerns when communication lags. Implication: councils must pair action with transparency, or their advantages erode.

Delegation forms the third layer, bridging raw token voting and insulated councils. The model gained prominence during Compound's governance expansion in 2020 and matured across protocols like ENS during its 2021 airdrop. Delegates act as sustained participants, offering continuity and context. They read proposals thoroughly, speak with contributors, and maintain voting patterns over months. But delegation works only when holders monitor it. When they do not, the system drifts into a quasi-representative regime where delegates accumulate influence by inertia rather than merit. A delegate with millions of voting units may face no effective accountability, especially if the underlying holders dispersed their governance tokens for reasons unrelated to civic interest. Show: delegate dashboards often reveal stark differences between voting power and engagement. Name: public analytics from platforms such as Tally in mid-2022 consistently displayed delegates with significant voting weight but sporadic activity. Explain: misalignment between delegated power and active stewardship. Implication: without periodic review, delegation hardens influence without guaranteeing judgement.

Where these three layers intersect lies the central puzzle of turnout versus capture. Turnout measures the breadth of participation; capture describes the concentration of power. A system may exhibit high turnout yet remain captured if a few large actors coordinate outcomes. Conversely, a system may avoid capture yet suffer low turnout, producing decisions that lack broad legitimacy even when technically sound. The motif returns: silence shapes outcomes as much as voice. This is not abstract. When Aave revised risk parameters for volatile assets in January 2022, turnout exceeded 20 per cent; the diversity of participating addresses restrained any single faction. When a smaller lending protocol altered its liquidity mining schedule in October 2021, two exchanges effectively dictated the result. In both cases, the mechanics were identical; the social layer made the difference.

The temptation is to assume that capture is always malign or that turnout always strengthens quality. Neither belief survives scrutiny. Coordinated whales can stabilise a protocol during stress—some prominent holders prevented a problematic collateral type from passing a debt ceiling increase in a 2022 MakerDAO vote. Conversely, mass turnout can amplify fads or momentum, especially when token holders conflate governance with speculation. The limitation is structural: token voting treats capital as a proxy for competence, attention, and alignment. Sometimes the proxy works. Often it does not. Yet no protocol can dispense with it entirely without abandoning the very decentralisation it seeks to maintain. Reconciliation lies in recognising that token voting is not a constitution but a substrate—one that requires supporting structures.

One such structure is quorum calibration. Another is time delay. A third is role segmentation: separating emergency powers, parameter updates, treasury allocations, and constitutional changes into different voting paths. The design mirrors political theory more than financial engineering. Show: Curve's implementation of separate gauges for emissions in 2021. Name: the gauge voting system explicitly segmented authority, distributing influence across hundreds of pools. Explain: segmentation reduces the scope for any single vote to wield disproportionate effect. Implication: capture becomes more difficult because influence must be exerted repeatedly across many decision points.

Limitations persist. A vivid counter-example emerged during SushiSwap's tumultuous governance debates in late 2020, when internal conflict, founder withdrawals, and unclear role boundaries produced a drift that neither token voting nor ad-hoc councils resolved. The system needed structure before it needed votes. Reconciliation came later, through well-defined roles, multisig oversight, and clearer processes. This underscores a broader point: governance machinery cannot compensate for foundational ambiguity. The motif of silence reappears—ambiguity invites it.

The deeper question remains unresolved: how does a decentralised protocol ensure that those who decide bear the consequences of their decisions? Token voting ties influence to capital exposure; delegation ties influence to reputational exposure; councils tie influence to operational accountability. Each path embodies a different theory of responsibility. The design challenge is not to choose among them but to interlock them such that failures in one do not cascade across the system.

The chapter cannot resolve this tension; it can only sharpen it. The forward test endures: when a contentious proposal emerges—an emissions change, a treasury swap, a collateral listing—what signals should a thoughtful participant examine first? Turnout, concentration, alignment, history. Do those who decide carry enough stake, context, and scrutiny to justify their weight? Or is silence doing the deciding again?

Incentive Compatibility

When Curve deployed its "gauge voting" mechanism in August 2020, a handful of early observers noticed a strange divergence. Liquidity providers on some pools earned annualised returns well above 50 per cent, yet several of those pools generated negligible trading fees. The rewards came almost entirely from token emissions rather than genuine economic activity. This imbalance produced a clear outcome by October: deep liquidity accumulated in places where no users traded, while genuinely needed pools struggled for depth. The token incentives worked mechanically, yet failed behaviourally. The system rewarded presence, not usefulness. A mechanism designed to allocate capital efficiently instead attracted arbitrageurs whose scripts harvested emissions with no interest in the protocol's underlying health. The episode caught the attention of researchers across Berlin and Singapore who chronicled it on public dashboards, marking a pivotal moment in the debate over incentive compatibility.

The motif emerged from that period and threads through this piece: *alignment is revealed in behaviour, not rhetoric.* Protocols can declare that rewards should strengthen the system, but users respond to what pays, not what is preached. The question is simple: do the incentives encourage actions that improve the protocol's resilience, or do they subsidise actions that inflate short-term metrics while hollowing out long-term viability? The gulf between these two regimes is where governance either matures or decays.

The starting point lies in distinguishing fee-sharing from inflationary bribes. Show: Uniswap's fee switch—tested in specific pools through governance discussions in 2022—tied rewards to actual trading revenue. Name: the trial involved votes in April and November, with heavy scrutiny from researchers at Gauntlet and independent delegates. Explain: fee-sharing links rewards directly to real utilisation, meaning liquidity providers and token holders earn only when traders pay. Implication: incentives stay grounded in usage, not token emissions, reducing the risk of speculative loops.

By contrast, inflationary incentives can detach from economic activity. Show: the 2021 emissions race on Avalanche where multiple protocols issued vast quantities of governance tokens to attract mercenary capital. Name: Trader Joe's liquidity campaigns between September and December 2021 illustrate the pattern, with triple-digit APRs driven primarily by token subsidies. Explain: when emissions dominate returns, capital behaves opportunistically, migrating as soon as a rival pool offers a higher nominal yield. Implication: protocols risk a brittle equilibrium—liquidity looks deep until incentives pause, after which depth collapses. The motif reappears: behaviour reveals alignment; capital that arrives for emissions leaves without warning.

The most telling examples come from protocols that recalibrated incentives to escape self-inflicted distortions. Balancer's 2022 fee weighting reforms, implemented after months of community debate, attempted to anchor emissions to performance metrics: trading volume, volatility bands, and stability measures. The reforms acknowledged a limitation: pure token-weighted incentives can inflate pools with little economic purpose. The redesign introduced granularity, making the incentives reflect usefulness rather than presence. The mechanism did not remove emissions; it made them conditional. This nuance matters. Incentive compatibility does not mean abolishing subsidies—it means ensuring subsidies steer behaviour towards collective benefit.

Yet exceptions remind us that no design is foolproof. A counter-example sits in the history of algorithmic stablecoin farms in early 2022—particularly the frantic accumulation of governance tokens for pools backing UST on Terra. The rewards encouraged participants to double down precisely as risk increased. Show: the Anchor Protocol's upward-only deposit rates from January to April 2022. Name: the system paid out APYs exceeding 19 per cent for deposits while relying on subsidies rather than income. Explain: the incentives encouraged users to expand exposure to an asset whose stability mechanism weakened. Implication: misaligned incentives can accelerate collapse by amplifying reflexive behaviour. But reconciliation is possible. When designs later adopted safeguards—fee-based subsidies, capped emissions, dynamic rates—they sought to ensure that rewards cooled behaviour when risk heated, rather than the reverse.

Incentive compatibility always forces designers to confront the lag between cause and visible effect. Many reward systems generate early success metrics—total value locked, headline APRs—while hiding long-tail liabilities. Behaviour supplies the clue. Sustainable incentives produce stable liquidity profiles, consistent governance participation, and predictable flows. Misaligned incentives produce churn, cliff-driven migration, and decaying attention. These signals are not abstract. They manifest as on-chain patterns: liquidity that spikes at epoch boundaries; voting power that concentrates around bribe cycles; governance discussions that balloon during reward debates but fall silent when structural proposals emerge. Show: the seasonal fluctuations on Convex during 2021–2022. Name: dashboards from Dune Analytics charted farm-to-farm flows with remarkable precision. Explain: bribe-dependent incentives generate cyclical capital rotations that erode long-term commitment. Implication: protocols become dependent on continual stimulus to maintain equilibrium.

The deeper challenge is that incentive compatibility must account for multiple constituencies simultaneously. Liquidity providers seek returns for capital; traders seek depth and low slippage; token holders seek value accrual; core contributors seek runway and operational continuity. No single reward mechanism satisfies all parties. Yet well-designed systems create reinforcing loops rather than competing loops. Fee-sharing that supports buybacks improves token value; higher token value improves governance distribution; better governance stabilises parameters; stable parameters attract traders; traders generate fees. Inflationary subsidies can do the reverse: emissions inflate token supply; diluted tokens weaken governance influence; weakened governance makes parameter changes reactive; reactivity increases risk; rising risk drives away traders; falling volume erodes fees; lower fees increase reliance on emissions. These loops are not theoretical—they describe the behavioural footprint of multiple DeFi cycles.

A striking example of harmonious incentive alignment came during Lido's 2023–2024 staking reforms. Show: Lido adjusted its node operator rewards and treasury routing following extended debate across research forums. Name: the drafts published in July 2023 and updated through early 2024. Explain: the changes attempted to harmonise three stakeholder groups—stakers, node operators, and treasury managers—by linking rewards to quality metrics such as validator performance and slashing risk. Implication: incentives that reward reliability reduce systemic fragility. The motif surfaces again: reward behaviour that strengthens the protocol, not just participation.

The limitation is that alignment is dynamic. Protocols evolve; markets cycle; user bases shift. Incentives that worked under one regime may distort behaviour under another. The path to reconciliation lies in feedback loops that correct rather than entrench misalignment. This is where governance merges with mechanism design. Systems that embed kill-switches, sunset clauses, and periodic reviews exhibit stronger adaptability. Show: Aave's risk parameter lifecycle, which includes recurring external audits from Gauntlet beginning in 2020. Name: monthly risk reports available publicly across 2020–2023. Explain: scheduled assessment forces incentives to be measured against outcomes rather than intentions. Implication: incentives that fail tests can be retired before they become liabilities.

Designers often aspire to create self-correcting reward systems, yet no model escapes strategic behaviour entirely. The question returns to the motif: what does the behaviour reveal? If liquidity disappears when emissions pause, the incentive was misaligned. If governance participation persists even without rewards, alignment deepened. If traders continue using a protocol despite reduced incentives for LPs, the utility is intrinsic. These behavioural diagnostics matter more than any marketing claim regarding decentralisation or sustainability.

The unresolved tension sits at the heart of all incentive design: should protocols reward what is *good for the system* or what is *popular with users*? The two overlap but rarely coincide fully. Fee-sharing rewards economically productive activity; inflationary incentives reward desired behaviour irrespective of its intrinsic value. Some protocols blend these forces; others rely entirely on one. But every mechanism eventually confronts the same test: when markets shift, which behaviours persist? And do those behaviours support or undermine the protocol's long-term health?

The forward question thus crystallises. When assessing a new reward mechanism—emissions schedule, fee switch, bribe market, or staking incentive—what pattern of behaviour will it reward six months from now, not just on day one? And if that pattern reveals misalignment, will the system adapt before the incentive becomes the problem itself?

Treasury Management

When MakerDAO voted through MIP65 in October 2022, the decision felt oddly traditional for a protocol long associated with radical experimentation. The DAO authorised up to USD 500 million of its reserves to be placed into short-dated US Treasury bills via a regulated asset manager based in Dublin. The outcome was concrete: by January 2023, Maker had shifted a meaningful share of its balance sheet into instruments yielding over 4 per cent, anchoring DAI's stability with government-backed cashflows rather than token incentives. The move marked a turning point. A DAO had chosen the dull reliability of sovereign debt over the glitter of on-chain yield, recognising that survival often demands prudence rather than innovation. The scene captured a quiet truth: a treasury is not a trophy cabinet; it is an operating buffer, a survival tool, and a governance lever.

That moment also foregrounded the motif that threads through this discussion: *discipline outlasts exuberance.* It is easy for decentralised organisations to inflate token balances or accumulate illiquid holdings during booms. It is far harder to structure a treasury that can fund its contributors through a two-year downturn, maintain liquidity during a depeg, and buy time when governance faces existential disputes. Maker's allocation demonstrated behaviour that outpaced rhetoric: it measured cashflows, defined runway targets, and acted before volatility forced its hand. Treasury management, at its core, is the art of converting protocol narrative into operational resilience.

The question that runs beneath every treasury decision is deceptively simple: what resources does the organisation need to continue delivering value, and how should it configure those resources across time, volatility and governance constraints? To answer it, DAOs must separate their ambitions from their balance sheets. Ambition is expansive; a balance sheet is finite. Treasury design forces priorities into the open.

The first major claim emerges from observing treasuries that treated tokens as perpetual assets rather than working capital. Show: the early Uniswap grants experiment of 2021, where the treasury contained billions in UNI but lacked a recurring mechanism to convert it into stable operational funds. Name: multiple governance discussions in May and

August 2021 raised this issue explicitly. Explain: a volatile governance token cannot reliably finance multi-year development unless converted or hedged. Implication: treasuries that rely solely on native tokens risk operational paralysis during price downturns, when funds shrink just as demands increase. The motif appears again: exuberant valuations seduce, but disciplined provisioning sustains.

Contrast this with protocols that created diversified, rules-based treasuries. Show: Gitcoin's 2022 diversification programme, executed through public auctions and OTC sales. Name: the DAO raised stablecoins and ETH at defined tranches in March and June 2022. Explain: by selling governance tokens during periods of strength, Gitcoin established a multi-year runway and stabilised contributor payments. Implication: diversification transforms governance tokens from accounting numbers into operational tools, creating predictable funding rather than speculative vulnerability.

Yet diversification is not a cure-all. A counter-example sits with DAOs that diversified poorly—allocating into correlated crypto assets during 2021's peak. Show: several NFT-focused DAOs bought vault-backed tokens and governance assets in late 2021, months before macro tightening. Name: public treasury dashboards from February–April 2022 reveal precipitous declines across these holdings. Explain: diversification across correlated assets offers the appearance, not the substance, of risk reduction. Implication: treasury stability requires correlation analysis, not mere asset count. Reconciliation lies in recognising timing and composition: diversification must be into assets with distinct risk regimes and verifiable cashflows, not simply different tickers.

Treasuries must also confront liquidity. A DAO with a billion-dollar balance sheet in illiquid governance tokens may have less practical flexibility than a DAO with thirty million in stable reserves and strict expenditure rules. Liquidity is behaviour, not theory. Show: Aave's Safety Module design from 2020–2023, which maintained a mix of native tokens and stable reserves accessible during stress. Name: Gauntlet's risk reports repeatedly emphasised liquidity coverage ratios. Explain: treasuries need assets that can be deployed within minutes, not weeks, during incidents. Implication: liquidity buffers are not optional; they are the difference between downtime and collapse. The motif returns: exuberant holdings impress; disciplined buffers save.

Another axis involves hedging. Many DAOs inherit directional exposure through their own tokens, making them functionally leveraged to crypto market cycles. Leaving that exposure unmanaged transforms treasuries into proxy trading desks. Show: dYdX community debates across 2021–2022 on delta hedging their treasury. Name: governance threads from October 2021 proposed using perpetual futures to offset token risk. Explain: hedging neutralises volatility that would otherwise distort budgeting. Implication: hedged treasuries make governance less reactive; unhedged treasuries make governance pro-cyclical, amplifying boom–bust dynamics.

Risk management extends into runway policy—the neglected bedrock of DAO survival. Traditional organisations maintain explicit runway targets; many DAOs rely on sentiment and token price. Maker's MIP65 crystallised a quantitative approach. So did Lido's 2023 treasury planning, which incorporated models for validator revenue, ETH volatility, and operational burn. Show: Lido's public financial simulations published in April 2023. Name: these documents modelled multi-scenario stress outcomes. Explain: formal runway modelling converts uncertainty into thresholds and triggers. Implication: DAOs that plan numerically make decisions before stress; DAOs that plan intuitively make decisions during stress—often too late.

Yet runway planning faces a limitation: rigid policies can stifle growth. A counter-example arises when DAOs over-optimise for survival at the cost of innovation. Some cultural DAOs in 2022 accumulated excessive stable reserves and spent little, resulting in stagnant contributor engagement. But reconciliation is possible. Treasuries must differentiate between *core* runway—funds that keep the protocol operational—and *discretionary* budgets that fuel experimentation. Clear separation prevents innovation from cannibalising survival while ensuring survival does not suffocate growth.

Treasury governance itself becomes a form of risk management. Who controls transfers? Who sets allocation rules? Do multi-sig signers act promptly during incidents? Show: Optimism's phased treasury expansion after its token launch in May 2022, which relied on a mix of council-approved budgets and delegate scrutiny. Name: the governance charters published from July to December 2022. Explain: layered controls reduce the chance of treasury capture; they also reduce the probability of rushed or politically influenced spending. Implication: treasury governance that distributes authority widely can absorb errors; centralised treasuries magnify them.

Operational mechanics matter as much as financial composition. A treasury is not merely a pot of assets; it is a workflow. Disbursement pipelines, audits, custody arrangements, and signers' security practices all shape the system's durability. Show: the multisig rotations executed by ENS DAO in 2023, where signers underwent external verification and security upgrades. Name: transactions recorded on-chain in March and September 2023. Explain: even a well-funded treasury can fail through operational negligence. Implication: treasury resilience demands process, not just capital.

The behavioural signature of a healthy treasury is distinctive. Spending patterns remain consistent across market regimes. Proposal quality stays high even when token prices fall. Liquidity buffers remain intact. Treasury reports appear regularly, not reactively. These behaviours communicate stability, which in turn shapes user trust and counterparty willingness. Notably, these are metrics that can be observed: frequency of treasury transactions, ratio of stable reserves to expenditure, proportion of predictable income to total runway, cadence of public reporting.

But the unresolved tension persists: should a DAO optimise its treasury for growth or durability? Excess durability can trap capital; excess growth can jeopardise survival. The next treasury decision—whether to diversify, hedge, stake, unbond, or raise buffers—forces every organisation to reveal its priorities. The forward test is therefore simple, but unforgiving: if markets turned hostile for six months, which parts of the treasury would still function, which would fail, and which decisions taken today would determine the difference?

Reading Proposals Critically

In May 2022, holders of Lido's governance token awoke to a proposal that seemed banal on the surface: a modest adjustment to stETH emission incentives. The document arrived through the usual channels, carried the familiar cadence of parameter tweaking, and offered projections that appeared self-evident. Yet within forty-eight hours the debate had fractured sharply, for a simple reason: the proposal omitted a sunset clause, did not quantify alternative options, and presented its justification as a set of assertions rather than testable metrics. The outcome was concrete. Delegates demanded revisions, a temporary vote was halted, and the revised version—submitted in June—introduced explicit ceilings, measurable targets, and an emergency rollback. What emerged from those weeks was not a dispute about incentives, but a lesson in scrutiny: governance thrives when proposals reveal their assumptions; it decays when they conceal them.

This tension between appearance and substance drives the motif running through this discussion: *clarity resists capture*. A proposal that looks complete but says little is more dangerous than a complex one that exposes its working. The Lido case showed it plainly. When a DAO faces volatile markets and dispersed stakeholders, the quality of its decision-making depends less on ideological alignment and more on the structure of the documents it evaluates. Reading proposals critically is not pedantry; it is a defence against fragility.

A governance proposal is a request for collective action. It competes for attention, authority, and execution bandwidth. To read it well, one must first surface its foundation: what problem is it trying to solve, and how precisely is that problem defined? Show: Curve's 2021 vote to adjust CRV emission weights following prolonged imbalance in pool utilisation. Name: the January 2021 governance thread that identified the issue with empirical data. Explain: by grounding the proposal in explicit performance metrics—relative volume, deposit share, and gauge scores—it made the problem visible even to delegates unfamiliar with the technicalities. Implication: proposals that quantify the underlying issue invite robust reasoning;

proposals that rely on narrative alone invite unexamined consensus.

The second major claim concerns the necessity of meaningful alternatives. Many proposals gesture at options but fail to articulate the trade-offs between them. Show: Aave's 2023 debate over reducing liquidation thresholds for long-tail assets. Name: the public risk assessment by Gauntlet in March 2023, which modelled multiple threshold paths, each with distinct insolvency probabilities. Explain: the presence of clear alternatives forced delegates to consider not only the recommended path but also the consequences of rejecting or modifying it. Implication: when options carry quantified outcomes, capture becomes harder, because persuasion must operate through evidence rather than influence. The motif returns: clarity resists capture.

Yet this requirement exposes a limitation. In some cases, the proposal's authors lack the data to construct meaningful alternatives. A counter-example lies in early 2020 governance experiments where DAOs proposed fee changes before robust revenue dashboards existed. Without data, options become guesses. Reconciliation depends on process discipline: when data is absent, proposals should explicitly declare uncertainty, specify required measurements, and sequence decisions accordingly. Ambiguity acknowledged is safer than ambiguity disguised.

Metrics form the third anchor of critical reading. A proposal without measurable outcomes is a request for blind trust. Show: Uniswap's retroactive grant framework of 2023, which required funded teams to publish KPIs tied to user adoption and audited usage. Name: the governance packet circulated in October 2023. Explain: by appending metrics to funding, the DAO could distinguish execution failure from market conditions. Implication: measurable proposals turn governance from a battleground of opinions into a feedback system. When metrics are absent, governance becomes theatre.

Kill-switches—rollback mechanisms, sunsets, and emergency conditions—serve as the final pillar. They reveal how seriously authors consider downside risk. Show: Balancer's June 2022 introduction of time-limited emissions for new gauges, accompanied by a built-in expiry unless renewed. Name: the gauge controller update published that month. Explain: including a sunset demands ongoing justification; excluding it buries future obligations. Implication: kill-switches transform proposals into commitments that must earn their continuation. They narrow the space for drift, inertia, and zombie policies.

But kill-switches bring their own tension. If overused, they can destabilise long-term planning. A counter-example appeared in several NFT DAOs in 2022 that attached short sunsets to nearly every budget line, forcing teams into constant renewal. Reconciliation lies in proportionality: core operational budgets require long horizons with periodic audits; tactical incentives benefit from tight sunsets and automatic reevaluation. The right balance preserves continuity while protecting against complacency.

With these pillars established, the deeper significance comes into view. Reading proposals critically is not merely a technical skill; it is a cultural posture. It treats governance as something continuous rather than episodic. The behaviours reveal themselves in patterns: delegates who request historical data before committing to incentives; authors who publish alternatives with quantified impacts; community members who flag vague objectives; signers who demand rollback logic before approving contracts. These are not abstractions—they are visible signals. You can measure them by tracking revision counts, comparing the ratio of data-backed proposals to narrative ones, and observing how often sunsets trigger actual review.

Two named examples reinforce this behavioural dimension. Show: Optimism's Series A governance upgrades of 2022, which introduced mandatory motivation statements, transparency standards, and ex ante success measures. Name: the governance documents published August 2022. Explain: these structures reduced the scope for proposals that lacked logic or accountability. Implication: structural clarity produces cultural clarity.

Another example: MakerDAO's "Endgame" debates from late 2022 to mid-2023. Name: the months-long sequence of public red teams and scenario analyses. Explain: while controversial, the process made assumptions explicit, invited scrutiny, and exposed internal disagreements. Implication: transparency cannot guarantee alignment, but it guarantees intelligibility—and intelligibility is the substrate for healthy governance.

The quiet motif again surfaces: clarity resists capture. A proposal with a defined problem, real alternatives, measurable outcomes, and a kill-switch is inherently harder to manipulate. It forces governance actors to persuade rather than pressure. It elongates the decision-making horizon, because evaluation continues after passage. It gives minority stakeholders tools to challenge drift. It converts what might otherwise be a popularity contest into an iterative reasoning system.

Yet a final tension remains unresolved. Too much structure risks bureaucratisation; too little structure risks capture. A DAO must decide not only *how* to govern, but *how tightly* to govern. And so the forward test emerges: when the next contentious proposal arrives—perhaps during volatility, perhaps during calm—what questions will you ask before reaching for the "Yes" button? Will you demand alternatives? Will you look for metrics? Will you check the kill-switch? Or will speed and sentiment win the moment, leaving clarity for later?

Chapter 9
Volatility, Sizing and Behaviour

The archive of Long-Term Capital Management is littered with immaculate spreadsheets. They sit in Yale University's Beinecke Library today, sealed in boxes labelled "Risk Models, 1997–1998", silent witnesses to the moment when intellectual brilliance collided with uncooperative markets. What stands out in those papers is not the mathematics but the scale. Positions were vast—too vast—because historical volatility looked tame, and models translated that calm into confidence. When Russia defaulted in August 1998 and spreads convulsed, the same position sizes that once looked elegant became existential. LTCM had extraordinary talent, Nobel laureates among them, yet it stumbled on a human constant: the temptation to treat volatility as a forecast rather than a warning.

That episode is no moral tale about hubris; it is a study in mis-sizing. The fund was not alone. During March 2020, as global markets convulsed under pandemic stress, several crypto trading desks found themselves trapped in leveraged positions that looked comfortable a week earlier. Slippage ballooned, liquidity thinned, and once-manageable exposures became forced liquidations. Screens showed numbers moving faster than hands could react. The underlying problem was familiar: position sizes built on yesterday's stability clashed with today's interruption. Volatility had shifted the ground, and portfolios built without slack had nowhere to stand.

Volatility is not a meter of chaos but a measure of fragility. It signals how violently a position might demand attention, how easily it can turn from asset to liability, how much behaviour it will extract from those who hold it. That becomes the quiet motif running through this chapter: *size shapes behaviour*. A portfolio that looks composed in calm weather can unravel under the slightest crosswind if its sizing reflects optimism instead of margin. And because the volatility of digital assets can turn in minutes, sizing becomes more than arithmetic; it becomes the architecture of survival.

From here, the thread unfurls. Volatility does not simply determine whether a token oscillates; it determines how large one can responsibly hold it. High-variance assets amplify both gains and mistakes. Long-tail tokens, with histories measured in months rather than years, move with a violence that established assets rarely match. Treating them as equals in size is not bold but reckless. This chapter delves into that translation process: how variance becomes allocation bands, how empirical movement becomes position rules, how sizing decisions cool the temperature of a portfolio rather than raise it. The aim is not to chase precision but to build proportionality. If an asset can halve in a week, its position should reflect that potential, not ignore it.

Time complicates everything. A position's horizon plays as great a role as its variance. A liquid token held for hours is entirely different from a locked LP stake that demands a calendar, not a clock. March 2023 provided a timely reminder when several DeFi pools on Arbitrum experienced fleeting imbalances during network congestion: those who needed to exit urgently discovered that timing is not a right but a luxury. This chapter examines that tension between horizon and liquidity—how lockups, exit windows, and market depth should shape how one commits capital. Forced selling is never a market event; it is a preparation failure.

Behaviour is the quiet engine beneath all of this. A portfolio is never just a set of positions; it is a set of commitments made by people under stress. Checklists matter because panic improvises badly. Clear max-loss levels, written before a trade, filter noise from necessity. Triggers clarify intent. Post-mortems prevent repetition. These tools may sound procedural, but they are behavioural guardrails, and that makes them indispensable. Even the most technical trading desks rely on them. When Alameda Research published fragments of its internal processes during 2021 conference panels, what emerged was not a story of limitless risk but a story of repeated procedure—frameworks that translated volatile environments into structured decisions. Process reduces drama.

And then there is communication: the overlooked but decisive variable. Small teams and emerging funds often stumble not because their models are weak but because their coordination is loose. A two-person review before upgrades sounds banal; in practice it prevents million-pound errors. Logging decisions may seem administrative; in reality it anchors accountability. In 2022, several DAO-aligned trading collectives discovered this painfully. One missed handoff during a weekend rotation left a large LP position unhedged, and a routine depeg turned into a permanent loss. The fix was trivial: a documented process. The cost of not having it was anything but.

What ties all of these threads together is the recognition that volatility does not merely move prices. It moves people. It shapes decisions. It tests preparation. This chapter approaches volatility not as an external force acting upon a portfolio but as a mirror that reflects how well-prepared its holders are. If size shapes behaviour, then behaviour shapes outcome. And the deeper one examines that loop, the clearer a question emerges, waiting at the threshold of every new position: when the market stutters, and the screen goes red, will your system still hold, or will your decisions expand, contract, and scramble with the randomness of the moment?

From Volatility to Position Size

The first numbers that caught regulators' attention in the collapse of Amaranth Advisors in September 2006 were not its losses but its scale. The fund's natural-gas book had swollen to more than five times the open interest of certain winter contracts on the New York Mercantile Exchange. When the market broke against its view, the volatility spike translated into a loss exceeding $6 billion within days. What destroyed Amaranth was not merely directional exposure; it was the mismatch between variance and position size. Volatility expanded. The positions did not shrink. The consequence was immediate and terminal. That contrast—between how fast markets can move and how slowly large positions can adapt—remains the centre of gravity for digital-asset portfolios. During the weekend of 12–13 March 2020, several crypto funds discovered that their allocations were far larger than their risk budgets had implied. Bitcoin's hourly volatility surged to levels not seen since 2013, and slippage on major exchanges widened by multiples. A position sized for yesterday's calm behaved like a lever in a gale. Some portfolios endured; others were liquidated in thin liquidity. The behavioural footprint was visible: traders who believed they were "hedged" found that the hedge could not be executed at the size they required. That gap—between expected variance and realised movement—is where position sizing becomes philosophy rather than arithmetic.

Volatility is movement. Position size is commitment. When those two diverge, the gap becomes a fault line. This subchapter treats that fault line with the seriousness it deserves, because allocation is not simply an optimisation problem; it is the architecture of survival. *How much can this asset demand from me when it wakes up?* That is the motif that returns several times, because volatility is not a forecast but a question.

Volatility does not merely widen a chart; it widens the emotional range of its holders. A token that can move 20 per cent in a day does not simply threaten a portfolio; it demands attention, and attention carries cost. Long-tail assets demonstrate this vividly. Their shorter histories, thinner markets, and faster reflexivity create movement patterns that dwarf those of the majors. A position that looks trivial in nominal terms can become the portfolio's gravitational centre under stress. The more an asset can move, the more modest its place within the portfolio should be. This is not caution. It is symmetry.

The clearest expression of this principle can be seen in how professional desks classify assets by historical variance. When the Chicago Mercantile Exchange published its volatility indices for bitcoin and ether in 2021, it provided a baseline against which to contrast the behaviour of altcoins whose movements frequently doubled or tripled those levels. The implication was straightforward: if the daily standard deviation of an asset is twice that of another, a position of equal size carries twice the agitation and twice the potential drawdown. Some DeFi-native funds applied this rule publicly. Framework Ventures noted during a 2022 panel that their allocations to younger governance tokens rarely exceeded low single digits of the portfolio, precisely because variance was elevated and liquidity uneven. They were not avoiding risk; they were pricing it.

Variance should not be treated as a static input. It expands and contracts with narrative, with liquidity, with structural changes in the market. Consider the behaviour of LUNA in late 2021. Its volatility compressed as a wave of demand for UST built reflexive flows, drawing in momentum strategies and widening liquidity pools. Position sizes grew across many discretionary portfolios because the movement appeared orderly. Yet the same compression masked fragility. When UST began drifting from its peg in May 2022, volatility reappeared with brutal speed. Some positions that were modest in percentage terms became immovable in practice because exit capacity vanished. The lesson was not that volatility forecasts failed but that volatility itself is path-dependent: tranquillity can be camouflage. When volatility contracts, the temptation is to expand size. That temptation must be resisted unless liquidity confirms the stability. Calm is not safety.

Liquidity therefore becomes the bridge between volatility and position sizing. A volatile token with deep markets can be managed. A volatile token in shallow markets becomes an anchor. Market depth, measured by executable volumes within acceptable slippage bands, determines how quickly a position can be reshaped when the numbers change. A study by Kaiko (April 2023) documented how several governance tokens maintained the appearance of liquidity in aggregated order books but could not absorb more than a few million dollars without double-digit slippage. A portfolio that ignores this metric commits to a fantasy: that it can exit at the mid-price. The reality is harsher. If a token's volatility is high and its depth thin, its position must be small. This is not fear. It is geometry.

One might counter with the example of stablecoins: volatility near zero, liquidity ample, behaviour predictable. Size should follow. Yet even here, nuance matters. During the USDC depeg of 11 March 2023, volatility expanded from near-zero to several per cent within hours. Liquidity thinned in specific pools, particularly on decentralised exchanges where redemption expectations lagged. While most portfolios treated stablecoin holdings as ballast, the sudden movement exposed concentration risk. The volatility-link to sizing had been ignored because historical data suggested permanence. The counter-example therefore reinforces the rule: volatility can erupt even in assets engineered to suppress it. Size must always anticipate variance, not assume its absence.

Once volatility has been measured and liquidity assessed, the next step is converting those observations into allocation bands. This is where behavioural discipline meets statistical reasoning. Some desks anchor their bands to percentile moves. A token that routinely exhibits 95th-percentile daily swings of 12 per cent will be granted a narrower allocation than one whose 95th percentile move is 4 per cent. The approach is simple: position size inversely proportional to movement risk. The mechanics vary—Kelly fractions, equal-risk contributions, or drawdown-based sizing—but the principle is constant. Exposure must not exceed tolerance.

A concrete example can be found in the public disclosures of Paradigm's research arm during 2021. They discussed using equal volatility contribution frameworks, allocating capital so that no single asset could dominate portfolio movement. In practice, this meant long-tail tokens rarely exceeded two to three per cent of gross exposure. Conversely, assets with deep liquidity and moderate variance absorbed double-digit allocations. The model did not eliminate risk; it distributed it.

Yet sizing frameworks face a limitation: they are backward-looking. Volatility models treat the past as teacher. Markets do not always oblige. The late stages of bull cycles often compress volatility before violent expansions. The early stages of bear markets often exaggerate variance before stabilisation. A static sizing rule cannot capture these shifts. The reconciliation lies in humility: position sizes should include buffers. If a sizing model suggests a 10 per cent position, reducing it to seven may be appropriate when regime uncertainty is high. The cost is reduced upside; the benefit is survivability. Every portfolio must choose which matters more.

Overlaying all of this is behaviour—the least modelled but most decisive input. A trader may tolerate a 15 per cent drawdown in theory yet panic at five per cent in practice. Position sizing therefore becomes a psychological contract as much as a mathematical one. A position that is too large will distort attention, trigger impulsive decisions, and crowd out processes. Several funds have shared this candidly in post-mortems after the 2022 deleveraging. One desk on Solana noted that its largest losing trade was not a function of faulty analysis but of emotional overload caused by size. They cut the position too late because the scale paralysed them. The implication is unavoidable: sizing rules must incorporate human behaviour. The portfolio should be built for the humans who run it, not the hypothetical agents imagined in risk models.

A final tension remains unresolved because it cannot be. Volatility invites precision, yet precision is fragile. Allocation bands create structure, yet structure can lull. Liquidity offers comfort, yet comfort can seduce. Size must adapt. Volatility must be respected. The market will move when it wants to move. The open question—the one that returns each time a position is entered—lingers: when the volatility regime changes without warning, as it has done countless times before, will the size you chose expand your options or collapse them?

Time Horizons and Liquidity

At the height of the market dislocation on 19 May 2021, a mid-sized fund in Singapore faced a problem that had nothing to do with its convictions and everything to do with its constraints. Its largest pool of capital sat in a 30-day lockup on a lending platform whose utilisation had spiked. The assets were sound, the collateral ratios intact, yet the redemption queue lengthened past its mandated window. Liquidity had vanished at precisely the moment the fund needed it. Within forty-eight hours the team executed a series of forced sales in unrelated holdings to meet external obligations. Their losses did not come from wrong analysis. They came from poor alignment between horizon and liquidity. They moved too slow.

A quieter example unfolded three years earlier. In October 2018 a desk in London, managing a structured product book with crypto underlyings, built sizeable positions in ether with the expectation of a prolonged accumulation phase. The market obliged, drifting sideways for months. But the positions sat in a multisig governed by operational procedures requiring three signatories, two of whom were travelling when volatility returned sharply. A routine de-risking exercise turned into a scramble. They reduced exposure, but not at prices they would have chosen. The delay was bureaucratic rather than market-driven. Yet the effect was the same: misaligned timing created involuntary trades. *Time is a constraint,* the recurring motif that threads this subchapter.

Liquidity, then, is not simply a property of markets; it is a property of the calendar. To treat liquidity as static is to ignore the rhythm of obligations, lockups, vesting schedules, and operational bottlenecks. The trader who sizes positions without mapping the time horizon behaves like a sailor ignoring tides. Movement is inevitable. The question is whether it will work with you or against you.

The core claim begins with something observable: assets move in bursts, but obligations are predictable. Show the mismatch. In March 2023, Kaiko data revealed that several governance tokens could absorb less than $2 million in sales before slippage exceeded eight per cent. Name the issue: liquidity depth is insufficient for portfolios with short-dated liabilities. Explain the mechanism: when a fund must honour withdrawals weekly, yet its holdings require days to unwind without punitive execution, the temporal mismatch creates forced selling. Implication: portfolios built without horizon alignment are designed for fragility. A counter-example resides in treasury management practices during 2020–2021. Several DAOs, including Aave (2021), migrated portions of their treasuries into laddered stablecoin positions on Curve and Balancer. These allocations were structured with staggered unlocks, enabling partial liquidity each week. Their behaviour showed how horizon engineering prevents pressure. Even during bouts of volatility, these treasuries met operational expenses without touching volatile assets. The implication is clear: when horizons support obligations, liquidity becomes a tool rather than a trap.

Yet even thoughtful structures face stress. Consider MakerDAO's handling of collateral auctions in March 2020. The protocol's mechanisms were sound, but market depth evaporated so rapidly that keepers struggled to participate. The time horizon here was measured not in days but in minutes; the auctions could not be paused. Maker's experience became a reference point for how designs that rely on instantaneous liquidity can falter when volatility outpaces execution. The limitation of horizon-dependent mechanisms is that they treat time as linear. Markets do not. They compress and expand unpredictably. Reconciliation requires buffers: designs that permit delays, wider windows, or emergency procedures. In human portfolios, that translates into maintaining liquidity tranches: dry powder explicitly reserved for irregular events, not optimised away for yield.

The next claim concerns behaviour: humans misjudge how long processes take. Show this through a concrete pattern. During the 2022 deleveraging cycle, desks frequently underestimated the time required to exit LP positions. Unstaking periods of seven days seemed manageable during calm markets. But under duress, those seven days felt like an eternity. Prices moved, liquidity rotated, and some pools experienced meaningful impermanent loss. Name the behavioural error: horizon neglect. Explain its effect: when investors treat unlock delays as incidental rather than structural, their mental models collapse under pressure. Implication: time horizons must be treated as risk factors, not administrative footnotes.

A second example underscores this point. In July 2022, Lido introduced stETH redemption mechanics that aligned withdrawal queues with validator exit rates on Ethereum. The design anchored the horizon to a predictable, protocol-level cadence. Yet many traders still treated stETH as a fully liquid instrument until the first liquidity shock revealed the structural lag. The mismatch caused panic-selling despite the mechanism functioning as intended. The implication: investors often assume instant liquidity where none exists. That assumption becomes a hazard during stress.

Time horizons have a second dimension: they determine how narratives evolve. A trade held for hours responds to microstructure; a trade held for months responds to fundamental changes. Sizing and planning must reflect this. Show the distinction. A quant desk in Zurich, running short-horizon strategies in 2023, sized positions based on intraday volatility and immediate liquidity. Their positions seldom exceeded a few hours; redemptions and lockups were irrelevant. By contrast, a discretionary fund in Berlin managing a concentrated DeFi portfolio used six- to twelve-month horizons. They preferred assets with predictable unlock schedules and deep, programmable liquidity. Name the principle: horizon dictates selection. Explain: different horizons require different liquidity profiles. Implication: mixing horizons within a single portfolio without explicit structure creates cross-contamination of risk.

One credible limitation deserves emphasis: short horizons impose liquidity demands that often reduce potential returns. Highly liquid assets offer tighter spreads but lower reward profiles. The reconciliation lies in accepting trade-offs. If a portfolio requires weekly liquidity, its asset universe shrinks. If it seeks higher returns in illiquid assets, it must extend its horizon and structure capital accordingly. Time cannot be cheated. The cost of ignoring this is forced liquidation; the cost of respecting it is opportunity cost. Every portfolio must choose.

The quiet motif returns: *time is a constraint.* It shapes everything from operational requirements to psychological endurance. A position that matures in ninety days asks different questions of its holder than one that can be exited in ninety seconds. The misalignment between those questions and the rest of the portfolio creates friction. Teams that thrive cultivate routines. They maintain calendars for unlocks. They schedule rebalancing windows. They ensure that multi-sig signatories remain reachable during expected volatility catalysts such as major CPI releases or protocol upgrades. These behaviours are not administrative. They are risk controls disguised as scheduling.

Two further examples illustrate how deliberate horizon design reduces distress. In 2021, several funds participating in Avalanche's liquidity mining programme structured laddered exits from LP positions. Rather than unbonding all liquidity simultaneously, they staged redemptions weekly. This prevented slippage spikes and insulated them from short-term noise. Another example comes from a DAO treasury that implemented a monthly rollover into liquid assets three days before governance votes involving large token flows. The foresight ensured that voting power remained available without forced swaps during volatility. In both cases, liquidity aligned with predictable needs.

The final tension cannot be resolved with formulas. Time horizons anchor discipline, but they introduce rigidity.

Liquidity grants freedom, but it can seduce investors into overtrading. A portfolio must navigate between these poles. Too much rigidity, and opportunities are missed. Too much liquidity, and impulses dominate. The unresolved question—the one that surfaces each quarter as unlocks, redemptions, or market cycles converge—is simple: when markets move faster than your processes, will your horizon protect your decisions or smother them?

Checklists Beat Feelings

At 14:07 on 12 March 2020, in a cramped office off Bishopsgate in London, a derivatives trader named Alex Morgan executed a position he would regret for years. Screens showed ether cascading through $100. Funding rates whipsawed. His desk's risk officer was on another call. Alex had no written plan—only the sensation that *this* was the moment to "buy the capitulation". He doubled his usual size. Within eight minutes the position was underwater by a further twenty per cent, and the forced unwind wiped out half his quarterly limits. Nothing about the trade was structurally unsound; the problem was the absence of a pre-defined checklist. A single decision, taken in a state of heightened emotion, contaminated an entire quarter of work. The silence that followed his liquidation felt heavier than the loss itself.

A different scene unfolded in Tokyo during November 2022. A small digital asset fund received notice that a major counterparty had halted withdrawals. Panic loomed, but the investment lead opened a binder labelled "Stress Protocols". It contained pre-trade theses, sizing rules, exit triggers, and review memos for every active position. The team didn't guess; they acted. They reduced exposures mechanically, documented assumptions, and prepared summaries for their LPs. The fund still absorbed losses, but its path was coherent. The checklist anchored their behaviour. It made them move with intent. In this subchapter, the quiet motif returns: *paper over pulse*. The contrast between Alex's improvisation and the Tokyo team's method shows the first claim: markets demand structure, not sensation. When stress rises, the unprepared lean on instinct. The prepared lean on process.

Show the behaviour. Traders under pressure tend to over-size positions or shift theses mid-trade. Name the concept: emotional drift. Explain the mechanism: without a written pre-trade checklist—thesis, catalysts, invalidation point, maximum loss—the trader's internal narrative mutates with every candle. Implication: the absence of a constraint system transforms volatility into confusion. A checkable example illustrates this. US equities regulators recorded similar behavioural distortions during the 2010 Flash Crash, when firms without automated trading halts executed orders far outside intended bands (SEC & CFTC, 2010). Automation wasn't the only advantage. Checklists that specified "halt criteria" prevented human error. A second example comes from Compound's USDC liquidation cascade in May 2020. Analysts with pre-defined collateral action plans fared better: their models contained explicit thresholds for unwind, so they acted early while liquidity remained healthy. The implication is simple: when the plan is clear, the decision becomes mechanical. A credible counter-example exists. In early-stage venture investing or thin DeFi pools, conditions shift too quickly for rigid pre-trade checklists. Some discretionary flexibility is necessary. Reconciliation lies in hybrid design: maintain fixed components—position size limits, maximum loss—and flexible components—entry timing or venue selection. Checklists do not eliminate discretion. They fence it.

Paper over pulse. The motif repeats because it exposes the second claim: writing forces clarity. Show its power. A pre-trade template requires articulation of a thesis in one or two sentences. Naming the claim: thesis compression. Explain: reducing the idea to its economic essence reveals whether the trade belongs in the portfolio. Implication: many trades die on the page, sparing capital.

Behavioural finance research from Daniel Kahneman and Gary Klein (2009) highlights that structured decision protocols reduce error variance. A crypto-specific echo occurred during the 2021 Solana congestion episodes, when trading firms that documented "latency risk" acted early to avoid liquidation queues. Writing made risks visible. A limitation deserves attention. Some practitioners argue that documenting every trade slows execution. In fast-moving markets, seconds matter. Yet the reconciliation is that slowness is the point. Checklists are not speed bumps;

they are filters. Trades that cannot survive two minutes of clarity rarely deserve capital.

The third major claim addresses post-mortems. Show their effect. A desk in Berlin adopted a practice in 2021: after every closed position, profitable or not, the analyst wrote a 200-word post-mortem. Name the process: retrospective calibration. Explain: these memos recorded entry rationale, deviation points, and whether exits matched triggers. The team then compiled monthly patterns—recurring errors like premature exits after minor drawdowns or repeated disregard for liquidity depth. Implication: post-mortems are mirrors that correct future sizing, selection, and process. A concrete example anchors this. A U.S. fund that traded NFT-related tokens in 2022 catalogued slippage metrics in every post-mortem. The result surprised them: slippage, not thesis accuracy, consumed a measurable percentage of P&L. They adjusted execution strategies accordingly. The counter-example arises from over-analysis. Some teams drown in documentation, adding friction to every action. The reconciliation is that post-mortems must remain concise, time-boxed, and focused on decisions—not narratives. Discipline, not verbosity.

The motif returns a third time: *paper over pulse.* This time it applies to triggers. Show how triggers matter. During the stETH discount episode in June 2022, desks that maintained trigger matrices—discount thresholds, curve pool imbalance limits, liquidity drains—acted with discipline, swapping or hedging based on pre-written cues. Name the tool: trigger maps. Explain: triggers convert uncertainty into discrete choices. Implication: triggers reduce reactive selling, especially during cascading narratives. Another example: volatility traders in Zurich created a "three-strike" rule during 2023's memecoin episodes. If a position hit three adverse liquidity events—spreads widening beyond preset limits—they exited automatically. The behaviour reflected their principle: execution quality trumps thesis ego. The triggers enforced humility. A limitation surfaces. Triggers that are too rigid can cause unnecessary churn. A price wick may hit a stop that wasn't thematically relevant. But reconciliation comes through layered triggers: hard stops for catastrophic loss, soft stops for thesis violation, informational triggers for re-evaluation. Checklists build these layers into muscle memory.

Show the fourth claim. Checklists safeguard communication within teams. A desk in Paris used shared templates during 2021–2022 to coordinate allocations across liquidity venues. Each template included expected slippage, max exposure, and execution routes. This prevented duplicated trades and hidden correlations. Name the concept: collective alignment. Explain: when every team member acts from the same written structure, ambiguity shrinks. Implication: shared checklists reduce operational risk.

A second example comes from a DAO with a multi-sig treasury in 2023. Its signatories used a standardised "approval slip" capturing rationale, risks, and alternative options before signing transactions. When one signatory spotted an unstated dependency on an oracle feed, the transaction paused. The checklist revealed the oversight. Here the limitation is cultural resistance. Some teams, particularly smaller or more informal ones, treat documentation as overkill. Their defence is agility. The reconciliation is that checklists scale with complexity: the more capital, counterparties, or venues involved, the more indispensable structured processes become.

The motif fades but leaves its question: *does your pulse drive your decisions, or does your paper hold you steady?* The trade-off is unresolved by design. Checklists impose structure but risk dulling intuition. Feelings inspire creativity but risk undermining discipline. As volatility rises and markets mutate, each team must choose which to privilege in moments that matter. When the next rapid, disorienting move arrives—and it will—the question is simple: will your process speak louder than your pulse?

Communication and Team Process

At 09:42 on 18 February 2021, a three-person crypto fund operating from a shared workspace in Shoreditch pushed a routine smart-contract upgrade to production. Their lead engineer, pressed for time and irritated by a failing test, bypassed the review step. The change went live with a single signature rather than the documented two. Forty minutes later, a liquidity management script misfired, draining a portion of the fund's stablecoin reserves into an incorrect address. The error was reversible only because the destination was a secondary wallet they controlled. The portfolio survived by luck, not design. No market mispriced their risk; their own communication failed them. Contrast this with an incident in Zürich in June 2023. A small digital asset desk identified an anomaly in an exchange's API feed. Their policy required a two-person sign-off before halting execution systems. They followed it without complaint. One trader captured logs; another notified counterparties; the operations lead drafted a short note for LPs. Every action occurred in under fifteen minutes. Their advantage wasn't size or technology. It was choreography. The same tools handled by the Shoreditch team produced opposite outcomes because the communication fabric was stronger. The quiet motif that threads through this subchapter is simple and unforgiving: *coordination equals survival.*

The first claim rests on visibility. Show the behaviour. Small teams often outsource structure to goodwill: someone "usually" reviews transactions, someone "normally" updates the risk sheet. Name the concept: implicit delegation. Explain: roles remain unwritten, so responsibility drifts to the path of least resistance. Implication: during moments of stress—API failures, oracle anomalies, liquidity crunches—no one knows who must act. Reaction time elongates. Errors compound. A checkable example reinforces the point. The 2020 loss at KuCoin, based in Singapore, illustrated how unclear internal workflows complicated the freeze of suspicious withdrawals. Although the incident involved a large organisation, its post-mortem (KuCoin, October 2020) emphasised the need for explicit roles in incident pipelines. When accountability is opaque, escalation lags. A second example sits closer to home: the June 2022 Optimism token misdelivery, in which a market maker inadvertently received tokens meant for a multisig upgrade. The resolution succeeded only because communication logs were thorough enough to reconstruct intent. Transparent logs saved reputations.

A counter-example exists. A nimble, tightly bonded team might argue that explicit roles slow them down. Familiarity, they insist, is its own process. The reconciliation is evidence: speed born of familiarity collapses precisely when unfamiliar events strike. Scaling complexity outpaces intuition. Structure matters most when novelty arrives. Coordination equals survival.

The second claim concerns sign-offs, the choreography's spine. Show the practice. A two-person review on contract upgrades, parameter changes, or treasury transactions creates friction by design. Name it: deliberate friction. Explain: the second pair of eyes reduces single-point-of-failure risk and interrupts impulsive execution. Implication: the fund trades capacity for durability; it accepts slower action in exchange for fewer catastrophic mistakes. Consider a concrete example. MakerDAO's Emergency Shutdown Module, introduced in 2020, requires multiple independent actors to trigger. While not a small fund, the design exemplifies rigorous approval structure: no single actor can compromise stability. Another example: Gnosis Safe's multisig adoption by small teams throughout 2021–2023. Teams that enforced a minimum two-of-three signature threshold saw materially fewer operational incidents than those using single-signer hot wallets, according to internal audits released by several DeFi protocols.

A limitation exists. During high-velocity market events—stablecoin depegs or liquidation cascades—the sign-off requirement may cost precious seconds. Here lies the reconciliation: dual-track procedures. High-severity, time-critical actions follow pre-signed playbooks with delegated authority; all other actions follow full sign-off. Coordination equals survival, but survival sometimes demands speed. Design both tracks before they are needed.

The third claim concerns logs—the memory and audit trail of a team. Show their utility. A log of trade intents, approval rationales, RPC failures, and post-mortem notes transforms chaos into a traceable narrative. Name it: operational memory. Explain: without logs, teams re-learn the same lessons repeatedly; with them, error patterns become visible and solvable. Implication: logs are multipliers. They amplify learning, reduce disputes, and sharpen risk assessments.

A checkable example occurred during the 2021 Polygon RPC outage. Teams that maintained execution logs could quickly confirm which trades failed, which needed resubmission, and which exposures remained unresolved. A second example comes from DeFi Saver's published transparency logs in 2022, documenting automation misfires and corrections. Their public logging allowed external analysts to verify claims, raising trust in their service.

A counter-example is noise. Obsessive logging turns repositories into clutter. Thousands of irrelevant entries bury important signals. The reconciliation lies in curation: logs must record decisions, not everything. Capture intent, rationale, and deviation—never background noise.

The fourth claim ties communication to behavioural discipline. Show the practice. A team that begins each week with a fifteen-minute coordination call—positions, risks, upgrades, expected liquidity events—reduces ambiguity. Name this: alignment cadence. Explain: repeated, structured touchpoints prevent assumptions from festering into blind spots. Implication: coordination reduces behavioural drift.

A checkable example stems from a London-based prop shop that traded altcoin pairs throughout 2022. Weekly alignment identified creeping correlation across their positions; by documenting exposures openly, they cut aggregate tail risk by measurable basis points. A second example: Lido's long-form governance calls during 2021–2023, archived and summarised, ensured stakeholders aligned on upgrade paths and validator incentives.

A limitation appears when meetings proliferate. Over-coordination wastes energy. The reconciliation is that cadence must be sparse but reliable. Short, consistent rituals beat sprawling ad-hoc discussions. Coordination equals survival, but survival requires restraint too.

The motif returns: *coordination equals survival*. When roles are unclear, when approvals drift, when logs vanish, small teams confuse motion with mastery. They believe they operate efficiently, yet their risk is latent. Processes replace guesswork. Written roles replace assumption. Dual-track sign-offs replace improvisation. Logs replace fading memory. Alignment cadence replaces emotional scatter. Yet a tension lingers unresolved. Too much structure stifles initiative; too little structure invites disaster. Each team must draw its own line between discipline and dynamism. When the next upgrade, exploit, or liquidity shock arrives—and it will—the question remains: will your coordination hold under pressure, or will you discover your process only in the moment it breaks?

Chapter 10
Building Your DeFi Playbook

Just after dusk on 13 March 2020, traders watched a strange pattern unfold across exchanges from Hong Kong to London. Ethereum gas fees spiked. Liquidations fired in relentless waves. And while screens flickered red, one small fund working out of a co-working hub near Farringdon did something unusual: they paused. Instead of improvising, they opened a laminated sheet they had printed months earlier—a personal "playbook" for market stress. The sheet mapped their exposures, ranked by code risk, liquidity depth, and counterparty dependence. It listed which positions could be unwound instantly, which required staggered exits, and which demanded oracle checks before action. Their responses were not fast. They were precise. While others sold blindly into collapsing liquidity, this team treated the chaos as a sequence of pre-written steps. The playbook did not save them from loss; it saved them from ruin.

A different tableau played out in November 2022, when rumours swirled around an exchange in The Bahamas. Some teams reacted with reflexive withdrawals, burning fees in frantic on-chain transactions. Others hesitated, paralysed by contradictory information. Yet a handful of desks executed almost mechanical routines: snapshot balances, verify on-chain proofs, escalate to cold storage, reassess per-position risk tiers. Those who had codified their response patterns—risk maps, alerts, and small reversible actions—moved early enough to matter. Their advantage emerged not from foresight but from preparation. The thread running through these events is almost banal yet continually overlooked: discipline beats clairvoyance.

The chapter begins with an idea that underpins every serious DeFi practice: risk is multi-dimensional, and until it is externalised—drawn, scored, colour-coded—it remains invisible. Code vulnerabilities feel different from liquidity traps or governance fragility, yet they interact. A stablecoin position that seems safe on paper can become fragile if its redemption window narrows or its oracle wobbles. A lending position that appears straightforward becomes precarious when incentives skew validator behaviour. A risk map captures these entanglements. It forces the uncomfortable recognition that no position stands alone. In the same way a pilot reviews instruments rather than gut feelings, a DeFi participant benefits from a visual field where vulnerabilities sit side by side.

The next layer is control—designing safeguards that correspond to each identified risk. If price feeds break, the trader receives a message on their phone within minutes. If a liquidity pool's TVL drops beneath a threshold, a dashboard flashes amber and forces a decision. If a validator set changes in a protocol's governance system, a weekly review flags it long before it becomes existential. Good controls do not merely restrain; they guide. They bring the abstract into the operational. They convert looming threats into bite-sized actions. The reason many teams falter is not lack of intelligence; it is the absence of links between insight and behaviour. The playbook closes the gap. But insight depends on input. Information quality, more than speed, shapes judgement. The teams that navigated the most volatile periods in 2021 and 2022 tended to consume information through intentional diets: a fixed cadence of reviews, trusted sources, and filters that separated noise from signals. They understood that raw feeds from social platforms distort perception and that dashboards, without context, breed overconfidence. The strongest operators viewed context as a rhythm—weekly cycles for metrics, monthly cycles for deeper strategic reviews, real-time alerts only for conditions they had pre-defined. This chapter examines how these patterns affect outcomes, and how the smallest tweaks—an added data source, a removed distraction—reshape decision quality.

Yet perhaps the most counter-intuitive element of any playbook is its embrace of small, reversible steps. In early DeFi cycles, many desks grew addicted to maximalist moves: full-size entries, speculative yield strategies, or aggressive purchases of long-tail assets on thin liquidity. When they were wrong, they stayed wrong. Reversibility offers something different: optionality. Pilot a strategy at one-tenth size. Test slippage on a minor tranche. Enter a lending market with a non-critical amount. These actions reveal truths that no simulation or governance forum can provide. And when conditions shift—contract upgrade, oracle anomaly, governance vote—the smallness of the step preserves optionality for the next decision.

Part of what makes DeFi demanding is the persistent mismatch between pace and comprehension. Protocols evolve quickly; humans evolve slowly. A playbook narrows that gap. It is not a guarantee of safety but a container for judgement. The risk map trains the eye. Controls translate intention into action. Information diets sharpen discernment. Small steps keep errors survivable. Together, they allow participants to face the market with clarity rather than bravado.

Still, the tension endures: codifying behaviour always risks rigidity. Markets reward the prepared, yet they also reward the adaptive. This chapter asks the reader to confront a subtle question at the heart of every resilient strategy: how much structure is enough to protect you, and how much flexibility is necessary to preserve edge? The answer lies not in doctrine but in design—your design.

The Risk Map

At 14:07 UTC on 6 April 2022, developers at Sky Mavis in Ho Chi Minh City sifted through logs that made little sense. The Ronin bridge should not, by design, allow five validator keys to sign withdrawals without human intervention. Yet a transfer worth roughly $540 million had cleared hours earlier with unnerving ease. The breach was not a single flaw; it was a convergence of code assumptions, validator key concentration, and social engineering. What struck investigators later was that the warning signals existed beforehand: a small cluster of validators controlled by one organisation, ambiguous operational boundaries, and a multi-signature threshold that offered the illusion—not the substance—of security. The pieces were visible, but no-one had placed them on the same page.

A contrasting scene unfolded in December 2023 at a co-working space in Lisbon, where a small quantitative crypto desk held its quarterly review. Instead of price charts, the screen displayed a grid: rows of protocol names, columns titled "Code Exposure", "Market Liquidity", and "Social Reliance". A colour scale ran from green to scarlet. One position—seemingly low-volatility, superficially conservative—burned bright red in the "Social Reliance" column. It depended on a single governance multisig whose members had not rotated keys for eighteen months. The traders reduced the position by half that same afternoon. Two weeks later, the project announced an emergency governance pause. Their decision had not been predictive; it had been procedural. They simply read the map. Risk, in DeFi, behaves like water. It seeps through cracks others do not notice and gathers in basins no dashboard highlights. The only way to understand its flow is to lay the entire landscape flat—to draw every relevant threat on a single canvas, regardless of its origin. A risk map is less a tool than a commitment to visibility. It forces the recognition that code audits mean little if a token's liquidity is thin, and that deep liquidity provides scant comfort if control of a protocol rests with a handful of delegates who rarely publish disclosures. The act of mapping—placing market depth beside governance concentration, or oracle reliability beside validator incentives—creates the perspective that raw intuition cannot. "See it together" becomes the motif, the refrain that turns scattered data into coherent risk.

To show how this perspective works in practice, consider the exploit that hit Curve Finance on 30 July 2023. The underlying vulnerability lay in a compiler bug affecting Vyper versions released in prior years. That was the code layer. But the losses materialised because large liquidity pools held assets that could not exit quickly once confidence broke—a market layer. And recovery was possible only because significant holders, including the Curve founder Michael Egorov, negotiated off-market debt resolutions to stabilise the system's collateral dynamics—a social layer. Code. Market. Social. Three planes, one event. Naming them separately clarifies how they intertwined. Explaining each layer reveals why isolating one domain leads to false comfort. The implication is stark: no DeFi position has a single risk; every position is a braid.
A second example reinforces this triad. When MakerDAO debated real-world asset collateral in mid-2022, the on-chain metrics—liquidation ratios, stability fees, oracle sources—dominated discussions. Yet the critical data point proved to be a different category: monthly attestation letters

from regulated custodians holding short-term U.S. Treasuries. Without these documents, market participants could not judge the reliability of the backing. The risk map for Maker positions thus included not only smart-contract parameters and DEX liquidity depth but also the legal clarity of off-chain custodial arrangements. Here, market and social factors constrained what the code could meaningfully guarantee. The implication again echoed the motif: only by "seeing it together" could participants form a realistic threat profile.

A credible counter-example deserves scrutiny. Some quantitative teams in 2021 argued that DeFi risk could be reduced to market data alone—volatility, correlation, liquidity decay curves, and liquidation schedules. They produced models showing impressive historical performance and insisted that structural factors such as governance capture or team credibility did not materially influence returns. The limitation of this approach surfaced during the collapse of LUNA and UST in May 2022. Market signals deteriorated within hours, yet the structural risk—the algorithmic stablecoin's reflexive design combined with opaque reserve mechanisms—had been evident for months. The models were not wrong; they were incomplete. Reconciliation lies in recognising that market data is indispensable for sizing, but insufficient for understanding how failure unfolds. Plotting market volatility alongside mechanism design flaws and reserve transparency would have altered allocations long before the decline accelerated.

Abstractions such as "confidence" and "vulnerability" only gain meaning when attached to behaviours or metrics. For code risk, the visible behaviours might be audit depth, bug-bounty participation, or the percentage of contracts upgradable without delay. For market risk, they might be 30-day average liquidity, the slippage at $1 million notional, or the number of independent oracle providers. For social risk, they appear in delegate turnout, multisig key rotation frequency, or governance distribution across jurisdictions. When these behaviours sit side by side, the map reveals misalignments. A protocol may boast three audits yet run with a two-of-three emergency multisig controlled by one founder. Another may have deep liquidity but rely on a single-price oracle. A third may have impeccable decentralisation yet negligible liquidity for redemptions above £500,000. By turning abstractions into observables, the map grounds decisions in structure rather than sentiment.

The map also reshapes time. Code risk tends to be concentrated at upgrade events and new releases. Market risk expands and contracts with liquidity cycles—weekends, post-announcement volatility, seasonal rotations. Social risk is slow-moving yet decisive, often visible only through months of governance data. A well-constructed risk map layers temporal signals: coloured cells darken or lighten according to cadence. For example, when Uniswap updated its governance cadence in 2021 to include regular delegate reports, social-risk indicators for related positions dimmed slightly on several desks' internal maps.

Conversely, when a smaller project's multisig stopped posting monthly attestations in autumn 2023, its cells drifted from green to amber long before anything dramatic occurred on-chain. The implication is that risk, once mapped, takes on a pulse, revealing its rhythms. The motif of "seeing it together" becomes even more powerful when applied across a portfolio. Consider a team holding five positions: a lending protocol with deep liquidity but concentrated governance; a stablecoin issuer with strong attestation but limited redemption windows; an AMM with robust code but fragile oracle integration; a liquid-staking token with variable lock-ups; and a yield strategy reliant on incentive emissions. If each position is analysed in isolation, the risks seem manageable. Draw them next to each other, however, and patterns emerge. Three depend on the same oracle network. Two share a single custodian. One protocol's governance token dominates multiple positions' collateral pools. The map reveals systemic overlap—the kind that triggers correlated losses. Once exposed, this overlap can be reduced, hedged, or accepted knowingly. Without the map, it remains invisible until crisis forces recognition.

A map, though, carries a subtle limitation: it tempts its users into false precision. Colour scales seduce. Numbers confer confidence. A row labelled "social risk: low" may lull a team into ignoring small signals of governance drift. Reconciling this limitation means treating the map not as a prediction engine but as a conversation starter. It should provoke questions: has this assumption changed? Is this data stale? What would flip this cell from green to red? The map works best when it is dynamic—redrawn monthly, debated, challenged. Static maps breed complacency. Living maps sharpen perception.

The power of a risk map lies not merely in its structure but in the discipline it enforces. It compels the operator to confront uncomfortable truths: a beloved protocol has brittle liquidity; a high-yield strategy depends on a small set of insiders; an asset considered "blue-chip" suffers from one-way redemption clauses. It turns preference into posture. It creates the habit of looking broadly before acting narrowly.

Yet the unresolved tension remains. A map can reveal every vulnerability, but action still demands trade-offs. If two positions share an oracle dependency, should one be reduced or both? If a protocol's governance appears stable but its liquidity thin, which risk outweighs the other? And perhaps the hardest question: how frequently should the map itself be redrawn without inducing paralysis by constant revision? The map does not answer these questions. It frames them. And that, more than any colour or metric, is what makes it indispensable.

Controls by Design

At 11:42 on 14 December 2020, engineers at Compound Labs in San Francisco watched their monitoring dashboard flash red. A sudden, unexplained spike appeared in the protocol's oracle feed for DAI: a price deviation large enough to trigger liquidations if left unchecked. The on-call engineer paused the protocol's price updates within minutes—not because they understood the full cause, but because the controls were already in place. A deviation alert fired at 0.5 per cent. A secondary oracle comparison flagged the mismatch. A cap on value-at-risk prevented any single market from cascading into the rest. The outcome was uneventful by design. No user funds were lost. No positions were forced closed. The drama sat in what *didn't* happen. Contrast this with the events of 7 October 2022, when Mango Markets on Solana experienced a manipulation-driven collapse. The attacker inflated the spot value of the MNGO token on thin liquidity, used this artificial valuation as collateral, and drained borrowable assets. No oracle deviation limit halted the reading. No position caps restricted leverage. No circuit breaker paused lending as utilisation surged. The protocol lacked the very constraints that had protected Compound two years earlier. The hole—roughly $114 million—was the measure of an absent control.

Controls in DeFi are not ornamental. They are the invisible scaffolding that shapes behaviour before anything breaks. A protocol or portfolio with weak controls resembles a building without fire doors: stable until the moment it is not. A team that "sees it together"—the motif that threads through this chapter—understands this instinctively. They do not rely on sentiment or vigilance. They build guardrails that operate even when they are tired, distracted, or too slow.

The first major claim emerges from these two cases. Effective controls start by showing where risk concentrates. In the Compound example, engineers saw a spike in DAI's oracle price. Naming the issue as "oracle variance" turned a vague discomfort into a defined category. Explaining why it mattered meant recognising that an incorrect oracle can liquidate positions at scale. The implication is obvious yet often overlooked: controls must sit closest to the failure point. Deviations must trigger alerts. Alerts must trigger evaluations. Evaluations must have authority to pause a subsystem. Without this chain, a team is left hoping the market behaves.

Visible metrics anchor these abstractions. An oracle control is not "robust"; it is configured to trigger at 0.3 per cent deviation for stablecoins and 1.2 per cent for volatile assets. A position limit is not "sensible"; it caps exposure at no more than 15 per cent of the protocol's total value locked (TVL). A diversification rule is not "balanced"; it enforces a maximum of 25 per cent of treasury assets in any single issuer or chain. These numbers—specific, measurable, revocable—turn intent into discipline.

The second claim centres on linking market risk to quantitative limits. A position that benefits from liquidity in quiet times may evaporate under stress. The 2021 congestion on Ethereum during NFT peaks showed this plainly. Gas costs spiked above 1,000 gwei on 7 September

2021, reducing the ability of users to unwind leveraged positions. Traders who had placed their own internal "gas caps" avoided forced selling. Those without limits found themselves priced out of the exits. Naming this behaviour as a liquidity control—"never enter a position whose exit cost exceeds X per cent of size"—makes it explicit. Explaining its effect reveals how controls convert structural fragility into contained damage. The implication is simple: size without exit conditions is speculation; size with clear exit limits is risk management.

A counter-example is instructive. Some desks argue that diversification alone is a sufficient control. They point to periods of market growth—summer 2020, early 2021—when spreading positions across ten or twelve protocols reduced drawdowns. But diversification without limits can compound systemic exposure. If half those protocols rely on the same oracle network or share similar liquidity pairs, diversification becomes illusion. Reconciliation lies in recognising that diversification is only a control when mapped against dependencies. Ten positions depending on one price feed is one position disguised as ten.

The third major claim concerns social risk embedded within technical systems. The Ronin bridge collapse in April 2022 illustrated this with painful clarity. Code audits existed. Market liquidity existed. What failed was the concentration of validator authority within a small cluster, several controlled by Sky Mavis itself. The visible behaviour was immutable: four of nine validators formed a threshold, and the attacker compromised them sequentially. Naming this as a governance-control failure reframes the incident. Explaining its relevance highlights that protocol safety derives not only from code, but from who controls upgrade paths and emergency actions. The implication is that multisig distribution, key rotation cadence, and delegate reporting are not process niceties—they are load-bearing structural controls.

Controls for social risk require observables. A multisig with seven signers across five independent organisations behaves differently from a multisig with five signers from one team. A governance protocol with turnout consistently above 10 per cent exhibits broader participation than one where 95 per cent of votes originate from three "delegation whales". These details belong on the control canvas. They turn soft concerns—*are we exposed to governance capture?*—into measurable thresholds.

The fourth claim turns to automated alerts. Alerts are the nervous system of a risk process. Without them, controls exist only on paper. Consider Chainlink's release of its low-latency oracles in May 2023. Teams integrating them gained the ability to compare feed values with decentralised exchange (DEX) mid-prices in near real time. The visible behaviour—an alert triggering when the difference exceeded a defined threshold—gave risk managers minutes rather than hours. Naming such a control as an "oracle differential alert" clarifies its purpose. Explaining its necessity reinforces that price feeds fail less often than liquidity, but when they fail, the damage compounds quickly. The implication is that teams must not merely monitor; they must automate detection.

Yet alerts bring their own limitation: alert fatigue. A system that fires twenty times a day becomes noise. Reconciling this means curating alerts deliberately: only those with direct action paths, only those tied to measurable thresholds. A balanced alerting system forces attention rather than diluting it.

Threading the motif of "seeing it together", controls take their strongest form when integrated. An alert without a limit breeds anxiety but no action. A limit without diversification narrows exposure but misses structural overlap. Diversification without observability risks masking hidden correlations. When combined, however, these controls enrich each other. A gas-cost alert tied to a position-exit limit ensures a team knows when its exit assumptions no longer hold. A TVL cap paired with diversification rules prevents overconcentration in yield farms that share counterparty risk. A multisig-distribution monitor paired with treasury allocation limits shields operational governance from dominating financial exposure. The map and the controls feed one another; the map reveals where controls belong, and the controls keep the map honest.

Controls by design embed foresight. They express the idea that risk is not only external but behavioural. A well-designed system prevents its operators from drifting into overconfidence. It enforces humility. This is why some funds require dual review on strategic changes. When Uniswap upgraded its governance modules in August 2022, several small funds implemented temporary two-person sign-off before adjusting liquidity positions. The visible behaviour—a second reviewer marking assumptions—became a control in its own right. It turned private conviction into shared responsibility.

Equally, some teams impose mandatory "cooling intervals" after large trades. If a position exceeds a size threshold—say, £250,000—no follow-up increase is allowed for 24 hours. This prevents momentum-driven sizing. It forces reflection, a behavioural control that reduces exposure to impulsive conviction. Controls that shape human behaviour are often the most valuable because they address the risk humans least like to admit: themselves.

The question of calibration remains. How strict should limits be? How sensitive should alerts remain? How much diversification is enough? The answer sits between two dangers: rigidity and complacency. A rigid control framework ignores new realities—protocol upgrades, liquidity changes, governance improvements. Complacent frameworks drift until they no longer reflect the system they oversee. Reconciling these poles requires cadence. Monthly reviews for limits. Quarterly reviews for diversification. Live updates for oracle thresholds. These cadences keep the framework alive without letting it mutate into noise.

And yet, even with thoughtfully designed controls, unresolved tension lingers. Controls constrain, but do they constrain the right things? A TVL cap protects against liquidity collapse, but at what opportunity cost when markets surge? A strict alert threshold prevents sudden losses, but does it prompt unnecessary pauses? A diversification rule spreads exposure, but does it dilute high-conviction strategies? Every control solves one problem while creating another.

The forward test is simple but difficult: which controls genuinely protect the portfolio's *structure,* and which merely soothe its operators? Answering that requires sustained discipline and a willingness to redraw the boundaries. Controls are never final. They are revised, not assumed. They demand commitment, not comfort. The map shows the risks. The controls shape the response. And between the two lies the art of staying solvent.

Information Diet

At 06:58 on 12 March 2020 in London, an analyst at a mid-sized crypto fund refreshed his terminal and watched liquidity evaporate in real time. ETH dropped more than 40 per cent within hours. MakerDAO's auctions stalled as gas fees surged. Telegram feeds dissolved into panic. Yet, in the noise, a small detail—posted quietly by Maker Foundation engineers on GitHub minutes earlier—clarified the situation: the oracle updates had lagged, collateral auctions were failing, and the system risked insolvency unless keepers returned. That single line, buried in a sea of low-signal commentary, shaped decisions that prevented the fund from compounding losses. The analyst acted not because he consumed *more* information than others, but because he consumed *less*, filtered harder, and relied on a disciplined ritual.

Compare this with the behaviour of a cohort of traders on Binance in the same week. Many spent hours cycling through Twitter threads, Discord rumours, and anonymous claims that "the peg was gone" or "ETH would hit zero by noon". The cognitive fog was visible in their trades: repeated entries and exits within minutes, contradicting positions, frantic messages begging for clarity. Their portfolios didn't fail because they lacked intelligence or tools. They failed because they lacked filters. The information firehose became a liability. What they needed was not insight, but *selection*.

The motif that threads through this subchapter—*signal over spectacle*—begins here. DeFi rewards those who can sift, not those who can scroll. A well-structured information diet acts as a risk control as decisive as caps, alerts, or diversification. It disciplines the mind before it disciplines the portfolio.

The first major claim is straightforward: without constraints, information becomes risk. Show this through the March 2020 chaos. Named sources like MakerDAO's GitHub repo provided measurable facts: time-stamped oracle delays, visible collateral deficits, quantifiable auction failures. Meanwhile, Twitter's stream produced zero metrics and abundant speculation. Explaining the difference reveals a structural truth: high-quality information has observable data behind it; low-quality information has only narrative. The implication is clear—risk is shaped by what you pay attention to. A fund that privileges verified metrics over opinion gains early clarity and avoids unnecessary churn.

Metrics anchor this distinction. An oracle lag can be measured in seconds. A liquidity depth change can be measured in basis points. A change in governance voting turnout can be measured as a percentage. Each metric is a handle for decision-making. Rumour offers nothing to grip.

The second claim concerns cadence. Information, like diet, becomes harmful when consumed constantly. Show this through Jump Trading's handling of the Wormhole exploit in February 2022. Within hours of discovering a 120,000 wETH hole, their internal teams drew from clear, pre-defined sources: core development channels, on-chain data, and direct communications with Solana validators. They did not immerse themselves in the hourly frenzy of social media. Their cadence was structured: incident update every 30 minutes, code verification in parallel, treasury assessment on a fixed rhythm. Explaining the methodology reveals a deeper principle: cadence protects cognition. It prevents overreaction and ensures that decisions reflect structured assessment rather than emotional oscillation. The implication is that teams must choose *when* they look, not only *where* they look.

A counter-example exposes the limitation of cadence without curation. The Squid Token collapse of November 2021 saw thousands of holders flood Reddit and Telegram for updates after the liquidity pool was drained. Their cadence was intense—refreshing channels every few minutes—but their sources were low-trust and unverifiable. Reconciliation lies in combining cadence with source integrity. Rhythm without quality becomes ritualised confusion.

The third claim centres on the construction of trusted sources. Trust must be earned through behaviour, not reputation. Show this by pointing to Lido's public validator performance dashboards, maintained consistently since mid-2021. The dashboards reveal missed attestation rates, slashing events, and withdrawal queue lengths in clear, visible metrics. Naming Lido's model as "transparent by construction" clarifies why it belongs in a risk-conscious information diet. Explaining how these dashboards support position sizing, withdrawal timing, and governance decisions demonstrates their value. The implication is that trusted sources are those that expose their internals, not those that cultivate mystique.

By contrast, some information channels—certain high-profile influencers on X—generate engagement but disclose no methodology, no verification trails, and no incentives for accuracy. Their updates may be timely, but they lack the minimum criterion of a credible source: verifiability. The limitation is that speed is often mistaken for quality.

Reconciling this means privileging sources with consistent, measurable accuracy over those with consistent visibility.

The fourth claim concerns noise filters. Noise is not random; it is patterned. It appears around funding announcements, airdrop rumours, token listings, bridge failures, and regulatory speculation. Show this through the Celsius withdrawal freeze on 12 June 2022. Minutes after withdrawals halted, dozens of Telegram groups erupted with claims ranging from insolvency to government seizure. Meanwhile, blockchain explorers showed something quieter and more concrete: stablecoins leaving Celsius-controlled wallets at a predictable cadence hours before the announcement. Naming the explorer data as "primary-source signal" reframes the situation. Explaining its significance demonstrates that noise can be filtered by choosing sources that cannot lie: on-chain flows, code repositories, governance proposals, exchange wallets. The implication is that a noise filter is not an abstract discipline—it is a selection of channels whose incentives align with truth.

The motif—signal over spectacle—returns here. Noise bursts loudly, but signal persists quietly.

The fifth claim examines the ritual of structured review. Weekly reviews, when done honestly, become an anchor of operational hygiene. Show this through the practice used by several small funds during 2023, where every Friday they reviewed five metrics: TVL distribution across chains, liquidity depth for exit positions, governance changes on active holdings, oracle deviation logs, and gas price medians. Naming this as a "review ritual" elevates it beyond habit. Explaining how this reduces cognitive load reveals a subtle dynamic: when information is sorted into rhythms, attention becomes sharper, not narrower. The implication is that the weekly ritual protects against the illusion of constant oversight.

A limitation emerges: a weekly cadence can miss rapid developments. For example, Curve's pool imbalance on 30 July 2023 worsened within hours after Vyper vulnerabilities were disclosed. Funds relying on weekly reviews would have acted too late. Reconciling this requires a hybrid approach: daily alerts for critical metrics, weekly reviews for strategic context. Ritual and immediacy must coexist.

The sixth claim deals with the social dimension of information. Teams do not merely consume information—they interpret it. Show this through the behaviour of a London-based trading desk in August 2022 during a major governance proposal on Aave's risk parameters. Rather than rely on individual interpretation, they used a short morning briefing to align on the facts: current utilisation, liquidation thresholds, and historical governance turnout. Naming this as "collective interpretation" clarifies what is often implicit. Explaining its significance reveals that information becomes useful when shared understanding forms. The implication is that an information diet is strengthened by conversation—not endless, meandering discussion but structured alignment on what matters.

The quiet motif finds new expression: seeing signal together is stronger than seeing it alone.

The seventh claim concerns mental bandwidth. Information diet is ultimately about protecting attention, the scarcest resource in volatile markets. Show this through a behavioural detail: some funds limit Slack channels, enforce quiet hours, or require a rationale for posting urgent market notes. Naming these as "attention controls" shifts them from preference to practice. Explaining why they matter reveals the mechanism: distraction increases reaction time and creates inconsistency in sizing, exits, and execution. The implication is profound—attention is a risk parameter. It must be managed like liquidity or leverage.

Toward the end of this subchapter, the tension surfaces. How much information is *enough*? Too little, and blind spots multiply. Too much, and clarity dissolves. Should one trust cues from explorers or updates from developers? Should one read everything or rely on summaries? At what point does filtering become ignorance?

The forward test remains open: if the information diet you follow shapes the decisions you make, do your filters reflect the risks you face—or merely your habits? The answer determines whether information serves as ballast or turbulence. And only those who master their diet can hope to master their decisions.

Small, Reversible Steps

On 5 May 2022, in Singapore, a small quantitative desk at QCP Capital faced a choice that would later define their reputation for composure. A new cross-chain yield strategy promised double-digit returns on paper, but it relied on a bridge contract audited only once and barely battle-tested under load. Instead of deploying the full allocation that traders informally pushed for, the team committed just 1 per cent of intended size for a seven-day pilot. When the Harmony Horizon bridge was exploited weeks later—24 June 2022—the desk's journals showed something striking: their pilot had already uncovered irregular settlement delays and inconsistent oracle updates. The strategy had been quietly shelved. The team's restraint saved millions. Their success was not prescience. It was *reversibility*. Contrast this with the behaviour of several retail collectives during that same summer, who poured the entirety of their treasuries into Terra's Anchor yields without staging or simulation. When UST began slipping from $1 on 7 May 2022, descending to $0.35 by 11 May, many of those treasuries had no reversible path left. They had gone all in. They had no circuit-breakers, no dry-runs, no trial allocations. Their loss was not merely financial; it was procedural. The difference is visible: one group treated decisions as experiments, the other as commitments.

This subchapter anchors itself in the modest motif of *footsteps rather than leaps*—a reminder that in DeFi, where information changes faster than conviction, the ability to backtrack cleanly is as valuable as the ability to advance.

The first major claim is that small size is not timidity; it is a diagnostic tool. Show this through the QCP pilot. They measured settlement times, variance in validator participation, and the frequency of cross-chain message retries. Each data point was a real-world metric, not a projected assumption. Naming this practice as "probative sizing" gives it conceptual clarity: position size becomes a probe into system behaviour. Explaining its value reveals a deeper truth—pilots reveal frictions, incentives, and failure modes long before dashboards or audits do. The implication is that sizing is not only about capital allocation but about information acquisition. A small step clarifies. A big step conceals.

The limitation is that pilots can give a false sense of safety. A bridge that behaves well at 1 per cent size may still fail catastrophically under aggregate network stress. Reconciling this requires distinguishing between *local* reliability (what your pilot sees) and *global* reliability (what the system can withstand). Pilots inform, but they do not guarantee. They are necessary, but never sufficient.

The second claim concerns reversibility as process design. Show this through the workflow of Gauntlet's risk simulations for Aave, widely cited during 2022–2023. Before any major parameter change, Gauntlet encouraged staged implementation: first adjust loan-to-value by a few percentage points, then pause, then observe user behaviour and liquidation metrics. Naming this as "progressive enactment" captures the structure. Explaining how the process prevents governance from inflicting sudden shocks—unexpected liquidations, liquidity cliffs, utilisation spikes—demonstrates why reversibility matters at institutional scale. The implication is that major changes should move in increments that allow for mid-course correction. Decisions become chains of small, observable steps, not single irreversible jumps.

A counter-example sharpens the point. In November 2021, several protocols implemented collateral factor increases for their governance tokens in a single motion, incentivised by short-term borrowing demand. Within weeks, utilisation whipsawed, liquidations spiked, and governance faced the unpleasant task of reversing parameters under duress. The reconciliation is straightforward: decisions that seem efficient when bundled often become brittle when conditions surprise. Efficiency without reversibility becomes fragility.

The third claim is that reversible decisions demand explicit exit conditions. Show this through the practice of a London-based crypto treasury in 2023. For every strategy they tested—options selling on Deribit, concentrated liquidity positions on Uniswap v3—they recorded three triggers: price deviation thresholds, volatility expansion markers, and utilisation changes on counterparties. Naming these as "reversal triggers" formalises what many treat informally. Explaining their purpose reveals a simple mechanism:

reversibility requires clarity about when to stop, not only when to start. The implication is powerful—decisions become safer when exits are architectural, not emotional. Yet trigger design has limits. Some signals fail gracefully, but others fail violently. A depeg event, for instance, may blow through every trigger before alerts even fire. Reconciling this requires humility: triggers are tools, not assurances. They must be paired with circuit-breakers and size limits that assume triggers may fail.

The fourth claim tackles emotional discipline. Small steps protect the mind from overcommitment. Show this through a behavioural pattern common among retail traders during liquidity mining booms of 2021: piling into opportunities at full size because to do otherwise "felt too slow". When rewards tapered or contracts malfunctioned, they faced not only financial loss but emotional entrapment—the sunk-cost fallacy amplified by the irreversibility of their position. Naming this pattern as "psychological lock-in" makes it legible. Explaining how incremental entry reduces psychological load clarifies a further truth: small steps preserve optionality in both capital and cognition. The implication is that discipline is designed upstream—into the entry process—not imposed downstream through willpower.

The fifth claim is operational: reversibility requires documentation. Show this through the operational logs maintained by a Paris-based DeFi team during 2022. They recorded every pilot allocation in a single shared document:

rationale, parameters, risks, exit triggers, expected duration. Naming this as a "pilot ledger" gives it structure. Explaining how it supported decision quality—surfacing inconsistencies, enabling post-mortems, revealing strategy drift—illustrates its practical utility. The implication is that reversibility must be visible. A step that cannot be audited cannot be reversed gracefully.

A limitation arises when documentation slows execution. Some teams resist pilots because "it takes too long to write things down". Reconciling this requires distinguishing between lightweight logs and bureaucratic prose. Proper documentation is not paperwork; it is memory.

The sixth claim concerns organisational culture. Teams that favour reversible steps tend to share power more effectively. Show this through the practice at Wintermute following the Optimism token mis-send in June 2022. After recovering from the incident, Wintermute introduced incremental deployment approvals: no new smart contract interactions above a defined threshold could proceed without second-party confirmation. Naming this as "distributed responsibility" highlights the cultural element. Explaining its impact reveals that reversibility becomes collective: decisions are made in pairs, not in silos. The implication is that reversible processes foster accountability not through punishment, but through structure.

The motif reappears: footsteps rather than leaps. Small steps create pause points. Pause points create clarity.

As the subchapter draws to its unresolved tension, a question emerges. How small is small enough? A pilot that is too small generates inadequate data; a pilot that is too large loses its reversibility. At what threshold does caution become paralysis? And how do teams decide when to scale from pilot to production?

The forward test remains live: if every decision you make could fail quietly rather than loudly, would your process look different? And what would you change today to ensure that every step you take is one you can always walk back from?

About the Author

Othman Verdan writes at the intersection of markets, code and human behaviour. He has worked alongside builders and risk teams across emerging financial technologies, translating complexity into plain decisions for operators and curious investors. His mission is simple: help readers replace hype and fear with clear mental models, practical controls and calmer time horizons. Raised on stories of medieval caravansaries and trust networks across North Africa and the Levant, he sees today's ledgers as the latest chapter in a long history of financial coordination. He believes good tools are boring, safeguards should be visible, and progress comes from disciplined iteration rather than bravado.

www.ingramcontent.com/pod-product-compliance
Lightning Source LLC
Chambersburg PA
CBHW031337230926
51848CB00002B/269
9789374598924